The Enforcer

The Enforcer

An IPS Officer's War on Crime in India's Badlands

Anirudhya Mitra

JUGGERNAUT BOOKS
C-I-128, First Floor, Sangam Vihar, Near Holi Chowk,
New Delhi 110080, India

First published by Juggernaut Books 2025

Copyright © Anirudhya Mitra 2025

10 9 8 7 6 5 4 3 2 1

P-ISBN: 9789353454333
E-ISBN: 9789353458065

The views and opinions expressed in this book are the author's own. The facts contained herein were reported to be true as on the date of publication by the author to the publishers of the book, and the publishers are not in any way liable for their accuracy or veracity.

All rights reserved. No part of this publication may be reproduced, transmitted, or stored in a retrieval system in any form or by any means without the written permission of the publisher.

Typeset in Adobe Caslon Pro by Mukul Chand

Printed at Thomson Press India Ltd

To my police fraternity…

*This book is dedicated to each one of you.
What you do is not just a job, it is a calling.*

And you have always responded to that call with grit, grace and unwavering commitment.

*To the constable who stood in the rain to manage traffic,
To the officer who cracked cases through sleepless nights,
To the teams that innovated when the odds were stacked against us –
You are the true soul of this force.*

This journey, and this book, would mean little without you.

– Prashant Kumar

Contents

Preface   ix

Part 1
Rooting Out Gangsters

1. The Night of the Ambush   3
2. The Infallible: End of Atiq Ahmed   27
3. The Last Supper of Mukhtar Ansari   51
4. Bullets, Billions and the Fall of the Mafias   71
5. The State Strikes Back   83
6. Justice Delivered   99

Part 2
Organizing the Greatest Mela on Earth

7. Faith, Flow and the Force   113
8. Poetry of Chaos   131

Part 3
The Making of a Policeman

9. Roots of a Warrior — 151
10. Red Dust and Silent Guns — 169

Part 4
Significant Cases

11. The Furnace of the West — 189
12. Promotion, Protest and the Missing File — 207
13. Transfers, Turmoil and a Prayer at Kailash — 227
14. The Assignment After — 243
15. From Lakhimpur Kheri to the Challenge of COVID — 265

Part 5
An Officer and a Gentleman

16. Not a Power Couple – Just Partners — 281
17. The Final Badge — 293

Acknowledgements — 319
Notes — 321

Preface

One morning, a distinguished filmmaker – someone I had known both as a colleague and a friend – called me out of the blue. His voice carried that unmistakable tone of intrigue, the kind that tells you something interesting is coming. 'Would you like to write a biography?' he asked.

My instinctive response: 'Whose?'

'An IPS officer. Prashant Kumar.'

I took a beat. 'Prashant Kumar, you mean…?'

Across the line, he clarified, 'He is in the UP Police. That big moustache.'

And just like that, the image clicked in my mind. 'Oh, you mean the top cop of UP? Yeah, of course, I know him … I mean, I keep seeing him on television.'

Every time there was an encounter in UP, there he was – Prashant Kumar, the moustachioed Indian Police Service (IPS) officer, staring unflinchingly at the news anchor, his sharp eyes unwavering as he laid out his version of events. He had a presence, an aura that made you believe that if anyone could take on the kind of criminals who had long ruled the state, it was him. You don't just need tactics to dismantle organized crime, you also need an attitude, a presence that makes men who believe themselves untouchable realize they are not.

I had seen him dominate television screens, his unwavering gaze locking horns with news anchors, his voice carrying the weight of law and order. He had an aura that made even the most hardened criminals rethink their bravado.

So, when I was asked to write his biography, there was only one answer. Yes. But nothing had prepared me for the man I was about to meet. The tiger in the room, the officer who seemed larger than life, turned out to be something else entirely.

It was mid-October. I had arrived early at his office. He landed sharp on time. No uniform, no insignia of rank or power. Instead, he walked in wearing steel-grey trousers and a crisp white half-sleeved bush shirt. The man who had loomed large on television screens, the no-nonsense cop with a stare that could unsettle the most seasoned criminals, now stood before me with a warm, almost disarming smile.

'How are you, sir?' he said, his voice polite, his demeanour humble. He extended his hand for a firm but welcoming handshake.

It threw me off, if I am being honest. In all my years as a crime reporter, having met and written about some of the most powerful and formidable police officers, I had never encountered one of his rank and stature who greeted me with such genuine warmth. The contrast between the man I had imagined and the one standing in front of me was striking.

I hesitated for a moment, waiting for him to take his seat first. But he gestured towards the chair opposite him and said, '*Pehle aap.*' You first.

That's when it hit me – I was in Lucknow. And here was Prashant Kumar – tough-as-nails, feared by gangsters, the man leading the charge in one of the most brutal crackdowns in UP's history – embodying that very essence of old-world politeness. In that moment, I realized something. However much I thought I knew about him, this was going to be a story full of surprises.

Power in UP comes wrapped in symbols – grand residences, armed security, offices buzzing with political and administrative clout. The DGP house in Lucknow is one such fortress, sprawling across 7 acres and boasting expansive rooms, guest houses, staff quarters, courts for badminton and tennis and massive gardens. It is a residence every senior officer dreams of.

But Prashant Kumar doesn't live there. He chose a different path. He stays in a house he built himself, on land he bought with his own money. His father had once told him a man should build his own home, not live in something borrowed, no matter how grand. I asked him why he didn't move into the DGP house like every other officer would.

'*Aadat bigad jaati hai*,' he said simply.

One day, while I was on my computer writing, a WhatsApp message popped up from Prashant Kumar. It contained an African proverb: 'Until the lion learns to write, every story will glorify the hunter.'

I told him it was an interesting proverb, no doubt, but what could be the context? Knowing Prashant Kumar, he had no time to waste with me. Then he clarified. He was curious: Why had I agreed to write his story when the media rarely shows interest in going deep into a cop's side of the story?

It struck a chord with me. This wasn't just a casual remark, it was also an insight into the mind of Prashant, a man who had spent his life on the frontlines of crime and law enforcement, watching how narratives were shaped, reshaped and sometimes hijacked.

Sometime later, I was in Lucknow to meet him. He called me at precisely 7 a.m., inquired about my well-being, laid out his day's packed schedule and informed me that he would meet me at 11 a.m. at his office in the DGP house. At five minutes to 11, a staff member escorted me to his office.

He sat behind his desk in full khaki uniform, the gallantry medals on his chest gleaming under the lights, his police cap set perfectly. Before anything else, he checked if I had been attended to properly. His staff could not have been more accommodating. Only after ensuring my comfort did he return to the stack of papers on his desk, signing documents while continuing to talk to me.

Multiple television screens lined the walls, displaying real-time updates from across UP. His phone rang non-stop, yet he balanced his attention effortlessly, shifting seamlessly between our conversation and the stream of updates requiring his attention. Amidst all this, I noticed something unexpected – he was signing birthday greeting cards. They weren't for high-ranking officials or bureaucrats but for his officers – every rank and file. Each one received a personal message from him.

He had just returned from a two-day DGP conference in Bhubaneswar, and his desk was flooded with pending files. Even as he navigated administrative tasks, visitors streamed in. Among them was a senior politician – a stalwart in his own right, now a member of the Bharatiya Janata Party (BJP). Dressed in a *bandhgala* suit instead of his old khadi attire, Kripashankar Singh had come not for a non-police matter but to ask for help in road construction. A four-time member of the Legislative Assembly (MLA) and former home minister of another state, and yet he had to request Prashant Kumar's assistance for something beyond policing. That was the extent of Prashant's influence. With composed politeness, he assured Singh that he would look into it.

Sitting in his office felt like riding in a police patrol van through a trouble-torn area. The difference? Instead of the crackle of a wireless set filling the air, it was his cell phone – ringing non-stop, an unrelenting stream of updates, crises and decisions waiting to be made.

He answered most calls without hesitation, knowing that only the most urgent, high-priority matters reach his personal number. Every call was a live case file, a developing situation somewhere in UP – some unfolding in real time, others simmering just beneath the surface. He navigated them with clinical precision, his responses crisp and to the point.

What fascinated me was how he instinctively decided which calls to put on speaker mode. Without intending to, he granted me a front-row seat to his world – letting me witness how he operated, how he unravelled a crisis, how the tension built and dissipated, how he pulled invisible strings to contain a volatile situation before it exploded into a law-and-order nightmare. It was like watching a real-time thriller unfold, except this one wasn't scripted.

At one point, I couldn't help but ask, 'What about the calls you don't put on speaker? Those must be the most interesting ones.' He looks at me, his lips curling into a half-smile. Then, as if to humour my curiosity, he says, 'No problem. From now on, all incoming calls will be on speaker mode.'

For a moment, I thought he was joking. Then his phone rang again, and true to his word, he answered it – on speaker. And just like that, I found myself eavesdropping on a world few outsiders ever get to hear.

Between these interruptions, our conversation continued – each break a reminder of how seamlessly he juggled roles. A deputy superintendent of police (DSP) sought intervention in an internal matter and a former army officer (his brother-in-law) stopped by; within moments, he shifted from law enforcement to a personal exchange without missing a beat.

As time slipped by, he glanced at the clock. 'Let's go,' he said. The setting changed as we arrived at the police headquarters (PHQ), but his routine did not. The files, the officers, the calls – they followed him everywhere. From the DGP house to PHQ, his day remained the same – piles of files, endless visitors. But at PHQ, the influx was larger – constables to additional director generals (ADGs), officers from different jurisdictions, all seeking his intervention. Some came for professional matters, others for personal concerns.

A fleet of IPS officers, vertical heads and senior officials lined up outside Prashant Kumar's office, waiting for their turn. They sought approvals, discussed career moves and handled operational matters. He treated each case with the same even-handed approach – no raised voices, no unnecessary delays. Even when a high-level political functionary called, sounding agitated over an unfolding political crisis, he remained unruffled. He briefed the veteran politician in his signature calm tone, explaining the brewing situation with clarity. His ability to stay composed in high-pressure moments was remarkable.

Yet his ability to maintain order in a state long accustomed to lawlessness has not come without controversy. His policing style, though undeniably effective, has drawn both admiration and sharp criticism. Depending on whom you ask, Prashant is either a fearless reformer or a symbol of authoritarian policing. The truth, as always, lies somewhere in between.

His tenure as DGP has been anything but conventional. His critics denounce his methods as 'draconian', accusing him of 'orchestrating encounters driven by caste and religious biases to appease political masters'.[1] Allegations of selective demolitions – bulldozers targeting specific communities – have fuelled fierce debates, with Opposition leaders branding him a mere enforcer of the ruling party's agenda.

Yet his supporters tell a different story. They argue that Prashant Kumar's no-nonsense approach has brought a long-overdue sense of order to a state once synonymous with lawlessness. Under his watch, UP saw a dramatic drop in crime rates, fostering an environment that attracted 400 times more investment from outside the state. His leadership redefined the ease of doing business in a region that once repelled investors with its culture of fear and instability.

For every charge of being 'trigger-happy' or politically motivated, there exists a counter-narrative – one of lives saved, communities rebuilt and an economy revitalized by stability.[2]

A second call from the government followed, this time regarding the Tikait situation – a sensitive farmer agitation at the Delhi–UP border. Rakesh Tikait, an Indian farmers' rights activist, wanted to lead a protest march to Delhi despite prohibitory orders. Without hesitation, Prashant Kumar called an officer who had a personal rapport with Tikait and gave detailed instructions on handling the matter delicately.

His ability to resolve delicate situations effectively was astonishing.

His juniors had immense faith in him, knowing that if they sought justice, they would receive it. When he called an officer about a particular case, the discussion naturally transitioned into personal matters. He knew not just the professional issues his officers faced but also their struggles outside work. That was one of his greatest qualities as a leader – his knowledge of his people. But there were boundaries he never crossed. A friend called about a fatal accident in which his son was an accused. Prashant's response was firm: 'How can anybody be helped when a life is lost?' However, after hearing out the details, he said he would look into it.

Shortly afterward, a large contingent of officers arrived. A senior police officer was retiring, and a farewell ceremony was underway.

Even after lunch, his phone continued to ring. Each call brought new problems – some trivial, some critical. A politician's domestic staff had an issue, and they expected Prashant Kumar to intervene. An officer wanted his transfer stalled. This was a common request from inspectors to inspectors general (IGs). Yet in every single instance, Prashant refused to misuse his power. He rationalized why transfers were necessary and why officers needed to accept government orders. He never picked up the phone to call in favours for anyone. His own career had been marked by frequent transfers, many of them politically motivated, but he had always accepted them without resistance. He had moved forward, even at the cost of staying away from his family for years.

Another call from the government in the evening. The issue this time? Sambhal. Pakistan-made cartridges had been recovered, and the situation was escalating. Prashant provided a debrief, explaining the latest developments with the assurance of 'Sir, situation is under control.'

Then came the fallout from the leader of Opposition (LoP) incident at the Delhi–Noida border in connection with the Sambhal unrest. Reportedly, the government was not happy, even as the LoP managed to get media footage – exactly what he had come for – alongside his newly elected member of Parliament (MP) sister, who too was a very high-profile politician.

Through all of this, Prashant Kumar remained calm, responding with precision.

His life is remarkably simple. His house, his car, his food – everything about him is stripped of excess. I have never seen an officer of his stature live such a modest life. He speaks so softly that I often had to remind him to raise his voice for clearer audio recordings. And yet for all his authority, he is a reluctant subject when it comes to discussing himself. He is shy about talking about his own achievements.

The same man could have been far wealthier, and not necessarily through corrupt means. There are plenty of legitimate ways to multiply one's wealth in a country whose economic progress is the talk of the world. I know many officers, both of his rank and junior to him, who are far wealthier. They lead extravagant lives filled with social events; playing golf at five-star resorts; owning lavish homes with swimming pools, snooker tables and imported cutlery; taking regular vacations in other countries; and providing prestigious university educations for their children abroad. Their evenings are often reserved for the finest single malts and, following the latest trend, Japanese whiskey – savoured in dimly lit bars of luxury hotels and private lounges.

He did none of that. Instead, he ate a simple lunch at home and then, in his characteristic quiet manner, asked me if I would like some homemade *gajar ka halwa*.

This was his world – structured, disciplined, yet constantly shifting beneath the weight of power dynamics, crisis control and political pressure. Sitting across from him, watching him navigate these complexities with quiet authority, I realized that Prashant Kumar was not just a cop dismantling the mafias in UP, he was also someone far more layered, more enigmatic.

A man who lets his actions speak louder than words, he remains reluctant to discuss his own achievements. Yet his work has reshaped the very landscape of law enforcement in the state. That is why his story must be told – for the general readers and for every police officer who sees him on television without truly knowing the man behind the uniform.

In a world where titles are handed out too easily and often worn too loosely, Prashant Kumar's journey stands apart – etched not in words but in the weight of every medal, every commendation and every quiet nod of respect earned through decades of unrelenting service.

His pursuit of excellence began not in uniform but in academia where, in 1988, he emerged as the top-ranking postgraduate student in MSc (Applied Geology) from the University of Delhi. A gold medal marked his early brush with distinction. Years later, another gold would grace his journey, this time in an MBA in Disaster Management from Guru Gobind Singh Indraprastha University, Delhi – proof that learning never ceased, and neither did the pursuit of mastery.

But the classroom could only prepare him so far. The real tests came in the field, among smoke, gunfire, mobs and missions few dared to lead. Here, Prashant Kumar's mettle was forged. And the Republic of India took note.

Four times, he was decorated with the Police Medal for Gallantry (PMG) – in 2020, 2021, 2022 and again in 2024 – each occasion honouring moments when courage overtook caution and leadership outpaced fear. The third and fourth medals bore additional bars – first and second bars to PMG – an honour earned only by those who have returned to the fire not once but again and again. On 26 January 2024, when he was awarded the Gallantry Medal, it wasn't just a ceremony, it was also the culmination of years spent walking into conflict zones while others walked away.

Recognition followed in quieter, less visible forms too. In 2014, he was awarded the President's Police Medal for Distinguished Service, and long before that, the Police Medal for Meritorious Service in 2007. He has worn the Parakram Medal (2020), the Kumbh Mela Padak (2025) and the Chief Minister's Medal for Outstanding Services (2018) – each a reminder of the many faces of duty: operational, ceremonial, humanitarian.

Specialized agencies didn't overlook his contributions either. The director general's commendation rolls and discs from the Indo-Tibetan Border Police (ITBP), Central Industrial Security Force (CISF) and Uttar Pradesh (UP) Police tell a story of inter-agency respect and regard. The Platinum Disc, the rarest of insignias, was conferred on him by the UP director general of police (DGP) on 15 August 2020 – an acknowledgement few in the force ever receive in a lifetime.

Beyond medals, there are moments that can't be hung on a wall yet speak volumes. In 2017, he was chosen as the liaison officer (LO) for the Kailash Mansarovar Yatra, a spiritual odyssey demanding both physical rigour and administrative acumen. He completed the treacherous journey with characteristic calm.

In 2022, amid a charged atmosphere during the General Assembly elections in UP, Prashant's coordination of multiple law enforcement agencies ensured not just order but also dignity, safety and fairness. The Election Commission of India acknowledged his leadership with the Annual State Award for Best Electoral Practices and a rare letter of appreciation from the union home secretary. He had not merely policed an election, he had also protected democracy.

The India News Shaurya Samman, conferred by the chief minister (CM) of UP, and the FSAI Bravery Award, are more than trophies – they are also public affirmations of his strategic brilliance in the darkest of times. In operations like the encounter of Chitrakoot's dreaded brigand Udaybhan Yadav alias Gauri Yadav, Prashant didn't just oversee tactics, he also embodied resolve. The reward that followed – ₹3 lakh, a service pistol and a letter of commendation from the CM – was less a prize, more a testament to the impact he had.

Over the years, Prashant has quietly amassed over 113 commendations and appreciation letters from senior officers across postings, each one a ripple from the deep well of trust he built within the system. These weren't casual endorsements. They were battle-hardened acknowledgments from those who witnessed his commitment firsthand.

And perhaps, most significantly, he never sought applause. Even the largest of his awards – like the Ati Utkrisht Seva Padak from the union home minister – were earned in silence and received with humility. He wore the medals but never let them wear him.

In the heart of every citation, there was no singular story. There were hundreds. Stories of floods averted, riots controlled, terrorists killed, institutions restored and, above all, a standard raised.

Because, for Prashant Kumar, greatness was never a destination. It was a responsibility. One lived, day by day, without compromise.

PART 1
Rooting Out Gangsters

1
The Night of the Ambush

In the early hours of 3 July 2020, the convoy of police vehicles sliced through the darkness, sirens off, headlights dimmed. The air was heavy with monsoon humidity as fifty heavily armed officers, drawn from three police stations in Kanpur district, made their way to Bikru village, a remote settlement 150 km from Lucknow. Their target? Vikas Dubey, one of the most feared gangsters in Uttar Pradesh (UP).

For three decades, Dubey had ruled Kanpur's world of crime with bloodied hands, his name whispered in fear through political corridors and police stations alike. Sixty criminal cases – murder, extortion, dacoity, kidnapping, rioting – but never a conviction that stuck. He had always walked free. Until now.

This time, it was different. Unlike in the past, the present government of UP was determined to bring him down. The political will had shifted, and there would be no escape route paved with influence and corruption. Acting on a new arrest warrant, the police were finally closing in. No political rescue, no corrupt officials pulling strings, no last-minute court stays. Or so they thought.

Because Dubey already knew they were coming.

Hours earlier, in the dead of night, a phone call changed everything. It was a whisper through the ranks, a mole inside the police force itself. Station House Officer (SHO) Vinay Tiwari of Chaubeypur Police Station – the very jurisdiction that controlled Bikru village – had tipped off Dubey. It wasn't the first time. For years, this was how Dubey had stayed one step ahead.

'The raid is happening tonight. Be ready.'

Dubey wasted no time. He had been preparing for this moment for years.

Electricity to the entire village was cut off, throwing Bikru into complete darkness. His men, already stationed on rooftops, gripped their INSAS rifles, pistols and shotguns – some purchased, others gifted by corrupt allies. By the time the first police vehicle rolled in, Bikru was no longer a village. The police expected resistance, but nothing had prepared them for what happened next. It was a battlefield.

A single gunshot cracked through the air. Then another. And another.

Suddenly, gunfire rained down from every direction. It was an ambush. Bullets ripped through the night, shattering windshields, splintering wooden doors, punching holes into bulletproof vests. The first officers fell instantly, collapsing before they could fire back.

At the heart of the bloodbath was Deputy Superintendent of Police (DSP) Devendra Mishra. He was one of the few officers who knew the full extent of Dubey's corruption network – and he had been vocal about it. Mishra had even written a letter to his seniors months ago, warning them about Dubey's deep ties with the Chaubeypur Police Station. The letter was ignored, and the DSP paid the price.

Mishra went down fighting, but the brutality didn't stop with bullets. Dubey's men rushed forward, axes in hand, hacking away at his body. His head was severed, his feet mutilated, his corpse defiled beyond recognition. Revenge wasn't enough for Dubey. He wanted to send a message. Maybe that's why his men's actions included snatching of an AK-47 and INSAS rifles from the police.

Nearby, other officers scrambled for cover, but there was none. Seven more policemen were shot dead.

Seven others lay bleeding in the mud, barely alive. Some tried to fire back, but their weapons had been snatched, their training no match for Dubey's ruthless planning.

As the smoke settled, the survivors saw something even more terrifying – SHO Vinay Tiwari, the officer in charge of the raid, fleeing the scene. He was one of Dubey's men, but he had never been on their side.

By the time reinforcements arrived, Dubey and his men were gone. The police had come to arrest a criminal. Instead, they had walked into a massacre. The morning of that fateful Friday was chaotic. Eight policemen dead, seven critically injured, and Dubey was still at large.

When news of the ambush broke, Prashant Kumar – the additional director general (ADG) of law and order – was already preparing to move. He had just been briefed by the superintendent of police (SP) from the district. Around the same time, a call came from Lucknow asking about his whereabouts. His response was immediate: he was on his way to the scene. It was clear that the state government wanted him to take charge directly from the ground and also to manage the media storm that was brewing. This was no longer a routine arrest. It had escalated into a full-scale crisis. What followed was a manhunt unlike anything UP had ever witnessed: roadblocks, raids and a relentless, state-wide pursuit.

By nightfall, the special task force (STF) had launched raids across Kanpur, storming Dubey's house in Lucknow's Krishnanagar area. But Dubey wasn't there.

Vikas Dubey had slipped through the cracks of a system he had manipulated for years. But this time, the game had changed. This time, he wasn't just another wanted man. He was the most hunted fugitive in India.

His safe houses were being raided one by one, his network scrutinized, his men hunted. For the first time, the system that had always protected Vikas Dubey had turned against him. But Dubey wasn't done yet. He had spent a lifetime outmanoeuvring the law. Everywhere the police went, they found nothing but empty rooms, erased footprints and silence. And Dubey still had one last escape plan.

By Friday afternoon, the weight of the Bikru massacre had sent shockwaves through UP and beyond. A gang of criminals had slaughtered eight policemen in cold blood, mutilated their bodies and vanished into the night with looted police weapons. The sheer audacity of the ambush was unlike anything seen before, shaking the entire law enforcement apparatus to its core. It wasn't just an attack on the police – it was also an attack on the authority of the state itself.

Realizing the magnitude of the crisis, UP Chief Minister (CM) Yogi Adityanath rushed to Kanpur on Friday, meeting the grieving families of the slain officers. Grim-faced, his voice steeled with resolve, he announced financial assistance of ₹1 crore for each bereaved family. But money alone wasn't justice.

He promised government jobs to one member from each victim's family and an extraordinary pension to secure their future.

'The government stands with you,' Adityanath assured the families. 'Justice will be done, and those responsible will be punished as per the law.'[3]

The ambush had left the administration humiliated. A gangster had outmanoeuvred and massacred the police on their own turf, exposing the deep-rooted nexus between crime and law enforcement. This wasn't just a case of one fugitive on the run – it was also a full-blown institutional crisis. Yogi Adityanath made it clear: this wouldn't go unanswered.

But inside the police force, there was no time for speeches. For Prashant Kumar and his team, words meant nothing without action. The hunt for Vikas Dubey had begun.

By the time 4 July rolled around, thirty-six hours had passed since the Bikru massacre, but Vikas Dubey was still missing. The scale of his escape was an insult to law enforcement. Fifty officers had gone to arrest him, and now, twenty-five police teams from forty stations across seventy-five districts were hunting him down. Every second he remained free was another blow to the system.

The police already had their suspicions – someone on the inside had betrayed them. By Saturday morning, those fears gained ground. Vinay Tiwari, the Station Officer of Chaubeypur Police Station, was suspended and arrested on charges of tipping off Vikas Dubey about the impending police raid. Investigators alleged that one phone call from him gave Dubey just enough time to orchestrate the ambush that claimed eight policemen. While the investigation was ongoing, the arrest sent a clear signal that internal complicity was no longer going to be ignored.[4]

Investigators grilled Tiwari and other suspected insiders at the STF headquarters. The evidence was damning. Call records placed Dubey in contact with twenty-four policemen, some of whom had conveniently vanished after the ambush. He wasn't protected – he was embedded in the system.

The interrogation of one of Dubey's aides, Dayashankar Agnihotri, revealed a chilling sequence of events. Dubey had received a call – likely from the police station itself – just minutes before the officers reached Bikru village. With military precision, he had summoned twenty-five to thirty of his men, positioning them near a garden on the outskirts of the village. The police never stood a chance.

As the bodies of the slain officers were given a tearful farewell, the Kanpur administration sent its own message. When the police stormed Dubey's house in Kanpur, they weren't expecting to find a fortress straight out of a war zone. But inside, buried beneath the concrete, was a fully stocked underground bunker.

Kanpur Inspector General (IG) Mohit Agarwal described the site as less of a home and more of a war zone – piles of weapons, explosives and ammunition stacked like a private armoury braced for siege. This wasn't a hideout built for escape. It was a battlefield command post. Forensic teams found evidence that between 200 and 300 rounds had been fired during the Bikru ambush, a scale of firepower rarely seen in civilian confrontations. Dubey, it was now clear, hadn't envisioned himself as just another gangster. He had cast himself as a warlord, prepared not to flee but to fight.

The illusion of that warlord began to collapse when Shashikant, a close aide of Dubey and one of the twenty-one accused in the 3 July ambush, was arrested. Acting on his confession, police recovered two looted service weapons from Bikru village – an AK-47 rifle hidden inside Dubey's house, and an INSAS rifle from Shashikant's home nearby. At a press briefing, ADG,

Law and Order, Prashant Kumar confirmed the breakthrough. 'The weapons were recovered based on information given by Shashikant during interrogation,' he told reporters. 'He admitted to his role in the attack on our policemen in Bikru.' The cache didn't just mark the recovery of arms, it also marked the beginning of justice, one weapon at a time.

On Saturday morning, bulldozers rolled into Bikru village. What had once been Dubey's fortress-like mansion – a symbol of unchecked power and impunity – was reduced to rubble. But this was no act of retaliation; it was a calculated move rooted in hard intelligence. Forensic teams had uncovered weapons, explosives and looted police firearms concealed within the structure and buried in walls, basements and underground cavities. The house had functioned not as a residence but as a fortified command centre – stockpiled, barricaded and battle-ready. With every room designed to aid resistance and every layer hiding instruments of terror, the demolition wasn't symbolic – it was strategic. Dubey had built a war machine. The state had come to dismantle it, brick by brick.

Even as the state went after Dubey, his own mother had already given up on him. Seated in her house in Lucknow, the don's mother, Sarla Devi, faced the media, her voice carrying none of the defiance that had once surrounded her son's name. There was no denial, no excuse – only resignation. 'He has done a terrible thing. He has killed innocent policemen.' Her voice wavered, but her words were firm. 'If the police find him, they should kill him. If he is caught, they should still kill him. My son should be punished.'[5]

It was a mother's curse, a final condemnation of a son who had become a monster.

She revealed the truth behind his rise – how politics had turned him into a criminal, how his obsession with power led him into the underworld. He had once dreamt of becoming an MLA, she said. But his real path had been written in blood.

'I haven't met him in four months. I live with my younger son now,' she added. 'He has brought nothing but shame to this family.'[6]

As 4 July came to an end, the search for Dubey had intensified. Some reports suggested he was planning to surrender in court, but there was no confirmation. Others feared he had fled to Nepal. The only certainty was that his time was running out.

The hunt for Vikas Dubey was now a war on multiple fronts – against his men, his informants and the corrupt officers who had shielded him for years. Every new piece of evidence pointed to the deep rot inside the system, revealing how Dubey had turned the police force itself into his safety net.

In the early hours of Sunday, 5 July, Dayashankar Agnihotri, one of Dubey's closest aides, was cornered and arrested in a pre-dawn raid in Kanpur. Under intense interrogation, he spilled the truth everyone had suspected but couldn't prove – Dubey had received a tip-off minutes before the police arrived in Bikru.

And then came the confirmation. 'It was Vinay Tiwari, the station officer.[7] He warned Dubey about the raid,' Agnihotri admitted. The man who was supposed to lead the operation had sold them out. The betrayal had cost eight officers their lives. Now, the police were finally turning their guns on their own.

The fallout of the Bikru massacre was now visible in the streets and in the very soil of Vikas Dubey's empire. The same earthmover that had been used by his gang to block the police raid on 3 July was now being used to wipe out his existence.

By Sunday morning, a large police contingent surrounded Dubey's mansion in Bikru village, ensuring that nothing and no one could interfere. The district administration had given the orders: his house was to be demolished. This was not about destroying property, it was about dismantling a legacy built on fear, corruption and murder.

Before the bulldozers tore through the walls, authorities evicted Dubey's father and a domestic help, ensuring there were no human casualties. Then, under the watchful eyes of heavily armed officers, the mansion crumbled to the ground, brick by brick, floor by floor.

The message was clear. There would be no shrine to Vikas Dubey. No monument to his power. No safe haven for his return. His empire had begun to fall. And he was next.

By Monday morning on 6 July, the UP Police moved quickly to contain the damage. Three more officers were suspended, bringing the total to four. Two sub-inspectors and a constable were also removed from duty after suspicions that they had leaked operational details to Dubey. Meanwhile, an explosive letter surfaced – one that could have prevented the entire massacre had it been taken seriously.

It was a damning report allegedly written by DSP Devendra Mishra months before he was killed. In the letter, Mishra had directly accused Vinay Tiwari of protecting Dubey. If the system had acted on it months ago, the eight officers might still have been alive. Now, it was too late.[8]

With corrupt officers being purged, the police force was now singularly focused on tracking down Dubey himself. There was only one problem. He had disappeared. Fearing that Dubey had already left the state, the UP Police launched a statewide alert. Posters with Dubey's face were plastered across toll plazas, highways and railway stations. The bounty on him was raised from ₹1 lakh to ₹2.5 lakh, making it clear that this was no longer a manhunt – it was an all-out war. Photographs and identities of fifteen key gang members were circulated across UP, ensuring no one could hide.

By Monday night, the police had one certainty – Vikas Dubey was running out of places to hide. The system that had once protected him was now hunting him down. The endgame was near.

For the UP Police, it was no longer just about hunting Vikas Dubey, it was also about cleansing the force that had enabled him for years. By Tuesday, Chaubeypur Police Station was dismantled in one sweeping action. All sixty-eight personnel from the station – the very unit that should have acted against Dubey long ago but instead shielded him – were shunted to the reserve police lines. In a rare move, an entire police station was disbanded over corruption allegations linked to a single criminal. The message was unmistakable: every officer who had abetted Dubey's reign of terror would be held accountable.

Even as the UP Police purged their own ranks, they continued tightening the noose around Dubey's remaining associates. On 7 July, three more individuals connected to Dubey's operations were arrested, further weakening his network. With each arrest, the walls were closing in on him.

The Bikru ambush had exposed a rot that ran deep – reaching not just constables and inspectors but also officers at senior levels of the force. By Tuesday, the crackdown expanded beyond the lower ranks. Anant Deo, who was serving as the deputy inspector general (DIG) of the STF on the day of the ambush, was transferred to the Provincial Armed Constabulary (PAC) in Moradabad. The move signalled that even senior officers were not above scrutiny. Anant's earlier tenure as SSP Kanpur had coincided with the period when Vikas Dubey's criminal empire was allowed to grow unchecked. Though no direct link was officially established, the transfer – and the long suspension that followed – left little doubt: the state was willing to hold senior officials accountable for institutional failures that enabled Dubey's reign.[9]

By now, Dubey was no longer just a fugitive – he was the most wanted man in India. His allies were being picked off, his political backing was crumbling, and the police force that once shielded him had turned into his greatest threat. The endgame was near. And by this time the next day, his face would be all over the news again.

On 8 July 2020, in Hamirpur, the UP STF made its first major strike. Amar Dubey, Vikas Dubey's shadow, bodyguard and most trusted enforcer, was cornered. He was more than an aide – he was the man who always carried Dubey's weapons, the executioner who pulled the trigger when the dreaded gangster didn't want to get his hands dirty. He had been there on 3 July, standing on the rooftops, firing down on the unsuspecting police officers in Bikru village. The STF had been tracking him for days, and when they finally cut off his escape route in Hamirpur, there was no negotiating. The encounter was swift. Gunshots. A body in the dirt.

The same day, the Haryana Police arrested one of Dubey's close aides in Faridabad, a man who had sheltered him in Sector 87 while the net was tightening. The police raided Sri Sasaram Hotel in Badkhal Chowk, where CCTV footage had captured Dubey's presence. But by the time they arrived, he was gone. The digital video recording (DVR) of the security footage was seized, leaving no doubt that Dubey was slipping through their fingers. But not for much longer.

Back in UP, the STF turned its sights inward. The investigation had uncovered the ugly truth: Dubey had moles inside the very force hunting him. As a result, Vinay Tiwari and Bikru beat in-charge K.K. Sharma were arrested and placed under interrogation.

In Madhya Pradesh, the STF made another move, detaining Dubey's brother-in-law, Raju Nigam, in Shahdol district. His foot soldiers were either dead or behind bars, his enforcers eliminated, his informants exposed. The noose was tightening.

Roadblocks. Raids. A relentless pursuit. Yet Dubey moved like a phantom, always a step ahead. From Kanpur, he had reportedly vanished in Shivli, hiding at an aide's house before slipping into Faridabad. The police were closing in, but he wasn't ready to be caught – not yet. Using a fake ID under the name Shubham, he crossed state lines, dodging police cordons and melting into the streets of Rajasthan. By the time authorities got their first real lead, he was already in Ujjain, Madhya Pradesh.

Ujjain, home to the sacred Shree Mahakaleshwar Temple, is a place of redemption for many. But for Vikas Dubey, it became the stage for his final act. He didn't sneak in under cover of darkness. He didn't attempt to disguise himself. Instead, on 9 July, he walked into the temple like a man with nothing to lose, head held high, arrogance still intact. He bought a VIP pass for ₹250 to skip the lines, showing security a second fake ID – this time under the name Naveen Pal. The deception might have worked had he not made a fatal mistake.

As he adjusted his mask, a flower vendor caught a glimpse of his face. There was something familiar, something unnerving about the way the man carried himself. The vendor alerted the temple guards, who kept a close eye on him. The moment they approached him, Dubey tried to bluff his way out. 'My name is Shubham,' he claimed. Then, 'I'm Naveen Pal.' But his words wavered, and his eyes darted around looking for an escape. The security team wasn't buying it. They stalled him and called the police, and as the first officer arrived, Dubey finally stopped running.

His voice, when he spoke, wasn't fearful. It wasn't panicked. It was defiant. *'Main Vikas Dubey hun, Kanpur-wala.* (I'm Kanpur's Vikas Dubey.)'

It wasn't a confession; it was a challenge – a final, arrogant display from a man who had spent his life defying the law. The police took no chances. Within minutes, he was in custody, surrounded by heavily armed officers, flashbulbs bursting as cameras captured the moment. The most wanted man in India had just walked into his own capture.

As the news of his arrest spread, debate erupted. Had he truly been caught? Or had he staged a surrender, knowing that a courtroom battle might be his only way out? Some said he had run out of allies. Others whispered that a deal had been struck in the shadows – that he was safer in police custody than roaming free.

The border between Madhya Pradesh and UP had turned into a theatre of high-stakes transfer. On one side stood the Madhya Pradesh Police, holding custody of Vikas Dubey, the most wanted man in India. On the other, a contingent of the UP STF was waiting to bring him home. But this wasn't a quiet, procedural handover. The air buzzed with tension. News crews, camera vans and SUVs packed with journalists had swarmed the border, turning the area into a media battleground.

The legal formalities of inter-state handover were hurriedly completed. But the real concern for the UP Police wasn't paperwork, it was visibility. The transfer was supposed to mark the arrival of justice. Instead, it became a rolling spectacle. The convoy carrying Dubey barely crossed into UP before the chase began. News vehicles tailed them relentlessly, headlights slicing through the dark, broadcasting every bump and turn in real time. From toll plazas to narrow highways, the gangster's return was no longer a matter of law. It had become live theatre.

At several points along the journey, the convoy tried to shake off its followers. Police vehicles blocked roads, seized car keys and created diversions, but the media kept catching up. At one bypass, a chase turned aggressive, with a high-speed vehicle nearly colliding with a press car. The roadblocks became more frequent. Reasons varied: routine checks, COVID-19 protocols, 'orders from above'. Yet none could hide the fact that the police seemed more concerned with the cameras than the man in their custody.

And then, the script flipped.

In the early morning of 10 July, the monsoon rain had turned the highway slick. As the STF convoy carrying Vikas Dubey entered Sachendi, on the outskirts of Kanpur, the nightmarish chase that had gripped India for a week was about to reach its violent conclusion. According to official accounts, it all started with a herd of cattle suddenly rushing onto the highway. The driver of the vehicle carrying Dubey swerved sharply, lost control and hit a cement divider. The car turned over, skidding onto its side.

For a moment, everything was still. Then chaos exploded. Taking advantage of the confusion, Dubey crawled out of the overturned vehicle, snatched a service pistol from injured Inspector Ramakant Pachauri and made a desperate dash towards an unpaved road. The STF officers in the vehicles behind rushed forward, shouting for him to surrender. But Dubey, a man who had spent his entire life defying the law, wasn't going to be captured alive. He turned, raised the stolen pistol and opened fire. Bullets cracked through the rain-soaked air. Two STF officers went down – Constables Shivendra Singh Sengar and Vimal Yadav – hit by Dubey's gunfire. Special Task Force DSP Tej Bahadur Singh, leading the chase, barked orders – this was no longer an arrest, it was a fight for survival. The police retaliated, unleashing a volley of bullets. Dubey staggered. A bullet struck his leg. Then another tore into his torso. He stumbled, his body collapsing onto the wet ground.

The man who had once walked into a police station and shot a minister in cold blood, the man who had ruled Kanpur's underworld with impunity, the man who had massacred eight policemen in an ambush was now lying in the mud, his blood mixing with the rain.

The police wasted no time in declaring Dubey dead. Inspector General Mohit Agarwal confirmed the news first. 'Gangster Vikas Dubey was killed in an encounter when he tried to flee after a road accident.'[10] Kanpur SP (West) Anil Kumar echoed the same statement. 'The gangster fired at the police. He was injured in retaliatory firing and died during treatment.'[11] It was textbook police procedure – except no one believed it.

Within minutes, social media erupted with conspiracy theories and allegations. Had Dubey really tried to run? Or had the chase, the spectacle, the pressure and the stakes become too heavy to let him speak another word? Why had only one vehicle overturned while the rest of the convoy remained intact? Why wasn't Dubey handcuffed if he was such a high-risk fugitive? How did a man who had supposedly 'surrendered' in Ujjain suddenly attempt an escape? Was this an encounter or an execution? Opposition leaders wasted no time in attacking the UP government. Congress leader Priyanka Gandhi Vadra hinted at a cover-up, questioning whether justice had been served or evidence had been erased. Jitin Prasada tweeted: 'People expect justice, not revenge.'[12] The debate raged on. The encounter that was supposed to bring closure had only opened more questions.

Amid the storm of criticism, Prashant Kumar stepped forward. Speaking to the press, he was unapologetic, direct and firm. 'The encounter was unavoidable,' he stated. 'Dubey fired at our men first. He injured two of our officers. What should we have done – stood there and let him kill more policemen?' He dismissed accusations of a staged killing, emphasizing that Dubey had already killed eight policemen just days earlier. His intent was clear. 'The police have done their job,' he declared, adding that the matter would also be probed by the People's Union for Civil Liberties (PUCL).

There would be no remorse. No regrets. The state had made its final move. Vikas Dubey was dead. His criminal empire had been crushed. But the questions he left behind would haunt India for years to come.

The killing of Vikas Dubey should have closed the book on contemporary India's most feared gangsters. Instead, it opened a Pandora's box of controversy, splitting the country into two fiercely opposing camps – those who saw justice and those who saw a cover-up. By the time the news broke, reactions poured in from across the political spectrum.

Critics wasted no time questioning the legitimacy of the encounter. Sharad Yadav of the Loktantrik Janata Dal (LJD) dismissed it as a staged execution, arguing that Dubey had been silenced before he could expose his political and police protectors. Akhilesh Yadav called the encounter an attempt to protect those in power, claiming that the car didn't topple – rather, the truth was buried before it could topple the government. Trinamool Congress (TMC) MP Mahua Moitra denounced UP's 'encounter raj', insisting that justice was the only thing truly killed that morning. Karti Chidambaram from Tamil Nadu went further, branding the UP Police as India's biggest mob, headed by a don. Former Jammu and Kashmir Chief Minister Omar Abdullah summed up the scepticism in one chilling phrase: 'Dead men tell no tales.'[13]

While Opposition leaders demanded accountability, many celebrated Dubey's end as overdue justice. Constable Ajay Kashyap, who had survived the Bikru ambush, admitted that the encounter brought him peace. Tirath Pal, father of slain constable Jitendra Pal Singh, expressed pride in the UP Police, stating that his son's sacrifice had not been in vain. Manoj Shukla, brother of murdered Bharatiya Janata Party (BJP) minister Santosh Shukla, said that it had taken nineteen years for justice to be served, but at last, it had been done.

Amidst the storm of controversy and political noise, Prashant stood his ground like a battle-hardened officer unfazed by the firestorm around him. Facing a media frenzy dissecting every moment of Vikas Dubey's encounter, he remained unyielding. 'The encounter was both general and genuine,' he declared with measured precision, shutting down whispers of foul play. His words weren't a defence. They were a statement of intent. 'Two of our officers sustained injuries while trying to contain Dubey, while five policemen were hurt in the accident.' The message was clear: this wasn't an orchestrated takedown but an unavoidable outcome of a gangster's last stand.

Anticipating the inevitable scrutiny from rights groups and Opposition leaders, Prashant Kumar ensured every protocol was followed to the letter. 'We have already informed the National Human Rights Commission and the State Human Rights Commission about the entire incident,' he stated, pre-empting allegations of extrajudicial action. There would be no loose ends, no gaps in the narrative that could be exploited.

Beyond the dust of the encounter, the real war continued. The killing of eight policemen in Bikru had set off a relentless crackdown, and Prashant made it clear that it wouldn't stop with Dubey's death. 'We are investigating the circumstances that led to the massacre of our officers. Twelve of his henchmen are still at large, and raids are being conducted to track them down. We will gather all evidence, file chargesheets and fast-track the legal process,' he asserted. The hunt wasn't over – it was just entering its next phase.

As the political fallout deepened, it was clear that the encounter wasn't just about the death of a gangster. It had turned into a battleground over governance, policing, and law and order. Congress leader Rahul Gandhi, in a cryptic statement, hinted that Dubey's silence spoke louder than the encounter itself. Bahujan Samaj Party (BSP) Chief Mayawati called for a Supreme Court-monitored probe, arguing that the entire case – from the Kanpur ambush to Dubey's death – needed to be independently investigated. Former Madhya Pradesh Chief Minister Kamal Nath questioned the authenticity of the police's claims, pointing out inconsistencies in the narrative and reminding everyone that Lord Mahakal never spared sinners.

As television channels dissected every frame of the encounter and Twitter (now X) battles raged, the truth remained as elusive as Dubey himself had been in life. Had the encounter been an execution to protect powerful figures, or was it the only way to end the reign of a gangster who had outlived the law for too long? The country remained divided. But one thing was certain: Vikas Dubey was gone. And with him, so were his secrets.

Vikas Dubey was not just a gangster, he was a phenomenon that thrived in the dark underbelly of UP's crime-infested politics. His rise was no accident. It was enabled by gaps in the system that was meant to contain him. He wasn't a lone wolf but a kingpin who built an empire of crime under the protection of political patronage and administrative inaction, while institutions around him struggled or failed to stop his ascent.

Born in Chaubeypur, Kanpur, Dubey grew up watching violence, corruption and political manoeuvring play out like a scripted drama. But unlike others, he refused to remain a spectator. His first act of defiance came in 1990, when a mere street brawl over an insult to his father ended with broken bones and police detention. He was just a teenager then, but even at that age, he understood the rules of survival in UP's hinterlands: fear is the ultimate currency, and power comes to those who dare.

Back then, Dubey didn't just get out of custody. He walked out without even a first information report (FIR) being registered. Why? Because he had already found his first godfathers in local politics – men who saw potential in his raw aggression and willingness to cross the lines others wouldn't. They didn't set him free out of kindness; they invested in him as an asset. A man who could settle scores, silence rivals and deliver votes was more useful than a loyal party worker.

By the early 1990s, he had built a loyal army of thugs, each one more ruthless than the last. Murder became a business transaction – one sanctioned by those who controlled power. By 1992, he was already a known name in Kanpur's underworld, facing his first murder charge. But that didn't slow him down. In every arrest, there was a bail. In every court case, a missing witness. In every crime, a loophole.

Dubey understood the game better than most. He didn't just use muscle power, he also played the political board like a grandmaster. He never aligned himself with just one party. He was a mercenary, shifting loyalties depending on who could offer him better protection.

His first major political mentor was Hari Krishna Srivastava, a seasoned politician who moved effortlessly between the Janata Dal, the BJP and the BSP – just like Dubey would later switch alliances to suit his needs. Under Srivastava's shadow, he learned how crime and politics were two sides of the same coin. By the mid-1990s, he officially entered politics, becoming a BSP member while still running a network of extortion, land grabbing and contract killings. By 2000, he wasn't just feared, he was also a necessity for those in power.[14]

The police knew who Dubey was. His criminal activities weren't hidden in the shadows. He operated in broad daylight, with the state machinery watching in silence.

He ruled over dozens of villages in Kanpur Dehat with the kind of absolute authority that elected officials could only dream of. He wasn't just a gangster, he was also the unofficial government. In these areas, there were no land deals, no elections, no police postings without his approval. His rise mirrored the era of UP's crime lords – men like Mukhtar Ansari, Atiq Ahmed and many more who had blurred the lines between gangsters and politicians. But Dubey was different.

While others used fear, he also used caste politics to his advantage. As a Brahmin strongman, he positioned himself as a protector for upper-caste interests. This wasn't about personal power – it was a caste-backed legitimacy that made it even harder for the state to move against him.

The moment that cemented Dubey's status as a legend came in 2001, when he murdered Santosh Shukla, a minister in the Rajnath Singh-led BJP government, inside a police station. Shukla had been a rising political rival and made the mistake of challenging Dubey's authority. He thought the law would protect him. It didn't.

On 11 November 2001, Shukla was chased into Shivli Police Station, begging for protection. But Vikas Dubey walked in after him, guns blazing. Twenty-five policemen stood frozen as bullets ripped through Shukla's body. Dubey walked out calmly, stepping over his victim's lifeless body. Not a single officer stopped him. Fear had already done its job.

A year later, he surrendered – only to be released on bail. During the trial, witnesses disappeared, evidence vanished and he was acquitted. This wasn't just a crime, it was also a statement. Dubey had proven that he was more powerful than the law itself.

For the next two decades, he operated as both a mafia boss and a political strategist. He controlled elections in his stronghold of Bikru and surrounding areas. No one contested without his approval. He decided who won and who lost. Even when he wasn't on the ballot, his men were.

From 2000 to 2015, he controlled the zilla panchayat seat of Ghimau, ensuring that his loyalists won unopposed. When the seat was reserved for women in 2015, he simply got his wife Richa Dubey elected without opposition. There were no campaigns, no speeches – just a message: vote for Richa or don't vote at all.

Dubey's greatest weapon was not a gun but his influence. Over 150 criminal cases were filed, yet he walked free every time. He had political backing from every major party at different times – BSP, Samajwadi Party and even BJP leaders sought his help. A network of corrupt police officers, judges and bureaucrats ensured he was never behind bars for long.

Fear controlled his territories where people whispered his name but never spoke against him.

His criminal enterprise was built on land-grabbing, extortion and political deals. No business ran, no land changed hands without his blessing.

By 2018, he had set his sights on contesting the 2022 UP Assembly elections. He had manipulated the system for decades, and now he wanted to legitimize his power. His gang was laying the groundwork for his political career, and he was negotiating entry into the BJP. Dubey was a gangster who had become the system, and that was what made him so feared, so brutal, so untouchable.

Long after Vikas Dubey's blood soaked into the highway, long after the debates dimmed and the outrage cooled, the most awaited verdict came not from politicians or prime-time anchors but from a courtroom. A three-member judicial commission set up by the Supreme Court and headed by retired Supreme Court Judge B.S. Chauhan, submitted an 825-page report that cut through the noise.[15]

The commission delivered two damning conclusions. First, that the ambush at Bikru village, in which eight police personnel, including a DSP were killed, was made possible by an entrenched nexus – Dubey had advance warning of the police raid, thanks to insiders within Chaubeypur Police Station. Officers who were supposed to lead the crackdown had in fact enabled the massacre. The report cited a 'total failure' of the intelligence unit in Kanpur in collecting information about Dubey's criminal activities and possession of sophisticated weapons, legal and illegal. The thirty-eight to forty officers who reached Bikru were ill-prepared: only eighteen were armed, the rest carried sticks, and only few wore bulletproof vests.

Second, the commission ruled that the encounter in which Dubey was killed was not fake. The post-mortem, conducted by Dr R.S. Mishra, confirmed that the bullet wounds were consistent with the police version – that they had fired in self-defence.

The commission noted that no independent eyewitness or member of the media had come forward to contradict this version. Richa Dubey had filed an affidavit calling the incident a fake encounter but had failed to appear before the panel. As such, there was no evidence filed in rebuttal.

Perhaps the most damning revelation in the report was the extent of systemic collapse. The commission confirmed that Vikas Dubey had long enjoyed the patronage of the police, revenue and administrative machinery. Authorities had helped him acquire arms licenses, passports, land and even ration shop permits in brazen violation of statutory rules. Some had maintained very good relations with him, despite his long history of serious criminal activity.

The report also exposed how justice was repeatedly denied. Cases against Dubey and his associates were never properly investigated. Government advocates never sincerely opposed his bail in court. In fact, the commission stated there was nothing on record to show that his cases had ever been contested seriously. The investigation into the murder of Santosh Shukla, a minister of state, was described as 'a total farce'.

While some depositions alleged Dubey's political ties to leaders from the Samajwadi Party and BSP, the commission noted that these claims were based on hearsay and media reports. No personal knowledge was presented to confirm political patronage. In the end, the commission's conclusion was unambiguous: Vikas Dubey was not an aberration. He was a monster built and shielded by the system. And when that same system finally turned on him, it acted within the bounds of the law.

With Vikas Dubey's encounter, the UP Police had sent a clear message to the underworld. In Prashant Kumar's words, 'Policemen are not being given arms just for decoration.' But crime in UP was not a one-man endeavour. It was a web, a tangle of politics, power and patronage, with many more kingpins still lurking in the shadows. Some scoffed at his declaration, believing the system would continue to protect them. Others, more cautious, began to watch their backs.

Yet in the underbelly of this lawless landscape, a new storm was brewing. The police had drawn first blood, but the underworld was ready to strike back.

The game was far from over.

2
The Infallible: End of Atiq Ahmed

The streets of Prayagraj (previously Allahabad) pulsed with tension as a convoy of police vehicles rumbled through narrow lanes, their flashing red-and-blue lights slicing through the darkness like warnings of impending doom. The atmosphere was dense with the scent of exhaust and dust, and the lingering traces of spice and oil from food stalls that had long since closed. At the centre of the procession, two figures moved forward, their white clothing standing in stark contrast to the night – Atiq Ahmed and his brother Ashraf.

Atiq, clad in an all-white kurta-pajama with a Pathani-style white turban wrapped tightly around his head, looked visibly drained, his face lined with the exhaustion of a man whose world had begun to crumble around him. Yet there was something defiant in his gait, something stubborn in the way his eyes darted at the swarm of media surrounding him. Beside him, Ashraf wore a black T-shirt with olive-green trousers and a matching white Pathani-style turban, his expression a grim mask, his lips pressed tightly together. The two walked side by side, their wrists shackled in steel, the glint of the metal reflecting the occasional camera flash.

Around them, journalists jostled for position, their cameras raised high, microphones pushed forward, their voices colliding into a cacophony of questions. Atiq and Ashraf had to push through the relentless swarm of media personnel, bombarded by an endless barrage of inquiries – some shouted, others murmured – all blending into a chaotic din. The flashing lights of cameras blinded them momentarily, their faces captured in every grim detail by the relentless press. The sodium-vapour streetlights cast long, exaggerated shadows, distorting figures, making them appear ghostly. The scene was surreal – two feared men, once kings of the underworld, reduced to prisoners paraded under the scrutiny of rolling news cameras. And yet even in their downfall, there was a sense that they did not entirely belong here. They had ruled these streets for decades, instilling terror, dictating who lived and who died.

The entrance to the Colvin Hospital in Prayagraj loomed ahead, a dull, yellow glow emanating from its old, weathered facade. The police escort tightened its grip, guiding the two men towards the entrance for their mandatory medical examination, a routine yet ominous procedure for prisoners of their stature. The crowd thickened. Among them, three young men edged closer, appearing every bit like professional reporters – badges proclaiming 'PRESS' prominently displayed on their chests, cameras slung over their shoulders, microphones in hand.

As they neared Atiq and Ashraf, the media bombardment intensified. '*Kuch kehna chahenge aap*? (Would you like to say something?)' one journalist shouted, shoving a microphone towards them. Another pressed, '*Aap log janaaze pe nahi gaye the*? (Why didn't you attend your son's funeral?)' Ashraf remained silent, his face expressionless, refusing to acknowledge the questions. But Atiq, ever the defiant figure, retained his attitude. With his mouth filled with gutkha, he smirked and muttered, '*Ab nahi gaye toh nahi gaye!* (So what if we didn't go?),' his voice thick and garbled. The response, casual yet loaded with arrogance, only fuelled the media frenzy further, as cameras flashed. The three disguised assassins manoeuvred even closer, waiting for the perfect moment to strike.

And then time fractured.

Like a scene out of a thriller, a gun-toting hand entered the frame from the right side, just millimetres away from Atiq's head. In an instant, his turban was knocked off, spinning away as the deafening crack of the first gunshot shattered the night, leaving everyone around speechless.

Atiq barely had time to react before the first bullet slammed into his head, his skull snapping back from the impact of the Turkish-made Zigana F semi-automatic pistol. His body jerked violently, his white kurta instantly blooming with red, life draining from his eyes even before his knees buckled. His body crumpled forward, hitting the cold pavement; his turban slipped from his head, exposing his damp, greying hair.

Beside him, Ashraf turned sharply, his face a mask of horror as he instinctively flinched. His lips parted – perhaps to scream, perhaps to call his brother's name – but the second bullet silenced him before he could make a sound. His black T-shirt absorbed the dark stain of death, his body staggering for half a second before collapsing next to his brother. A final shot ensured there would be no survivors.

The entire execution unfolded in seconds. The air, once filled with the frenzied clamour of reporters, was now suspended in stunned silence.

Then, chaos erupted. A cacophony of shouts, screams and gunfire filled the air, merging into an indistinguishable roar.

At least one of the shooters bellowed '*Jai Shri Ram*', perhaps to garner public sympathy in a state where such chants resonated deeply. The rapid succession of gunshots drowned out everything else, their relentless blasts echoing off the hospital walls. In the confusion, no one could determine who had spoken, who had fired first or how many bullets had been unleashed. The only certainty was the grim finality of the attack.

Police officers lunged forward, their weapons drawn belatedly, but the killers had already raised their hands in surrender. The young assassins stood motionless, their expressions eerily composed, as if they had simply completed a task. Their blood-splattered clothes clung to their bodies, their eyes unblinking, their hands steady. The police wrestled them down, pinning them to the ground as the first officers on the scene barked urgent commands into their radios.

The cameras had captured everything.

Atiq Ahmed, who had eluded justice for decades, was executed along with his brother Ashraf in full view of the world, in a manner more brutal, more theatrical than anything even their worst enemies could have envisioned.

The crime scene was instantly sealed off, yet the crowd surged forward, desperate to glimpse the fallen don. Forensic teams rushed in, their gloved hands reaching for the discarded microphones-turned-murder-weapons and the dummy cameras left abandoned on the ground. The realization dawned too late – the assassins had never been journalists. Their press IDs were fake, their cameras hollow props. They had walked straight into the most secure police perimeter in Prayagraj and executed two among India's most feared criminals at point-blank range.

Blood had begun to pool on the uneven concrete, dark and thick, seeping into the cracks as if the ground itself sought to consume the remnants of two lives that had been steeped in crime. A police constable, Maan Singh, clutched his injured hand, a minor wound sustained in the melee, but his eyes were locked on the bodies. He, like everyone else present, knew that history had just been rewritten before his eyes.

The killers – later identified as Lavlesh Tiwari, Sunny and Arun Maurya – were dragged away, their faces eerily blank. There was no regret, no remorse. The audacity of their act had stunned even the police officers handling them. Had they been sent by someone? Had they acted alone? Was this retribution or a carefully orchestrated coup?

The response was swift and merciless. Uttar Pradesh was plunged into a state of high alert.

Section 144 was imposed immediately. The city's streets, which had just moments ago witnessed an execution in real time, were now crawling with riot police, their shields up, batons ready. The Rapid Action Force (RAF) was deployed across sensitive zones, an acknowledgment that this assassination could ignite something far bigger.

In Lucknow, Chief Minister Yogi Adityanath convened an emergency meeting, summoning the highest-ranking police officials to his residence. Prashant Kumar arrived at the command centre, the tension in the air suffocating. This was not just an execution, it was a statement, a declaration that the rules had changed, that those who once wielded power with impunity could be erased at a moment's notice.

Meanwhile, the bodies of Atiq and Ashraf were transported to the morgue, the cold, clinical environment a sharp contrast to the bloody chaos of their final moments. In the corridors of power, discussions swirled: Who had truly orchestrated this? Was this justice, revenge or something even more sinister?

For decades, Atiq Ahmed had been the nightmare of UP, a man whose empire had thrived on fear, extortion and political manipulation. He had walked through life believing he was untouchable, escaping conviction time and again, manoeuvring through the cracks of the legal system. But in the end, the law had not claimed him. The courts had not condemned him. Bullets had. And they had done so in the most public, most spectacular way possible.

As his lifeless body lay in a freezer at the mortuary, the world outside debated his fate. Some called it karma. Some called it a hit job. Others saw it as a new chapter in the ever-evolving power struggle of India's criminal and political underbelly.

Had justice been served, or had something far more dangerous been set in motion? Because if a man as powerful as Atiq Ahmed could be executed in police custody, under the full glare of live cameras, one question loomed larger than all the rest: who was truly in control?

They weren't journalists chasing a scoop. They were executioners in disguise, trained, composed and charged with a suicidal kind of courage, the kind that belongs more to fanatics than contract killers. The weapons they carried – Turkish-made Zigana F semi-automatic pistols – weren't just rare, they were designed for operations. Each capable of firing fifteen rounds of 9 mm bullets in a single burst and costing upwards of ₹6 lakh in India, these were not local street guns. The inner story later revealed that the weapons had made their way in from Punjab, allegedly trafficked via drone drops from across the Pakistan border – a known route for drugs and arms smuggling.

According to sources, all signs pointed to the Lawrence Bishnoi network. They claimed a trusted lieutenant in his syndicate had handed out the contract. The mission: kill Atiq Ahmed. And when the trigger was finally pulled, it was done under the glare of live television, in full view of the world. The man who once held UP in a chokehold, who had ministers on speed dial and the

The Infallible: End of Atiq Ahmed 33

police at his feet, was silenced by men no one had heard of, using weapons no one was supposed to have, in a plot that felt more like a cinematic ambush than real life. But it was real. And Atiq never saw it coming.

What was the motive? 'To become famous,' the shooters claimed. But then boys from modest backgrounds don't afford Turkish pistols, hotel stays and motorbikes for days. Someone else had clearly funded the killings.

According to the FIR registered at Shahganj Police Station, Atiq Ahmed, in a statement recorded under court orders, had openly confessed to links with Pakistan's ISI and terror outfit Lashkar-e-Taiba (LeT). The statement read like a script from a spy thriller, but every word was deadly real. 'The ISI, using drones, would drop weapons in Punjab. Someone associated with them would collect the cache – some arms went to LeT, some to Khalistani separatists. Weapons like the .45 bore pistol, AK-47s, and even RDX were routed to me ... and I paid for them,' Atiq reportedly told investigators.[16] It wasn't just a confession, it was a crack in the wall, revealing how deeply India's most feared gangster was entrenched in a shadowy cross-border arms network.

The theory was simple and chilling: Atiq had outlived his usefulness. As he got closer to being transferred from Sabarmati to Prayagraj Jail and as investigative agencies circled closer to his alleged foreign-arms connections and massive illegal wealth, someone hit the panic button.

For forty years, he had ruled with an iron grip. His name sent shivers down the spines of cops, judges and rivals alike. He was more than just another UP *bahubali* – he was an empire unto himself: untouchable, invincible. Over a hundred cases shadowed his name, yet the gavel never struck him down. Politicians courted him, the law cowered before him and the streets of UP whispered his legend in fear.

Until now.

On 28 March 2023, a Prayagraj court shattered the illusion of Atiq Ahmed's invincibility, sentencing him to life imprisonment for the 2006 kidnapping of Umesh Pal – a man whose name would become both his obsession and his undoing. But this was no ordinary conviction. This was the first crack in the unbreakable fortress of a man who had built his life on blood, betrayal and absolute power. His downfall had begun, but the nightmare wasn't over yet.

But to understand how a boy born to a *tanga* (horse cart) driver in the forests of Kasari Masari came to command ministers and mobs, you have to go back, back to where it all began, to see how history doesn't just repeat itself … It reloads.

Atiq's affair with crime began in his teenage years, when he drove the car of a local corporator and muscleman, Chand Baba, who doubled as a politician with a Congress ticket. Sitting behind the wheel, watching his boss command fear and loyalty, Atiq began to dream. He didn't want to be like Chand Baba – he wanted to surpass him.

When Chand Baba got the Congress ticket once again, Atiq decided to challenge him, not just politically but also fatally. Contesting as an independent from the same constituency, Atiq knew he wasn't going to win the old-fashioned way. On the night of the vote counting, as numbers rolled in – Chandbaba at No. 1, reportedly with Atiq trailing at No. 2 – he got up from a tea stall, walked into his mentor's den and killed him. That same night, the final count flipped: Atiq won. Locals roared, 'MLA Atiq Ahmed *zindabad!*' The gangster was now an elected leader, and his throne was soaked in blood.

But Atiq wasn't done. Two of Chand Baba's loyalists had fled to Mumbai. He had them dragged back to UP, tortured, skinned alive and dumped in the Kasari Masari jungle – the same patch of earth that had birthed him. Then, with twisted theatre, he called the police and complained about 'dead bodies causing foul smell' in his area. As his power grew, so did his political reach. He aligned with Apna Dal, then the Samajwadi Party. Who could forget the controversial image of Mulayam Singh Yadav shaking hands, not just with Atiq but also with Atiq's dog?

Atiq wasn't winning elections just for himself. He was getting others to win too too, using a mix of fear and loyalty. He was a five-time MLA who then became an MP.

When his MLA seat fell vacant, he wanted his brother Ashraf to contest. But BSP Chief Mayawati had other plans – she picked Raju Pal, once Atiq's deputy. Atiq warned Raju to step aside. The latter didn't. He won, and sealed his fate.

Raju Pal was no innocent. A Class 8 dropout from the Neewa area of Prayagraj, he had risen through the alleys as a local goon before his name began surfacing in police records. By 1992, he had his first criminal case registered. Over the next decade, Raju became a dominant force in Neewa and its surrounding pockets. His circle included hardened criminals, some of whom were close to Atiq's inner network. That proximity brought Raju into Atiq's world, first as a subordinate, later as a challenger.

By 2002, his name had surfaced in two high-profile murder cases, including that of Anees Pehalwan, the father of one of Raju's future killers. Another case involved the killing of his own maternal uncle. By 2004, he had over twenty-five criminal cases to his name, including two for murder. Yet his popularity among his caste group and the command he held over his constituency made him an asset too valuable to ignore. That same year, the BSP handed him a ticket to contest the bypoll for City West, the very seat Atiq had vacated after winning the Lok Sabha seat from Phulpur.

It was a direct confrontation. Atiq fielded his younger brother, Khalid Azeem alias Ashraf, to retain control over the seat. But Raju Pal refused to back down. Behind him stood Atiq's political rivals, including Rizwan Neewa, all united by a common goal: to fracture Atiq's grip on the region. Against all odds, Raju Pal defeated Ashraf. It was more than an electoral loss. It was public humiliation.

Atiq didn't forget. And he certainly didn't forgive.

In the shadows, the plotting began. Sudhanshu Tripathi, better known as Balli Pandit, nursed a personal grudge against Raju, one born of vengeance after Raju allegedly assaulted Balli's father, a Central Bureau of Investigation (CBI) officer. Just two weeks before the eventual assassination, Balli fired on Raju's SUV in a failed attempt. He was arrested and jailed, but the message was clear: Raju Pal had been marked.

When Balli failed, Atiq went bigger. He exploited old rivalries. Mohammad Farhan and Ranjeet Pal – both of whom had their own blood debts to settle with Raju – were recruited. Atiq offered them not just protection but also a common cause. He united vengeance, politics and criminal muscle into one devastating strike.

And then, the hammer fell.

It was just past 3 p.m. on 25 January 2005, when Raju Pal, newly elected BSP MLA from Allahabad West, was driving back to his home in Neewa, Dhoomanganj. He had just stepped out

The Infallible: End of Atiq Ahmed

of the post-mortem department at SRN Hospital, where he had gone to pay respects and show solidarity after the killing of a student from his constituency. With him were two SUVs – one was his own and a second trailed close behind.

Pal was behind the wheel. Beside him sat Rukhsana, the wife of a friend, whom he had offered a ride home. Supporters Sandeep Yadav and Devi Lal occupied the backseat. In the second SUV were Mahendra Patel, Omprakash and Saif – all loyalists from Neewa, Pal's bastion. Each vehicle had a police constable for protection. It wasn't enough.

As the two SUVs crossed Sulemsarai on the Grand Trunk Road, two vehicles closed in – one in front, one behind – cutting off any chance of escape. Before anyone could react, a storm of bullets erupted from all sides. Pal swung open the driver's door and tried to flee. But the shooters were professionals. They pursued him, relentless and focused. Bullets tore through the air – and through Raju Pal. He collapsed. His aides rushed to pull him into a car and drive him to the hospital. But the killers weren't done. As Pal's bleeding body was rushed through the city, the gunmen followed and opened fire again. For nearly 5 km, the chase continued. Before they could reach the hospital, Raju Pal was dead with nineteen bullets in him. But the shooters didn't stop. They continued to fire several rounds into the dead body of Pal.

Ashraf contested the by-elections in the wake of Raju Pal's murder. He won.

A sitting MLA had been assassinated in broad daylight on one of the busiest roads in the city. It was a statement, not simply a murder. And the man everyone suspected of orchestrating it – Atiq Ahmed – was nowhere to be seen.

But the bullet that ended Raju Pal's life did not end the war. It lit a fuse that would burn slowly, insidiously, across years.

Raju was dead, but Umesh Pal lived. He remained the thorn in Atiq's side, the one witness who could bring the don to his knees. He had been kidnapped once, tortured into silence, but he refused to vanish.

Umesh Pal's murder, exactly after eighteen years, wasn't just another event in Atiq Ahmed's blood-soaked empire. Umesh was Raju Pal's younger brother and the last living witness – the final thread tying Atiq to one of the most brazen political assassinations in UP's modern history. Umesh had been kidnapped once, tortured into silence, but he refused to vanish. In the end, though, his murder was a chilling echo of Raju Pal's fate.

On 24 February 2023, the streets of Prayagraj bore witness to an eerie spectacle that would mark the culmination of a vendetta spanning nearly two decades. A CCTV camera captured the harrowing sequence: Umesh stepping out of his white SUV, only to be ambushed by a barrage of bullets and crude bombs. The assailants, identified as members of Atiq Ahmed's gang, executed the attack with military precision. Among them was Asad Ahmed, Atiq's own son, leading the charge alongside notorious operatives like Guddu Muslim, Arman and Sabir.

Nearby, a young girl, startled by the sudden barrage of gunfire, appeared in the frame. She hesitated for a brief moment, watching the horror unfold before her, before running back to alert Umesh's family.

What stood out and horrified viewers across the country was the sight of Guddu Muslim, a master bomb-maker, throwing crude bombs one after another, right in the middle of the street. Witnesses later recalled his chilling words as he shouted, '*Itna bomb phenko taki charo tarf sirf dhuan hi dhuan ho!*' – create smoke all around! The intention was clear: disorient, terrify and ensure no one dared intervene. The narrow bylanes of Sulem Sarai were

The Infallible: End of Atiq Ahmed

blanketed in smoke and panic. And in that engineered chaos, Umesh Pal was finished.

The assailants fled the scene within seconds, leaving behind a trail of bodies and a city gripped by fear. Along with Umesh, his two police gunners were also killed, despite being armed. The attack had been so swift, so meticulously planned, that it left the police scrambling for answers – and suspects.

The murder sent shockwaves through UP, prompting an intense manhunt. Within weeks, several accused, including Asad and his aide Ghulam, were killed in police encounters. Others, like Guddu Muslim, remained elusive, their names etched on wanted lists with hefty bounties. Some said Guddu Muslim had fled to Bangladesh.

This brazen assassination underscored the lengths to which Atiq Ahmed's network would go to protect its legacy and eliminate threats. The courts still had their trials, but the real verdict had already been delivered – Atiq Ahmed was the untamed beast of UP, and no witness would live to tell the tale. Yet trying to tie all loose ends led to a chain of events that would culminate in the public, on-camera execution of Atiq Ahmed and Ashraf just weeks later.

Atiq's origins were as grimy as the alleys he once roamed. Born into poverty on 10 August 1962, he was just another boy trying to survive in the slums of Prayagraj. His father was a tanga-wallah, barely making ends meet. He dropped out of school after failing his high school exams, with no future beyond the rickety carts and coal-stained fingers of his father's world. But Atiq saw a different path for himself – the path of crime.

His first crimes were small, involving the theft of coal from trains, intimidation of local shopkeepers and extortion from struggling businesses. But as he realized the true power of terror, he escalated to large-scale land grabbing and contract killings. He committed his first murder in 1979, and by the mid-1980s, he was an unstoppable force of destruction.

Atiq Ahmed began to carve Prayagraj into his personal kingdom. He demanded money from businessmen, landlords, contractors and even common citizens. Those who refused faced brutal retribution, including torture, public beatings and execution. Victims spoke in whispers if they spoke at all. Witnesses disappeared; police officers were bribed, transferred or killed; and judges refused to hear cases against him out of fear for their lives.

Atiq led the 'IS-227' or the 'Inter-State Gang 227', a network of murderers, extortionists, kidnappers and terrorists with over 100 officially registered criminal cases. Former top cop Lalji Shukla summed it up best: 'For every crime attributed to Atiq, there were at least a hundred more that went unreported. He had the city in his iron grip.'[17]

But Atiq knew that raw power wasn't enough. He needed political protection too. In 1989, he won his first MLA seat from Allahabad West as an independent candidate. Over the next five consecutive terms, he held onto his position, jumping between Samajwadi Party and Apna Dal whenever it suited him.

By 2004, he reached the pinnacle of political power, winning a Lok Sabha seat from Phulpur, a constituency once held by Jawaharlal Nehru. A cold-blooded killer now sat in Parliament. Atiq played the game well. His political rallies were filled with talk of social justice and equality, while his men kidnapped businessmen and raped women in the shadows.

The Infallible: End of Atiq Ahmed

Even behind bars, he continued to rule. In 2008, the government had to temporarily release him from jail so he could vote in a crucial no-confidence motion in Parliament. The image of a mafia don walking into the halls of Indian democracy under police protection became an enduring symbol of the deep rot in the system.

When Atiq sought to contest elections in 2012, ten high court judges recused themselves from hearing the petition out of fear for their lives before the eleventh granted him bail. In 2018, businessman Mohit Jaiswal was kidnapped and taken inside Deoria Jail, where Atiq and his men beat him and forced him to sign over his property. But it was the murder of Umesh Pal, the last standing witness against him, that sealed his fate.

Atiq Ahmed had been locked away for years, but his true downfall began in 2017 as the tides turned. UP's new chief minister, Yogi Adityanath, launched an aggressive campaign against organized crime. Atiq's illegal properties worth about ₹10,000 crore were seized. His gang's financial backbone was systematically dismantled. In 2019, he was transferred to Gujarat's Sabarmati Jail to prevent him from running his syndicate from within UP's prison system.

Initially, his legacy of violence still bled through on the streets of Prayagraj. His men who carried out the killings – those still breathing – became the state's most wanted fugitives. Among them was his own son, Asad Ahmed – a name that now carried as much weight as his father's in terms of the blood on his hands. The police had apprehended Atiq, but Asad was determined that the story would not end there. Along with Asad, four others – Arman, Gulam, Guddu Muslim and Sabir – remained on the run, slipping through the cracks of the system Atiq had once manipulated so effortlessly.

However, the police had already begun closing in. The UP Police announced a cash reward for information leading to Asad's capture, raising the bounty from ₹2.5 lakh to ₹5 lakh, signalling just how desperate they were to bring the fugitives to justice. In the span of just a few weeks, two alleged gunmen – Arbaaz and Vijay Chowdhary alias Usman – were gunned down in encounters, their deaths further fuelling speculation about whether justice was being served or if a more calculated operation was underway.

But Asad was not waiting – he was moving, even with a price on his head. ₹5 lakh for a corpse. He was still in the wind, still armed, still consumed by vengeance. The law had claimed the father, but the son was now its next meal. As the UP Police tightened its net, one thing was certain – the streets of Prayagraj had not yet seen their final bloodbath.

For fifty days, the chase stretched across cities – a relentless, unforgiving pursuit that took the police through abandoned hideouts, secret safehouses and whispers in the underworld. Asad Ahmed, the son of the fallen kingpin, was running out of places to hide. Every day on the run brought him closer to the inevitable. He was not just fleeing; he was plotting, waiting, searching for a way to strike back.

But the UP STF was closing in. The walls were collapsing around him just as they had around his father. Every phone call, every movement, every breath could be his last.

And then, Jhansi became his grave.

On 13 April 2023, a stretch of desolate road near Baragaon and Chirgaon, 30 km from Jhansi, turned into a battlefield. The STF found him. Acting on intelligence gathered from captured associates, the officers intercepted Asad and his aide, Ghulam, near Parichha on the Jhansi–Kanpur National Highway.

The Infallible: End of Atiq Ahmed

The noon sun burned high, casting long shadows of trees across the dust-coated road. The tension was thick, the silence heavier than the heat. As the first siren blared, Asad and Ghulam knew the end had come.

'Surrender!'

The order rang out across the empty highway. The only answer was gunfire.

The moment the first bullet cut through the air, the encounter began. The STF, led by DSP Navendu Naveen and DSP Vimal Singh, had twelve highly trained officers with them. There would be no escape.

Asad fired first, his weapon cracking through the midday quiet. The STF retaliated. A storm of bullets tore through the dust, gunfire ricocheting off asphalt and metal. Asad ducked behind an abandoned vehicle, firing in desperation, his heart hammering in his chest.

For all his father's power, for all the blood he had spilled, this was how it ended – alone on a roadside, with nowhere left to run.

Within minutes, it was over.

A single shot shattered Asad's resistance. His body slumped to the ground, his pistol slipping from his fingers, blood seeping into the dirt. Beside him, Ghulam lay motionless, his weapon useless in his cold grip. The STF had fired only in retaliation – a clean, precise execution of the law.

When the smoke cleared, the bodies of Asad Ahmed and Ghulam lay still, their reign of terror extinguished in a hail of bullets.

The bodies were searched, their weapons – a British Bull Dog revolver and a Walther pistol – retrieved. Along with them, cell phones and SIM cards, possibly containing secrets that could unravel the final layers of Atiq Ahmed's crumbling syndicate.

The encounter sent shockwaves through the underworld. The men who had once been feared were now falling like dominoes one by one, hunted down, erased. Four of the shooters involved in Umesh Pal's murder had now been killed.

Back in Prayagraj, Atiq Ahmed sat behind bars, receiving the news that his son had been executed. The very fate he had feared for himself had now come for his blood.

The encounter of Asad Ahmed had triggered a political storm, with Opposition leaders, activists and BSP supremo Mayawati demanding a high-level inquiry. The echoes of Vikas Dubey's controversial killing were fresh in the public memory, and many believed history was repeating itself. But for the UP Police, this was not an act of retribution. It was an operation necessitated by imminent danger.

Standing before a press corps hungry for answers, Prashant Kumar did not waver. His voice was measured, his stance firm. This was not an extrajudicial execution but the culmination of a long, intelligence-driven pursuit, he explained.

'The UP Police had credible inputs that an attack was being planned on the police convoy transporting Atiq Ahmed and his brother Ashraf. Asad Ahmed and his associates were orchestrating a violent rescue mission – one designed to ambush law enforcement and free his father.'

The plot was uncovered during surveillance and tracking operations. The escape plan was audacious – highly armed assailants, possibly carrying automatic weapons and explosives, intended to strike while the convoy was in transit. Had the attack taken place, it could have led to casualties among police personnel and a resurgence of the very lawlessness the administration had vowed to eradicate.

'Let me make this clear,' Prashant Kumar continued, his voice cutting through the speculation and accusations. 'This was not a staged event. This was an armed confrontation initiated by the fugitives themselves. When ordered to surrender, they opened fire. Our officers responded in self-defence. There was no choice.' The encounter had not been a matter of vendetta, but of survival and law enforcement. 'The government has adopted a zero-tolerance policy against the mafias. The results of that policy are before everyone today,' he stated emphatically. There was no apology in his tone, nor any room for doubt.

Asad Ahmed was no helpless victim. He had not been cornered in a back alley, nor had he been dragged out of hiding and executed. He had been a fugitive, actively plotting to unleash chaos upon the state. For Prashant, the message was clear: this was not about silencing criminals, it was about protecting the rule of law. The press clamoured with follow-up questions, but Prashant Kumar had said all he needed to. Justice was served in the open, where every bullet fired had been an answer to an attack on law and order.

Atiq, being under strict watch behind the bars, was unaware of his son's movements. But the news didn't take long to reach him – his third son, Asad, had been killed in an encounter. He cried, he shouted and then he sat in silence. The weight of it all bore down on him, and somewhere in that quiet, a realization must have crept in – his son's blood was on his hands. Asad had walked this path for him, for his empire. Now, he had paid the price.

Maybe that was why Atiq never asked to attend Asad's funeral. Maybe that was why, even when he was finally taken out of prison and escorted to the hospital two days later, the media hounded him with the same question: why hadn't he gone? The cameras, the microphones, the relentless press – it was too much. And this time, Atiq shot back, 'So what if I didn't go?'

Was it defiance? Resignation? Or guilt finally speaking? We would never know. Because within seconds, a hand entered the frame – a gun at point-blank range. A deafening shot rang out, and his head snapped back, his white turban spinning into the air. The second bullet ensured there would be no last words. The don who had once believed himself untouchable had finally been erased. His story had ended the only way it ever could – not in power, but in ruin.

Within twenty-four hours, Chief Minister Yogi Adityanath issued a notification for setting up a three-member judicial commission that would probe the murders of Atiq Ahmed and his brother. Set up under the Commission of Inquiry Act, 1952, the panel was headed by retired high court judge Arvind Kumar Tripathi and comprised retired director general (DG) Subesh Kumar Singh and retired district judge Brijesh Kumar Soni. The commission was to submit its report within two months.

Despite massive controversies from politicians and activists, and cases being filed in various courts – including the Supreme Court – questioning the UP Police's actions, Prashant was on a mission. The calm, soft-spoken cop understood the public mood better than anyone else. No one chooses to live under the shadow of gangsters, but for decades the people of UP had had no choice. With Atiq Ahmed dead, the war against organized crime was far from over. As special DG, Law and Order, Prashant had been at the forefront of the state's most decisive crackdown in years. This wasn't just about encounters – it was about dismantling an entire system where criminals operated like shadow governments, controlling businesses, politics and entire communities.

For those unfamiliar with him, Prashant Kumar could be surprisingly unassuming, until one noticed his signature moustache and those penetrating eyes. His quiet demeanour

The Infallible: End of Atiq Ahmed

masked a relentless force of nature, a man who led not with rhetoric but with action. Beneath the uniform adorned with gallantry medals was a cop who had spent decades in the field, a strategist, a tactician and, above all, a man who believed that law and order must be enforced at any cost.

Prashant made it clear – the police had been given a free hand, and they would use it. There was no political interference, no bureaucratic red tape, only relentless action. 'For too long, people in UP lived by the saying "*Sab chalta hai* (Anything goes)". That has changed now. Gangsters can no longer terrorize the state. They will be crushed – legally, economically and operationally.' His words were not rhetoric, they were a warning to every criminal who still thought they could play the old game.

Under Chief Minister Yogi Adityanath, the police had been empowered like never before. 'When the chief minister said, "*Mafia ko mitti me mila denge* (We will reduce the mafias to dust)", he meant it,' Prashant stated. And he was the man executing that mission. Every law enforcement officer under his command was held to the highest standards of accountability, and only those who could deliver results were given key positions in the state's law-and-order machinery.

With each encounter, each crackdown, the criminal networks that had infiltrated UP's industries – construction, mining, tenders – were systematically dismantled. 'Earlier, a major company couldn't even bid for a contract without paying off these gangsters. Today, that has changed,' Prashant asserted. Fear had shifted from the people to the criminals.

When critics questioned the encounters, Prashant Kumar remained unfazed. 'The ultimate beneficiary is society. We are fighting for law-abiding citizens, for businesses and for the future of this state. There is no space for criminals here anymore,' he stated firmly.

He categorically dismissed allegations of bias or foul play. Atiq Ahmed, he pointed out, had travelled to UP from Gujarat's Sabarmati Jail at least three times in the past to attend court hearings and was always provided full security. Even on the night of his killing, Prashant said, the police managed to pin down one of the assailants immediately after the shots were fired. Some critics questioned why the attackers weren't shot at by the police. He countered, 'Had we fired, wouldn't the same people have claimed the whole thing was staged? It's always easy to pass judgement after the incident, without knowing the ground reality.'

He also dismissed doomsday predictions about the fallout of Atiq's killing. 'People even claimed the state would go up in flames, that communal riots would erupt. Has anything like that happened in the last seven years?' he shot back, before laying out the numbers – 183 criminals killed, over 5,000 arrested and thirteen police officers martyred in the line of duty.

'We do not distinguish by caste, creed or community,' he said. 'A criminal is a criminal, and we treat them as such.'

This was the new UP. A state where law and order was no longer negotiable, where justice moved at the speed of a bullet if necessary and where men like Prashant led the charge – not from behind a desk but from the frontlines.

A new order was taking shape. UP was no longer a safe haven for criminals who once operated with impunity. Prashant Kumar was a man on a mission, and in the wake of the relentless crackdown, the very landscape of the state underwent a transformation. The days when mafia dons walked freely, their power unchecked, were fading fast. The shift wasn't just in statistics or arrests, it was in the very psyche of the state.

The National Crime Record Bureau (NCRB) data for 2022 reflected this transformation. Despite being the most populous

The Infallible: End of Atiq Ahmed

state in India, UP's crime rate had plummeted below the national average – a shift many had once thought impossible. Of the 35 lakh criminal cases registered across India, only 4.01 lakh were from UP. The murder rate in the state was just 1.5 per cent, significantly lower than crime-heavy regions like Jharkhand (4 per cent) and Chhattisgarh (3.4 per cent). Even in heinous crimes like rape, robbery and extortion, UP ranked far below states traditionally seen as safer.[18]

But numbers alone didn't define the shift.

Prashant was not just tackling criminals, he was also dismantling the systems that had kept them in power. Emergency response services had been overhauled, cutting response time from twelve minutes to eight minutes in cities, and from fifteen minutes to nine minutes in rural areas. In just one year, 65 lakh citizens had received immediate police assistance, an unprecedented feat.[19]

Crime syndicates that had once dictated terms in business, land deals and infrastructure contracts were now powerless. In an UP where no company could previously win a major tender without paying off a local don, businesses now operated without fear of extortion.

The encounters, the crackdowns, the demolitions – they drew scrutiny, outrage and resistance from certain quarters. But to Prashant, the numbers told a story louder than any criticism.

The old ways were gone. The age of crime was over. Justice was no longer a slow-moving process shackled by bureaucracy. It was a storm, sweeping through UP, making sure that gangsters would never rule again.

Just when UP seemed to be settling into its new order, another storm brewed. Mukhtar Ansari, the last of the old-guard mafia dons, was gone. Officially, he died of cardiac arrest. Yet the end of such a towering criminal figure inevitably brought with it a swirl of speculation. His family alleged foul play, claiming he had been poisoned in jail. His network of loyalists, sympathizers and quiet beneficiaries stirred uncomfortably, their unease simmering across pockets of the state.

As news of his death spread, security forces across UP went on high alert, anticipating public backlash or unrest. But the more complex challenge was not on the streets – it was within the system. Once again, Prashant Kumar found himself at the center of institutional scrutiny, as fresh inquiries unfolded. The state had lost one of its most feared ganglords, but the entrenched power structures that once enabled such figures were still very much alive. The war, clearly, was not yet over.

3

The Last Supper of Mukhtar Ansari

Banda, a district in UP, is famous for its Shajar gemstones, a prized mineral used in intricate jewellery. But in recent years, the district was known for another kind of gem – one that carried an air of notoriety, fear and bloodshed. Banda's most talked-about resident wasn't a jeweller, businessman or politician – it was Mukhtar Ansari, one of India's most feared mafia dons, a man whose very name sent chills through the law enforcement agencies of UP and beyond.

For close to three decades, Mukhtar Ansari had ruled the criminal underworld, his influence extending beyond mere extortion rackets and contract killings. He was more than just a gangster – he was a political figure, a lawmaker who thrived in the very system that was supposed to dismantle men like him. Imprisoned since 2005 in Banda District Jail, he was an empire behind bars, still pulling the strings of his vast criminal syndicate from his cell.

Yet for a man with sixty-five criminal cases, ranging from murder, extortion and rioting to kidnapping and violations under the Gangsters Act, the wheels of justice moved at a painfully slow pace. The first FIR against him was registered in 1978, but his first conviction came only in September 2022 – a glaring testament to his deep political ties, his ability to manipulate the system and the sheer terror he commanded over those who dared to testify against him.

It was the month of Ramadan – a time of reflection, restraint and faith. But for Mukhtar Ansari, the feared mafia don, the evening of 28 March 2024 was anything but serene.

Seated inside his Banda Jail cell, he had just broken his *roza* with dry fruits and saffron-infused milk. The meal before him was elaborate – a spread fit for a king, even within the confines of prison. Plates of mutton korma, fragrant biryani, kebabs and fresh naan awaited him. But before he could take his first bite, uneasiness crept in.

A dull pain tightened around the left side of his chest, spreading swiftly to his shoulder and forearm. Beads of sweat formed across his forehead and temples, soaking into the collar of his crisp white kurta. His breath grew shallow.

The prison staff noticed immediately. The towering figure of the underworld, who had once dictated the fate of countless men, now clutched his chest, his fingers trembling ever so slightly. Panic surged through the jail corridors.

The jail doctors were summoned in haste. After a brief examination, their verdict was clear – he needed to be shifted immediately. This was not an ordinary ailment. The notorious don of UP had to be rushed to a hospital with advanced facilities.

Within minutes, Banda District Jail authorities swung into action. A high-security convoy was scrambled, sirens piercing the evening air. The destination: Rani Durgavati Medical College Hospital, the best facility in the city, the only place equipped to handle a man of Mukhtar Ansari's stature and ailments.

The Last Supper of Mukhtar Ansari

As the police escort sped through the darkening streets of Banda, whispers had already begun to spread. Was this just a medical emergency? Or was something far more sinister at play?

By the time the ambulance carrying Mukhtar Ansari screeched to a halt outside the emergency ward of Rani Durgavati Medical College Hospital, the clock read 8.25 p.m. Inside the vehicle, the once-feared don lay motionless, his pulse weak, his breath shallow. Somewhere between the prison gates and the hospital entrance, consciousness had slipped away.

The moment the stretcher rolled in, the hospital corridors buzzed with tension. Mukhtar Ansari was no ordinary patient. His reach and influence extended far beyond these walls, and everyone in the room understood that his life – or death – would have consequences.

A panel of nine doctors was assembled in haste – the best hands the hospital could provide. No protocol was skipped, no delay entertained. They worked swiftly, checking vitals, administering oxygen, injecting pain relief, running an ECG and preparing for an angiography. But before the procedure could even begin, Mukhtar Ansari flatlined.

At 8.45 p.m., the monitors emitted a single, long, unbroken beep.

He was gone.

For a man who had outmanoeuvred the law for decades, who had escaped conviction for years, who had built an empire of fear and political clout, the end had come suddenly, without fanfare, without resistance. One moment he was the invincible don, the next, a lifeless body under the hospital's harsh white lights.

A hushed silence filled the room. The doctors exchanged looks, some clinical, some uncertain. But everyone knew one thing for sure – this was no ordinary death. It would send shockwaves through the political and criminal underworld alike.

Just two days before his death, on 26 March, Mukhtar Ansari had already shown signs of deteriorating health. That evening, he was rushed to the hospital, complaining of severe abdominal pain. Given his history of ailments, the prison authorities took no chances.

Upon examination, the doctors had diagnosed him with urinary tract infection (UTI) and admitted him to the intensive care unit (ICU). His condition, while serious, was deemed manageable, and surgery was recommended to prevent further complications.

Lying in the hospital bed, Mukhtar Ansari listened quietly as the doctors explained his medical condition. He was not a man easily rattled, and true to his nature, he did not immediately commit to the surgery. Instead, he asked for time – time to consider his options, to decide on the next step.

But fate had already decided for him.

No one – not the doctors, not the jail officials, not even Mukhtar himself – could have imagined that something far more fatal was waiting just around the corner.

His final hours had begun ticking away, and yet no one saw the storm approaching.

In fact, days before his death, while being produced before a Barabanki court, Mukhtar Ansari had made a chilling claim – he was being poisoned in prison. He told the judge that the food served to him had been laced with poison, hinting at a conspiracy to kill him. His plea was dismissed, no investigation was ordered and life moved on. But now, with his sudden and mysterious death, those words seemed less like paranoia and more like a warning no one took seriously.

The Last Supper of Mukhtar Ansari 55

The first move by Prashant Kumar's police force after Ansari's death was swift and decisive – prohibitory orders under Section 144 of the Criminal Procedure Code (CrPC) was imposed across UP, banning large gatherings to prevent any unrest following Mukhtar Ansari's death. Security was tightened in Banda, Mau, Ghazipur and Varanasi, the strongholds of his influence.

To the ever-relentless media, Prashant made it clear – the convict's death had occurred in judicial custody, not under police control. He emphasized that Mukhtar Ansari had been convicted eight times over the past one-and-a-half years. He was identified as one of the main mafia figures and had a forty-year-long criminal history. Whenever Mukhtar required medical attention in jail, he was provided with the necessary care. He was admitted to the best available medical facility. Additionally, court records confirm that he suffered from a heart condition, and his death had occurred due to cardiac arrest.

But the timing couldn't have been worse. With general elections around the corner and UP being the most crucial battleground, the fallout of Mukhtar's sudden death was only going to escalate.

The news of Mukhtar Ansari's death had barely settled when the political chessboard shifted. The air was thick with condolences, accusations and demands for justice – each statement carefully crafted, each word carrying an undertone of deeper political manoeuvring.

The Samajwadi Party was among the first to react, releasing a formal statement: 'Sad demise of former MLA Shri Mukhtar Ansari. May his soul rest in peace. May the bereaved family members get the strength to bear this immense sorrow. Humble tribute!'[20]

While some debated whether the party's tribute to a mafia don was a routine condolence or a subtle political signal, a sharp reaction came from his family: 'We are waiting for the truth behind his death to come to light. Until then, our sorrow is mixed with suspicion.' In such a situation, it is only natural for his family to grieve with unease.[21]

The implication of the words was clear: BSP supremo Mayawati had turned the conversation toward scepticism. In a post on X, she wrote: 'The persistent apprehensions and serious allegations made by Mukhtar Ansari's family regarding his death in jail require a high-level investigation so that the true facts of his death can be revealed. In such a situation, it is natural for his family to be sad. May nature give them the strength to bear this sorrow'. There was now unmistakable suspicion around the circumstances of Mukhtar's death. And with general elections just around the corner, it was no longer merely a law-and-order issue – it had become a full-blown political flashpoint. In the power corridors of Uttar Pradesh, battle lines were being drawn.[22]

The state government, sensing the growing controversy, quickly ordered a magisterial inquiry, but Akhilesh Yadav wasn't satisfied. Dismissing it as inadequate, he called for a high-level investigation under the supervision of a Supreme Court judge. His attack on the state government was direct and scathing: 'UP is going through the worst phase of government anarchy.'[23]

Meanwhile, Mukhtar Ansari's son Umar Ansari added to the need of a thorough investigation by escalating the accusations, claiming his father had been 'slow-poisoned' inside Banda Jail. 'My father wrote to the courts and said he was being subjected to slow poisoning. The entire country now knows about it,' he declared.[24] The allegations weren't just emotional outbursts – they were fuel for an already raging fire. The battle over Mukhtar Ansari's death was turning into a high-stakes war of narratives, power and control.

Director General of Police Prashant Kumar remained unfazed in the face of the allegations made by Mukhtar Ansari's family. 'This is a democracy – anyone can say anything. But I don't think there's any room for doubt in this case. How long a person stays in the hospital is decided by doctors, not by any official. If anyone has any doubts, the investigation is underway – they should come forward and record their statement.'

It is true that the noose around Mukhtar Ansari began tightening the moment the BJP government took charge in UP in 2017. For decades, he had manoeuvred through the cracks of the system, but now, the ground beneath his feet was shifting. The first real tremor came a year later when his closest aide, Prem Prakash Singh alias Munna Bajrangi, was executed inside Baghpat Jail. On 9 July 2018, just a day after being transferred from Jhansi Jail, Bajrangi was shot dead by another gangster, Sunil Rathi. The murder wasn't just an internal gang war, it was also a signal, a warning that the old order was collapsing.

Mukhtar Ansari had ruled the streets with fear, but inside Banda Jail, he was not untouchable. Senior police officials later revealed that after Bajrangi's murder, Mukhtar became visibly uneasy. He knew what was coming. His lawyers began making frantic efforts to get him shifted outside UP, citing security concerns. In January 2019, the plan worked. He was moved to Ropar Jail in Punjab in connection with an extortion case. For almost two years, despite twenty-three reminders from the UP government, the then Congress-led Punjab government, under Captain Amarinder Singh, refused to send him back, citing his medical condition.[25] It was an escape, but not forever. In April 2021, the Supreme Court finally intervened, ordering his transfer back to Banda Jail.

What followed was a wave of bloodshed. Just weeks after Mukhtar's return, his two trusted aides, Merajuddin and Mukeem Kala, were gunned down inside Chitrakoot Jail by another gangster, Anshu Dixit. As a swift police response, Dixit was also killed, leaving behind a trail of unanswered questions and a growing sense of inevitability around Mukhtar's fate. It didn't end there. In June 2023, another of his key men, Sanjeev Maheshwari alias Jeeva, was assassinated inside a Lucknow court in broad daylight. With twenty-six criminal cases against him, including the murder of BJP MLA Brahm Dutt Dwivedi, Jeeva had been one of Mukhtar's closest confidants. Alongside Munna Bajrangi, he had also been a co-accused with Mukhtar in the murder of sitting BJP MLA Krishnanand Rai.

The systematic elimination of his inner circle wasn't lost on Mukhtar's family. His son Umar Ansari took the battle to the Supreme Court, filing a writ petition in December 2023. He alleged that the state government was planning his father's assassination inside Banda Jail and demanded that Mukhtar be transferred out of UP. The UP government, in response, assured the court on 15 December that necessary security enhancements would be made to ensure that no harm came to Mukhtar while in custody. But outside the courtroom, the crackdown was relentless. The police tightened their grip, dismantling the remnants of Mukhtar's empire. Action was taken against 292 individuals linked to him. Many were booked under the Gangsters Act, and by December 2023, 186 had been arrested.

For years, Mukhtar had thrived in the shadows of politics and crime, evading consequences at every turn. But now, the walls were closing in. His men were falling one by one, and his influence was fading fast. No amount of legal manoeuvring or political shielding could stop what was coming. His time was running out.

Mukhtar Ansari was never supposed to be a criminal. His story, if it had followed the path of his ancestors, would have been one of leadership, patriotism and public service. Instead, it became a tale soaked in blood, power and an unchallenged reign of terror that spanned decades.

Born on 30 June 1963, in Ghazipur, UP, Mukhtar carried the weight of a family name that was once revered across India. His paternal grandfather, Dr Mukhtar Ahmed Ansari, had been a towering figure in the Indian freedom struggle, president of the Indian National Congress in 1927 and a man who shaped national policies before Independence.

On the other side of his lineage, his maternal grandfather, Brigadier Mohammad Usman, was a decorated war hero, posthumously awarded the Maha Vir Chakra for his sacrifice in the Indo-Pakistan conflict of 1948. Mukhtar's father, Haji Subhanullah Ansari, dabbled in communist politics, ensuring that the family remained politically connected. But Mukhtar did not inherit their ideals or their noble intentions. He inherited something far more dangerous – an insatiable thirst for dominance. He was reportedly a brilliant athlete in his youth, known for his prowess in cricket and shooting, a sharp-eyed marksman whose skills would later serve him well in a different battlefield. He studied at Banaras Hindu University (BHU) and PG College in Ghazipur, but his real education happened in the streets, among men who didn't shake hands but sealed agreements with loaded revolvers. The 1980s in UP were a time of chaos, when criminal syndicates operated with impunity, filling the power vacuum left by a weak administration. The police were either corrupt or terrified, and the real governance was handled by those who controlled contracts, land and loyalty through force.

Mukhtar entered the world of crime strategically, aligning himself first with the Makhanu Singh gang, which ran extortion rackets across Varanasi, Jaunpur and Ghazipur. He observed, learned and waited. When the time was right, he broke away and formed his own network, bringing in trusted enforcers and setting up an empire that would eventually overshadow all others. His biggest enemy emerged in the form of Brijesh Singh, a rival mafia boss with an equal thirst for power. What followed was a brutal, decades-long war for dominance over Purvanchal, a war fought not in courtrooms or assembly halls but in the streets, through assassinations, ambushes and betrayals that would leave a trail of bodies across eastern UP.

Mukhtar understood one thing better than his rivals – power wasn't just about fear, it was also about presence. His convoy, a fleet of twenty to thirty black SUVs, all bearing the number 786, became a symbol of his untouchable status. People cleared roads when his fleet passed. Shopkeepers shut their stores. Eyes turned away. He was no longer a gangster; he was a living, breathing legend, a man whose name was spoken in hushed tones even in police stations.

As his grip tightened over Purvanchal, he expanded beyond extortion. He took over government contracts, railway tenders, mining leases and land grabbing, amassing a fortune while making sure that those who opposed him simply ceased to exist. The system, which should have crushed him, instead legitimized him. By the mid-1990s, Mukhtar realized that to remain invincible, he needed something more than guns and money – he needed political power.

His first taste of electoral victory came in 1996, when he won the Mau Sadar seat on a BSP ticket. It was a masterstroke. No longer just a fugitive or a gangster, he was now a legislator, operating his criminal empire directly from the UP Assembly.

He knew that politics would give him immunity, and it did. He continued winning elections, becoming a five-time MLA, even when he was behind bars. It didn't matter where he was, Mukhtar's word was law. Inside jail, he lived like a king, running his operations through loyalists, making sure every contract, every extortion demand and every hit job was executed with precision.

Yet even kings have enemies. And Mukhtar had made a powerful one in Krishnanand Rai, a BJP MLA from Mohammadabad. The two men couldn't have been more different – Rai represented everything Mukhtar despised. He was a political force that threatened Mukhtar's syndicate. In 2002, Rai did the unthinkable – he defeated Mukhtar's brother, Afzal Ansari, in the elections. It wasn't just a political loss; it was also a personal insult, a direct challenge to Mukhtar's supremacy in his home turf.

On a cold November afternoon in 2005, the challenge was answered in the only way Mukhtar knew – through sheer, unrelenting violence. As Rai's convoy passed through Basaniya Chatti, an ambush was waiting. Gunmen armed with six AK-47 rifles stepped out of a waiting SUV and opened fire. Five hundred rounds were fired in a ruthless, calculated onslaught and sixty-seven bullets were later recovered from the bodies. It was more than an execution; it was a massacre. Mukhtar, ever the meticulous planner, allegedly ordered that Rai's *choti*, the scared braid, be chopped off and sent as proof of the kill, a trophy from a war won in blood.

And then came the call.

What they didn't know was that a sharp-eared operative from the UP STF was listening in. The voices crackling over the line belonged to two men locked up in separate jails – Mukhtar Ansari in Ghazipur and his trusted hitman Abhay Singh in Faizabad. The distance between them was irrelevant. Power, after all, was a signal that never lost strength behind bars. The STF recorded the call. Later, the one-minute-eight-second audio clip was handed over to the CBI. What it revealed was nothing short of chilling – a real-time glimpse into the minds of those who orchestrated and celebrated death like a festival.

Abhay Singh: '*Hum Abhay Singh bol rahe hain.* (This is Abhay Singh speaking.)'

Mukhtar Ansari: '*Bolo, Thakur.* (Speak, Thakur.)'

Abhay: '*Bhaiya, ek o zameen thi – jisme Rizwan Bhai se wahan baat hui thi. Sab log wahan par aaye hue the. Usme vo beech mein mamla bigad gaya tha.* (Bhaiya, that land deal – Rizwan bhai had spoken to them. Everyone was there. But things got messy.)'

Mukhtar: '*Haan… haan… haan. Thoda badmashi kiya hai. Sab chhodo abhi. Yahan par vo ho gaya hai. Pata chala halla ho raha hai ki goli chal rahi hai Munna Bajrangi aur Krishnanand Rai mein.* (Yes… yes… yes. Some mischief happened. Forget it now. Something big's going down here. Word is, there's gunfire between Munna Bajrangi and Krishnanand Rai.)'

Abhay: '*Accha?* (Really?)'

Mukhtar: '*Ye sunne mein aaya hai.* (That's what I'm hearing.)'

Abhay: '*Achha, kahan par?* (Where exactly?)'

Mukhtar: '*Krishnanand Rai ke gaon par dono taraf se mukabla chal raha hai.* (Rai's village. Both sides are in a shoot-out.)'

Abhay: '*Haan, haan, baraabar goli chal rahi hai.* (Yes, yes, gunfire's flying.)'

Mukhtar: '*Haan.* (Hmm.)'

Abhay: '*Ek tarfa.* (One-sided, though.)'

Mukhtar (with chilling calm): 'Jai Shri Ram…'

The Last Supper of Mukhtar Ansari

Abhay: 'Okay.'
Mukhtar: 'Hello?'
Abhay: '*Haan, haan.* (Yes, yes.)'
Mukhtar: '*Kaat leenh.* (We've snipped it [referring to the braid].)'
Abhay: '*Thik hai.* (Got it.)'
Mukhtar: '*Mutthi mein.* (Now it's in our fist.)'
Abhay: '*Haan, thik hai, thik hai, rakh rahe hain. Baad mein baat hogi.* (Okay, okay, I'm hanging up, we'll speak later.)'
Mukhtar: 'Namaste.'[26]

There was no remorse, no hesitation – only coded satisfaction, like soldiers reporting a mission accomplished.

That phone call – intercepted by chance – would become one of the most damning pieces of circumstantial evidence ever recorded against Mukhtar Ansari. It offered a window into the cold, strategic cruelty of a man who ran a criminal empire from behind bars, where shoot-outs were discussed like weather and murder was reduced to a metaphor: 'The braid is in our fist.'

Despite the brutality of the attack, Mukhtar remained untouchable. Witnesses vanished, the case crumbled in court and he walked free. But his days of unchecked dominance were numbered.

Another powerful enemy had emerged – Yogi Adityanath.

The tension escalated in 2008, when Yogi's convoy was ambushed in Azamgarh. His forty-vehicle cavalcade was attacked with stones, petrol bombs and gunfire. One man was killed and six were injured, but Yogi narrowly escaped due to a last-minute decision to switch cars. The situation was so volatile that to bring it under control, Indian Police Service (IPS) officer Brij Lal had to be airdropped from a chopper carrying an AK-47 to control the violence.

When Yogi Adityanath became chief minister in 2017, his first order of business was to target gangster-turned-politicians, and he had one name at the top of his list. In a relentless crackdown, Mukhtar's aides were executed one by one – Munna Bajrangi, Jeeva, Merajuddin and Mukeem Kala, all killed inside jails or in orchestrated encounters. Mukhtar, once the master of Purvanchal, was reduced to a prisoner, fighting legal battles as his properties worth ₹500 crores were seized.

By 28 March 2024, when Mukhtar collapsed in Banda jail, clutching his chest as pain shot through his left arm, the man who had ruled with absolute power for four decades was merely a frail, wheelchair-bound figure, his body broken, his empire gone. They said he was poisoned, they said it was fate; in truth, Mukhtar Ansari had always known how this story would end.

The don who had controlled Purvanchal with an iron grip, whose name once inspired fear in the police force itself, had finally met the one enemy he couldn't outsmart – death.

In the narrow lanes of Ghazipur and Mau, Mukhtar Ansari's name continues to echo in whispers. Because in places where crime and politics are inseparable, legends never die. However, they do get rewritten.

And that was exactly what began to happen. Mukhtar's family cried foul, claiming he had been slowly poisoned inside Banda jail. His food, they said, had been tampered with – laced with something lethal, killing him bit by bit. The accusations sparked a political storm, igniting speculation and dragging his death into the realm of conspiracy. His son Umar demanded a post-mortem by AIIMS doctors in Delhi and called for a judicial probe. The weight of history, vendettas and power struggles wrapped itself around Mukhtar's death like an inescapable noose, ensuring that his story would not rest as easily as his body.

But when the investigation concluded, the findings told a different story. The district magistrate's report reaffirmed what the post-mortem had already stated – Mukhtar Ansari had died of a cardiac arrest. A panel of five doctors conducted the autopsy, their conclusions leaving no room for speculation. No toxins were found in his system, no trace of slow poisoning. Forensic analysis of samples of food found in Mukhtar's barrack – salt, jaggery, chickpeas – yielded nothing unusual. Statements of every security officer stationed outside his barrack, every doctor who examined him, every member of the medical team that attempted to save his life, all pointed in one direction.

Yet even as these official findings were released, the firestorm refused to die down. The timing of the election season ensured that Mukhtar's name would not be buried so easily. The Forensic Science Lab confirmed the absence of poison in Mukhtar's viscera. But rather than putting the controversy to rest, it only fanned the flames further. The report's speed – barely a month after his death – became ammunition for the sceptics.

'We do not trust either the post-mortem or the viscera reports,' declared Afzal Ansari, Mukhtar's brother, standing before a rally in Ghazipur, garlanded, his voice carried by the charged murmurs of the crowd.[27] His doubts ran deep. He alleged that crucial nail and hair samples had never been taken – key evidence that could have detected slow-acting toxins. More than that, he questioned the credibility of the forensic process, alleging that the viscera sample had not been handled properly, that a different officer had been assigned the task instead of the designated one.

'In any death, whether in the country or the state, a viscera report usually takes between six months to a year to be released.

Here, it has come out in just one month,' Afzal claimed, his voice thick with suspicion.[28]

But officials dismissed these accusations. They believed in the post-mortem report, the forensic report and the statements of the doctors and security personnel, all pointing to the same conclusion: cardiac arrest.

Mukhtar's death commanded a final procession that played out like the closing scene of a gangster epic. A long convoy of vehicles snaked its way out of Banda that evening, carrying the body of the once-feared don back to his home turf in Ghazipur. Under the faint glow of streetlights, the procession moved through the silent, watchful towns, the weight of his legacy pressing down on the air like an unspoken truth. By Saturday morning, Mukhtar Ansari – once the most feared name in Purvanchal – was buried. But in the minds of his followers, his enemies and the political forces still using his name, Mukhtar Ansari wasn't truly gone. Not yet. He was making ripples in New Delhi.

The battlefield had shifted from Banda to the highest court of the land, and the fight over what his death meant had just begun. Senior advocate Kapil Sibal wasted no time. Representing Umar Ansari, he took the fight straight to the Supreme Court, challenging the UP government's handling of Mukhtar Ansari's death. Standing before a bench comprising Justices Hrishikesh Roy and S.V.N. Bhatti, Sibal demanded answers. The medical and magisterial inquiry reports – documents that could either silence the speculation or fuel it further – had not been furnished to the family.

Umar had already moved the Supreme Court months before his father's death, in December 2023, pleading for his transfer to a

The Last Supper of Mukhtar Ansari

jail outside UP, fearing exactly this outcome. The state government had then assured the court it would enhance Mukhtar's security inside Banda Jail if needed. Now, with the gangster-politician dead, that assurance seemed hollow.

The Supreme Court, however, did not waste words. A post-mortem had been conducted. A judicial inquiry had taken place. And so, the bench ordered the UP government to hand over the reports to Umar Ansari within two weeks. If he wished to contest the findings, he could file his response within three weeks thereafter.

The political fault lines in eastern UP had already been drawn, but now they were deepening. In Ghazipur, Mau and Azamgarh, where Mukhtar Ansari's name had once commanded both fear and loyalty, the ruling BJP had seen an opportunity, one that could cement their claim that the old order – where mafia dons dictated terms – was now a thing of the past. A BJP leader from the region was quick to frame Mukhtar's death as a turning point, declaring that the days of 'Goonda Raj' had finally ended. The message was clear: what had once flourished under the cover of political patronage had now been dismantled, brick by brick, encounter by encounter.

But the timing of it all was impossible to ignore. With the 2024 Lok Sabha elections looming, the battle for Ghazipur had taken on a new intensity. Mukhtar's brother, Afzal Ansari, the sitting MP from the constituency, had switched from the BSP to the Samajwadi Party, attempting to hold onto his family's grip over the region. His campaign, whether he admitted it or not, was steeped in Mukhtar's legacy. For the BJP, this was the perfect chance to turn that legacy into a liability. Their strategy was already in motion – Mukhtar became a reminder of why, according to them, Yogi Adityanath's crackdown on crime had been necessary in the first place.

The numbers supported their claim. Official state records showed that, in just six years of the Yogi government, 10,713 encounters had been carried out, leading to the arrest of 5,967 criminals.[29] It was the kind of data that reinforced the ruling party's message – law and order had been restored, and the state had no place for gangsters who once ran parallel governments.

For Afzal Ansari, however, this was more than just an election. His brother's name had long been his greatest strength, but now it risked becoming his heaviest burden. The BJP's campaign had already woven Mukhtar's downfall into Yogi Adityanath's larger promise of a crime-free UP. Every speech, every rally, every statement from party leaders repeated the same refrain – the days of fear were over. And yet in the narrow lanes of Ghazipur, whispers refused to die down. For some, Mukhtar was a villain, for others, a protector. But for everyone, he remained a presence that refused to fade, even in death.

The UP Police had never been known for restraint. But under Prashant Kumar's command, the force had transformed into something else entirely – a war machine against crime, built on precision, aggression and an unshakable doctrine: Fear must belong to the law, not the lawless. the numbers told their own tale. Over 10,900 encounters had unfolded across the state since March 2017 till January 2025, a staggering statistic that had earned UP its unofficial moniker – The Encounter State.[30]

Yet behind every police bullet fired, behind every gangster buried six feet under, a larger battle raged. Critics called it state-sponsored execution, a systematic purge masked as justice. The Opposition cried foul, claiming the encounters disproportionately targeted specific communities. But Prashant, the man in charge, dismissed such accusations with the precision of a surgeon wielding a scalpel. 'A cop doesn't carry a weapon as an ornament. When a criminal fires, we fire back,' he stated coldly. 'Casualties can happen on either side. It's a professional hazard.'

Prashant Kumar was no stranger to controversy, nor was he one to flinch in its face. Every time a gangster dropped dead in a police shoot-out, an investigation followed. Every encounter was scrutinized. Reports were filed, autopsies conducted and official statements issued. Yet the bullets kept flying. The law-and-order model of UP turned into a spectacle – ruthless, efficient and merciless in its execution.

And it was working.

Foreign investment in UP surged by 400 times in the past five years, a staggering contrast to the fifteen years prior.[31] Factories, multinational businesses and startups were pouring in, no longer held hostage by extortionists, land mafias and kidnappers. 'This shows the confidence of investors in UP,' Prashant Kumar noted. 'And the main factor is the better law-and-order situation.' The state's ease-of-doing-business ranking had improved significantly. Investors no longer feared for their safety. The law was finally in control.

But who controlled the law?

As encounter killings stacked up like dominoes, whispers grew louder. Was there an invisible hand guiding this purge? A force moving beyond law, beyond due process, executing criminals before the courts even had a chance to try them? Prashant Kumar's response to these was unflinching. 'There are guidelines in place for every police action,' he explained. 'All legal formalities are followed. It's like walking a tightrope – one mistake, and it brings a bad name to us.'

For him, the battle wasn't just against criminals – it was also against perception, against the system that had, for decades, allowed gangsters to run parallel governments, evade justice and mock the rule of law. Men like Mukhtar Ansari and Atiq Ahmed, whose criminal empires had thrived for forty years, had never known true fear – not from the courts, not from politicians and certainly not from the police. But now, that fear had changed sides.

Still, the war was not truly over. The names may have changed, the faces different, but the fight between law and lawlessness would never truly end. 'Criminals who once ran a parallel government are now facing convictions for the first time,' Prashant Kumar remarked. In the past eighteen months, UP had witnessed over 31,000 gangster-related convictions. Thirty-one of them ended in capital punishment.[32] It was unprecedented. In a state where criminals had spent lifetimes walking free, men who had evaded the law for decades were now shackled in courtroom docks, staring down the sentences they never thought they'd face. Yet even as the UP Police tightened its grip, Prashant Kumar understood the stakes. 'In a democracy, there have to be checks and balances,' he admitted. 'We work under the purview of all Supreme Court guidelines, as well as national and state human rights commissions.' The message was clear: justice must take place, but within the purview of the law.

For now, the police has the upper hand. Criminal syndicates have dismantled, gangsters have been wiped out and their heirs are either languished in prison or living in exile, watching their old dominions turn to dust. But UP had seen enough to know that power never truly disappears – it only changes hands.

Prashant Kumar's war with crime wasn't over with Mukhtar Ansari's death. It had only just begun.

4

Bullets, Billions and the Fall of the Mafias

Prashant Kumar knew better than anyone that encounters and arrests were just the visible end of the battle. The real war was being fought behind closed doors, in high-security meetings, war rooms where strategies were drawn and policy briefings where every move was calculated.

From 2020, a radical shift in governance was underway. The UP government, in collaboration with the police department, had committed itself to an ambitious mission – to make the state mafia-free. For decades, criminals had dictated terms, police officers had feared the consequences of action and the public had remained silent spectators, too terrified to speak out. That changed. The chief minister's mandate was clear and non-negotiable: eradicate organized crime, dismantle the fear that criminals had long wielded over the people and reverse the equation.

At the core of this mission was Prashant Kumar.

As one of the key architects of this new strategy, he wasn't just implementing orders, he was also helping shape them. Policy-making meetings in Lucknow had turned into war councils. The chief minister demanded results, not reports. Every senior officer at the table knew that they were no longer dealing with just gangsters. They were taking on an entire ecosystem that had allowed these criminals to flourish unchecked for decades.

The zero-tolerance against crime was born from these war-room deliberations, and Prashant Kumar was among those who saw exactly how it needed to be executed on the ground. There was no room for half-measures. Crime families that had been thriving for generations had to be uprooted, their influence neutralized.

The first step in this battle was identification.

A classified dossier was prepared – a hit list of UP's sixty-eight most notorious mafia bosses, each name meticulously investigated, each criminal marked for legal action. This wasn't just about arrests. It was about breaking their support networks, their financial backbones, their political shields.

For Prashant Kumar, this wasn't just about signing orders and reviewing intelligence files from the comfort of his office. He was in the field. He visited police stations, personally reviewed case files, interrogated informants and stood at the nerve centre of every major operation.

While bureaucrats and politicians debated strategies, he was the one ensuring that those strategies translated into swift, uncompromising action. If an officer in a remote district dragged his feet, Prashant Kumar called him directly. If a gangster's property was to be seized, he ensured it wasn't just symbolic action but a real message. A bulldozer rolling over an illegal mansion wasn't demolition; it was the funeral of an era of impunity.

This was no longer a state where the police feared criminals. Now, the criminals feared the police.

The fight against organized crime in UP was never meant to be a single strike – it was designed to be a systematic, unforgiving purge in phases. No longer would the police play defence. This was an offensive war, one that required precision, patience and ruthless efficiency.

The first official strike came in the form of a government order issued on 1 November 2019. Inside the police headquarters (PHQ) in Lucknow, a confidential file was laid open on desk. It contained twenty-five names – men who had, for decades, walked through UP's power corridors with impunity. These were not mere criminals, they were institutions unto themselves, protected by money, politics and a deep-rooted fear that had seeped into the bones of the state's people.

Prashant Kumar, leaning back in his chair, ran a finger along the first name on the list. Simultaneously, he was also studying battle plans. He knew that going after these men required more than brute force. Arrests weren't enough. Encounters weren't always possible. The real war had to be waged in courtrooms.

He had seen how history treated untouchables. The case of Al Capone loomed in his mind. The Chicago mob boss, too powerful to be arrested for murder or extortion, had eventually been taken down through a seemingly simple crime: tax-evasion. This would be UP's own version of that takedown. If a gangster couldn't be caught on the street, he would be crushed financially, legally and structurally. This time, the war wouldn't be fought with just batons or bullets but with laws, ledgers and lethal paperwork.

By mid-2020, the strategy was set. The mafia empires had been thriving on land encroachments, illegal businesses and black money. Teams were formed. Surveillance was intensified.

Bank accounts, properties, benami assets and offshore holdings were put under scrutiny. The order was clear and chilling: 'Don't just arrest them. Destroy them.'

By March 2022, the crackdown had gained such momentum that it became one of the largest crime-purging exercises in the history of Indian policing. Yet Prashant Kumar wasn't satisfied. Inside the high-security conference hall of the PHQ, amid the hum of air-conditioning and the faint aroma of freshly brewed tea, he sat at the head of the long mahogany table. Around him were the additional chief secretary (ACS), Home; the DGP; senior officers from the STF; and zonal police chiefs.

A blueprint for the future was spread across the table. The walls were lined with LED screens, displaying crime heat maps of UP – pockets where mafia dominance still thrived. The faces of hardened criminals flashed on the screen, accompanied by financial records, phone surveillance logs and reports from intelligence operatives.

'This is not a law enforcement issue anymore,' Prashant Kumar's voice cut through the room. 'This is a war to reclaim the state. If we leave even one of them standing, they will return stronger. We must eliminate their influence, their resources, their very ability to breathe freely.'

A final list of fifty names was drawn up, each handpicked after exhaustive input from every police zone, commissionerate and STF unit in the state. Each name on that list represented not just a criminal but also a syndicate built on extortion, land-grabbing, illegal mining and contract killings. The moment that list was approved, the war escalated.

In the weeks that followed, properties worth thousands of crores were seized. Illegal constructions were demolished, bank accounts were frozen and shell companies collapsed under forensic audits. UP's most feared mafia bosses weren't hiding from bullets anymore – they were running from tax notices, scrambling to find lawyers, watching their financial networks crumble before their eyes.[33]

By 9 January 2023, inside the operations control room at PHQ, a fresh dossier was opened. The crackdown had reached unprecedented heights, but the battle was still incomplete. Sixty-six names were now on the mafia list, each under continuous surveillance.

The meeting room was alive with reports from the field – bank transactions, satellite images of mafia hideouts, intercepted phone calls. New criminals had emerged, filling the vacuum left behind by those who had fallen. The list was revised again, expanded to sixty-nine.

As the crackdown intensified, eleven of these names disappeared forever – four shot dead in police encounters, others falling to the very law they once manipulated.

Each day, as the sun rose over UP, another layer of organized crime was stripped away. The mafia bosses who once roamed with convoys of SUVs, draped in gold chains, flanked by gunmen, were now either behind bars or buried under the weight of their past crimes.

This wasn't just policing anymore, this was warfare. Call it 'Operation Conviction' – the legal war against the mafias.

The battle against organized crime was never meant to be fought solely in the streets. Encounters, raids and demolitions could only do so much. The real deathblow to the mafias had to be delivered where they least expected it – inside the courtrooms.

For decades, UP's most feared crime lords had played the judicial system like a rigged game. Witnesses vanished overnight, judges recused themselves, case files gathered dust in back offices and trials dragged on for years until the accused walked free, often returning stronger than before. This cycle had to be broken.

Inside Prashant Kumar's office at the PHQ, a new kind of battle plan was unfolding. His desk was cluttered with legal dossiers, case files marked 'high priority' and forensic reports that would be used to bring down the men who had ruled the state from the shadows. 'If we want real change, convictions must happen – fast and without compromise,' Prashant Kumar had declared in one of the high-level strategy meetings, his voice carrying the weight of a man who had spent years witnessing criminals walk free due to loopholes in the system.

With his backing, UP's legal machinery was set into motion like never before. Prosecutors and legal experts were brought together in an unprecedented effort to ensure that members of the mafias didn't just get arrested but that they stayed behind bars for good.

One by one, the names of UP's most notorious criminals began surfacing in courtrooms across the state: Mukhtar Ansari (deceased), Vijay Mishra, Atiq Ahmed (deceased), Yogesh Bhadauda, Munir (deceased), Saleem, Rustam, Sohrab, Ajit Singh alias Happu, Aakash Jaat, Sinharaj Bhati, Sundar Bhati, Mulayam Yadav, Dhruv Kumar Singh alias Kuntu Singh, Amit Kasana, Ejaaz, Anil Dujana (deceased), Yakub Qureshi, Bachchu Yadav, Dharmendra Keerthal, Randeep Bhati, Sanjay Singh Singla (deceased), Anupam Dubey, Vikrant alias Vicky, Udham Singh, Rakesh Yadav and Shyam Babu Pasi.

For each of them, the state assembled ironclad cases, reinforced by meticulous investigations and undisputable evidence. There would be no room for manipulation, no missing files, no hostile witnesses.

Each courtroom showdown felt like a final reckoning. The once-feared mafia bosses who had walked into courtrooms with smirks and sunglasses now sat in silence, their realms crumbling with every sentence pronounced.

The results were unprecedented. Seventy-two cases resulted in convictions.

Thirty-one mafia leaders and sixty-nine of their key operatives were sentenced. Two criminals were handed the death penalty – the ultimate statement that the law had finally turned merciless. Others faced life imprisonment, decades of rigorous jail terms and crushing fines that bled their fortunes dry. With each conviction, the streets of UP felt one step closer to freedom.[34]

For the first time in decades, the law had not just caught up with the mafias, but had also overtaken, outmanoeuvred and crushed them under its weight.

This wasn't just a crackdown anymore. It was a revolution.

Justice in UP was no longer a slow-moving process riddled with bureaucratic delays and legal loopholes. The system had caught up with the crime lords who once treated the law as a mere inconvenience. The courtrooms had become battlegrounds where decades of unchecked power were being shattered, one conviction at a time.

The case files weren't just documents. They were the final verdicts on once-feared empires.

The fall of Mukhtar Ansari's criminal enterprise began despite the fact that, for years, he had ruled from behind bars, his influence undiminished by incarceration. Politicians had courted him, businessmen had feared him and the streets had whispered his name in hushed tones. But the law had turned into a relentless force that gave him no escape.

Eight convictions. Life imprisonment. Rigorous jail terms. Fines that stripped his empire to its bones. Even the lieutenants who had carried out his orders in the shadows weren't spared.

Four of his key gang members faced identical fates, ensuring that his criminal syndicate wasn't just weakened, it was eradicated.

The message was clear: UP was no longer a place where crime bosses could rule from inside prison walls.

If Mukhtar Ansari's downfall was the dismantling of a criminal empire, Atiq Ahmed's conviction was a reckoning decades in the making. A name synonymous with fear and political clout, Atiq had defied justice for far too long, manipulating the system, silencing witnesses and killing rivals with absolute impunity. But his reign ended the moment the courtroom doors closed behind him.

Ten of his closest associates fell with him.

Sentences were unforgiving – life imprisonment, rigorous jail terms and financial penalties so severe that even his deeply entrenched network could not recover. There was no second chance. No appeals that would buy time. The courtroom, once a place where his lawyers played legal gymnastics, had turned into the execution chamber of his criminal legacy.

Among the most significant convictions was Vijay Mishra, a man whose reputation had loomed over UP's power corridors for years. With four cases pinned against him, there was no way out. The verdict was swift – rigorous imprisonment and heavy fines that crippled the financial backbone of his empire.

In an even stronger blow to organized crime, Randeep Bhati and Sundar Bhati – men who had once commanded absolute obedience through fear – were sentenced to life imprisonment. Eleven of their top enforcers followed them into darkness, their criminal networks reduced to scattered remnants. The fines imposed – ₹1.8 lakh per convict – were a clear message that crime would not just cost freedom but also wealth, influence and control.

Bullets, Billions and the Fall of the Mafias

The list of fallen names continued to grow, each conviction breaking the spine of UP's criminal underworld. Ajit Singh alias Happu received prison sentences and financial penalties in three cases, his once-flourishing network dismantled in one legal stroke. Saleem, Sohrab and Rustam, alongside their close associate Raju Mohammed alias Sanu, were found guilty in two cases and sentenced to prison terms with heavy fines.

With every conviction, the ground beneath UP's underworld cracked further. The days when crime lords walked into police stations as VIPs and walked out untouched were gone. The message was hammered into the very fabric of the state. The courtrooms had become extensions of the law enforcement crackdown, ensuring that no powerful surname or political connection could alter the course of justice.

One by one, the pillars of organized crime collapsed, their influence dissolving under the weight of swift prosecution and relentless sentencing. This wasn't just policing. This wasn't just governance. This was a permanent shift in the power dynamics of UP.

But the real shockwave came with the rarest and most severe of judicial rulings – capital punishment.

Munir and his accomplice, Raiyan, were convicted in two cases, including Case No. 166/13 from Syohara Police Station in Bijnor. They had walked into the courtroom with the hope of yet another delay, yet another loophole. Instead, they walked out with death sentences.

Even the deeply entrenched syndicates weren't spared. Mulayam Yadav (not to be confused with the former UP CM Mulayam Singh Yadav), another name synonymous with violent rule, was convicted and imprisoned, marking yet another high-profile downfall.[35]

But some networks were far larger, their reach deeper, the law struck them even harder.

Dhruv Kumar alias Kuntu Singh and his twelve associates were sentenced in two cases, with verdicts ranging from life imprisonment to rigorous jail terms and financial penalties. The same fate awaited Yogesh Bhadauda and his six enforcers, all convicted in six cases, receiving life sentences that ensured their dominance ended permanently.

The net continued to tighten. Amit Kasana, Ejaaz and their associates faced convictions across multiple cases, their prison terms sealing their fate. Anil Dujana, a name once whispered in fear, faced conviction in a case registered at Badalpur Police Station in Gautam Buddha Nagar Commissionerate. His death in an earlier police encounter had ended his personal reign of terror. In his absence, his empire was torn apart by the judicial system. Four of Anil Dujana's closest aides were convicted in two cases, sentenced to rigorous imprisonment and heavy fines.

There was no longer a refuge for these criminals – not in the streets, not in the courts, not in the corridors of power. For decades, the mafias had dictated how justice functioned in UP. Now, the law dictated their fate, and this time, there was no escape.

The fall of Aditya Rana in an encounter in Bijnor was a resounding blow to organized crime in the state. Vishal, one of the gang's key enforcers, found himself convicted in five cases, his prison sentence accompanied by financial penalties that stripped away his last remnants of power.

Meanwhile, Haji Yaqoob Qureshi, a name that once held strong political connections, was convicted in a high-profile case registered at Kotwali Police Station, Meerut. His once-unshakable influence was now reduced to courtroom rulings and heavy fines.

Bachchu Yadav, another mafia figure with deep networks, was found guilty in two cases, his sentence including significant monetary penalties.

Dharmendra and his two associates, long known for their violent methods, were convicted in a case from Baghpat, all of them sentenced to prison terms and fines.

Even those who had already met their violent end weren't exempt from the wheels of justice. Sanjay Singh Singla, who had been killed in an earlier police operation, was handed a prison sentence and fines for his past crimes even after his death, ensuring that his criminal record did not fade into history without consequence.

In another landmark ruling, Anupam Dubey, convicted in a case at GRP Police Station, Farrukhabad, was sentenced to life imprisonment and slapped with a ₹1 lakh fine, severing his financial empire.

Udham Singh, a notorious name in western UP, found himself guilty in a case at Sarurpur Police Station, Meerut. The prison sentence that followed was more than a personal loss. It was the end of an era where his name alone had once kept people silent.

The courtroom reckoning continued. Vikrant alias Vicky and his two accomplices, men who had once run extortion rackets with impunity, were sentenced to ten years of imprisonment in a case registered at Kotwali Police Station, Baghpat.

Meanwhile, Rakesh Yadav, a man whose criminal dealings spanned multiple districts, was convicted in a case from Kotwali Police Station, Gorakhpur. The five-year prison term and fines imposed on him left his once-powerful network in complete disarray.

The crackdown was merciless in its pursuit. Sunil Rathi and his three associates, a faction long feared in UP's rural strongholds, were found guilty in two cases, sentenced to imprisonment and financial penalties. The same fate awaited Sudhir Singh, whose conviction in a case registered at Cantt Police Station, Gorakhpur, ensured that his chapter of crime ended with a cold prison cell.

No name, no legacy, no past influence could shield these men anymore.

5
The State Strikes Back

Even in Lucknow, once considered impenetrable territory of the underworld, the law closed in with full force. Harvinder Singh, known as Jugnu Balia, was convicted in a case at Alambagh Police Station. His sentence – prison and monetary penalties – was yet another nail in the coffin of UP's mafia rule.

The wave of convictions continued unabated, ensuring that no don, no matter how feared, could walk free. The state had been reclaimed, one judgment at a time.

With every conviction, the legal foundations of UP's underworld crumbled further. The courts were no longer places where criminals found loopholes or delayed their fate.

There was no room left for technicalities, backdoor settlements or political shields. The justice system had turned into a machine of accountability, ensuring that every mafia figure, regardless of his past influence or connections, met the full force of the law.

The message was loud and irreversible – UP was no longer a land where the mafias ruled the streets. The golden era of crime lords had ended.

The police and the administration stood as one relentless force, dismantling the organized crime networks that had thrived for decades.

But the state understood that to truly erase the mafias, it wasn't enough to imprison the men who ran the syndicates. The next strike had to be against what made them untouchable – their wealth.

The fall of another key syndicate came when Sharif and his six accomplices were convicted in a high-profile case from Kotwali Police Station, Meerut. The verdict? Rigorous imprisonment and heavy fines, ensuring that their network of crime collapsed not just in manpower but also in financial strength.

This was just the beginning. The real war was about to be fought on a completely different battlefield – against the very fortunes that had kept the mafias afloat for generations.

If there was one thing the mafias relied on as much as their muscle power, it was their money. Illegally acquired wealth had protected them, funded their crimes and allowed them to build political connections. But now, the very source of their power had turned into their greatest vulnerability.

Recognizing that the wealth of the mafias was their last line of defence, the UP government, in collaboration with multiple enforcement agencies, launched a crackdown unlike anything seen before.

This wasn't just about seizing bank accounts or freezing assets. It was also about erasing the very foundation of organized crime.

₹4,059.57 crore. That was the staggering worth of confiscated and demolished properties – ₹40.59 billion in illegally acquired wealth stripped away from the mafias' grip.[36]

And these were not just numbers on a report. Entire mansions, commercial complexes, land parcels and benami properties – once symbols of untouchable crime syndicates – were now either in government custody, bulldozed to the ground or reclaimed by the law.

What had once been fortresses of fear – lavish estates where gangsters hosted meetings, laundered money and controlled their networks – were reduced to dust, wiped from existence.

There was no rebuilding from this. The mafias had lost their freedom, financial immunity, safehouses and last strongholds. This was the final death knell of organized crime in UP.

But seizing property alone was not enough. The state went a step further – initiating legal proceedings to permanently transfer these assets to government ownership. This meant that for the first time in UP's history of crime, properties once considered untouchable strongholds of the mafias were now legally absorbed into the state's coffers, beyond the reach of their former owners.

With the legal framework set, the crackdown expanded further, leaving no district untouched. The next phase saw an even more ambitious target – ₹14,000 crore (₹140 billion) worth of illegally acquired assets placed under confiscation and legal takeover procedures. No syndicate, no mafia stronghold was spared. The network that once funded political connections, ran extortion rackets and facilitated underground businesses was being dismantled, brick by brick, rupee by rupee.

Among the most high-profile seizures was that of Atiq Ahmed, a mafia figure whose reign of terror had been rooted in deep financial control over Prayagraj's underworld. His ₹50 crore worth of properties were officially transferred to the state government, cutting off his family's financial resources as well as delivering a strong message to crime syndicates across the state.[37] This was not just about law enforcement anymore – this was also about economic justice, about ensuring that crime did not just result in prison sentences but in complete financial ruin.

The confiscation drive was a structured, legally-backed effort to ensure that the mafias' fortunes could never be reclaimed, never be transferred to a new generation of criminals, never be resurrected in another name. With every seized plot of land, every confiscated bank account and every demolished illegal mansion, the era of untouchable mafia dynasties was being erased from UP's history.

Justice in UP was no longer simply about punishing past crimes, it was also about preventing future empires from rising. The war against the mafias was a long-term strategy to ensure that the void left by fallen gangsters wasn't filled by their protégés or former associates.

The law and order division of the UP Police took preemptive control over the entire organized crime network in the state. Sixty-eight high-profile mafia leaders and their extended networks were placed under continuous surveillance, their movements monitored, their financial transactions tracked and their communication networks infiltrated.

This was a methodical, intelligence-driven operation designed to identify and dismantle any remnants of mafia influence before they could regroup. Preventive legal measures were put into place to block parole applications, revoke bail approvals and keep known offenders from returning to criminal operations under different guises.

The mafias were losing their freedom and future. The funding pipelines had been cut off, their influence networks destroyed and their legal loopholes permanently closed. The message was unambiguous. Crime would no longer pay in UP. There would be no resurgence, no second wave of dominance, no return to power.

What had started as a series of high-profile raids and encounters had now escalated into a war that spanned years, ensuring there were no cracks left for the underworld to slip through. This was not a temporary clean-up. This was an irreversible shift in power.

The streets that were once ruled by gang lords, where the common man feared speaking against criminals, were now reclaimed by the law. UP had undergone a transformation that was not just visible in the crime statistics but in the very psyche of its people.

There was no room left for escape.

The fight against organized crime in UP had reached its most decisive phase. This was no longer a series of isolated operations – it was a full-scale war waged against the state's most dangerous mafia bosses and their criminal networks. Under direct orders from the state administration, the UP Police initiated an unprecedented assault on sixty-eight identified mafia dons and their associates, shaking the very foundation of organized crime in the state. For decades, these names had been synonymous with unchecked power, ruling territories through violence, extortion and political manipulation.

Now, the balance had shifted, and the law was closing in with unrelenting force.

The results were nothing short of staggering.

Across UP, 1,359 criminals tied to these organized crime syndicates were subjected to legal action. The crackdown was swift and unforgiving. Around 775 criminal cases were registered, leading to the arrests of 611 key offenders – men who once operated above the law, now reduced to inmates awaiting their fate.[38]

But not every criminal had the luxury of standing trial.

Nineteen gangsters, including four of the most high-profile mafia bosses and fifteen of their enforcers, were killed in police encounters. These were men who had terrorized cities, built entire criminal empires and manipulated the system for decades. Their downfall sent a clear message – there would be no negotiations, no bargains, no escape routes.

The Gangsters Act became one of the sharpest legal weapons in this war, ensuring that mafia figures were not just arrested but permanently incapacitated from rebuilding their networks. In total, 752 gangsters were booked under its stringent provisions, their assets frozen, their operations dismantled.

For those whose criminal reach extended into national security threats, the state invoked the National Security Act (NSA), detaining eighteen hardcore offenders who posed a direct threat to public order.

To further cripple the organized crime structure, police identified 113 active gangs, registering them as criminal groups and placing every member under surveillance. No longer could they operate from the shadows, their names officially recorded in law enforcement databases, ensuring their activities were monitored, disrupted and ultimately killed.

The crackdown extended beyond arrests. It focused on stripping the mafias of all means of power. Legal firearm licenses were revoked, district-wide bans were imposed and history-sheets were opened for repeat offenders. Twenty-nine criminals lost their bail protections, ninety-six offenders were expelled from their respective districts and 358 licensed weapons were seized, ensuring that the mafias' access to legally sanctioned firearms was completely severed.

To cement this permanent shift in power, law enforcement introduced new legal provisions under Section 129 of the Bharatiya Nyaya Samhita (BNS; 110G CrPC) in 2023, resulting in 429 criminals being booked under its purview. Simultaneously, history-sheets were opened for 457 hardened criminals, branding them as repeat offenders under constant police scrutiny.

The State Strikes Back

The entire ecosystem of organized crime was being systematically dismantled, ensuring that even those who had escaped punishment for years found themselves backed into a corner.

This was not a short-lived crackdown – it had been in motion since 20 March 2017, an all-out assault on the most hardened criminals in the state. The numbers reflected the scale and intensity of this battle.

Over the years, 210 criminals were killed in police encounters, while 7,510 others were wounded in direct armed confrontations with law enforcement.

But the war on organized crime came at a steep, human cost. It wasn't just a battle of laws and bullets. It was a war fought with blood, grit and silent courage. Seventeen brave police officers laid down their lives in the line of duty, staring down gunfire and danger with nothing but their uniform and resolve. They didn't flinch. They didn't retreat. Alongside them, 1,626 officers were wounded in brutal clashes – flesh torn, bones shattered, but spirit unbroken. These were not mere statistics. They were the pulse behind a campaign that crushed syndicates once thought invincible. Their sacrifices didn't just uphold the law. They lit the fire that turned a state's resolve into an unstoppable force.

At the sharp edge of UP's war on organized crime stood a force feared by gangsters and revered by citizens – the STF. A shadow unit trained for surgical precision, the STF didn't knock, it struck. In 52 high-voltage encounters, they hunted down the most wanted trigger-happy warlords, extortionists and mob lieutenants who had long evaded the grasp of law. Each mission was a silent thunderclap, planned in secrecy, executed with ruthless efficiency. When the STF moved, it wasn't just a police operation, it was also an unmistakable message to every mafia kingpin in the state: your empire ends where our crosshairs begin.

The fight extended to rewarded criminals, those whose notoriety had grown to such an extent that the government had placed bounties on their heads.

As many as 19,631 criminals with cash rewards were arrested and sent to jail, stripping the underworld of its most-wanted fugitives. Among them, 17,570 criminals, each carrying a ₹25,000 bounty, were captured and imprisoned; 1,845 offenders with rewards between ₹25,000 and ₹50,000 were tracked down and taken into custody; 216 high-value criminals, whose bounties exceeded ₹50,000, were hunted, arrested and permanently removed from the streets.[39]

This was a total reconstruction of law and order in UP. Crime syndicates that had once operated like parallel governments, wielding influence over politics, law enforcement and business, now lay in ruins.

The streets no longer belonged to the underworld. The final tally of arrests, encounters and asset seizures stood as a testament to a war that left no room for resurgence. This was the new UP. A state where the mafias had finally met their reckoning.

The financial backbone of UP's underworld was shattered through one of the most aggressive asset seizures in the state's history. The Gangsters Act became the scalpel that carved out every layer of their illicit fortunes, leaving them crippled, vulnerable and unable to rebuild.

The numbers alone painted a picture of total destruction.

Under the National Security Act (NSA), 923 criminals were detained, ensuring that those who posed the most immediate threats to public safety were placed under high-security custody. The Gangsters Act, designed to strip crime syndicates of their wealth and influence, was invoked in a staggering 24,983 cases, leading to the arrests of 78,143 criminals. Each arrest was a strike against the financial pillars of the mafias, bringing down the networks that had sustained organized crime for generations.

The final and most decisive blow came through the unprecedented confiscation of assets.

In 4,847 cases filed under Section 14(1) of the Gangsters Act, a record-breaking ₹14,040 crore (₹140.40 billion) worth of movable and immovable properties were seized – palatial homes, benami plots, luxury hotels, commercial complexes and front businesses that had long served as the financial lifeblood of UP's most dangerous crime syndicates. This wasn't just a wave of routine confiscations, it was also a ruthless economic war. The police dismantled the network that sustained the gangsters. With each seizure and demolition, the state tore through the underworld's economic spine, striking at the very heart of their power. These were calculated, high-impact blows delivered with surgical precision. For the first time in India's law-enforcement history, crime was punished with prison and stripped of its profit. It was justice with an economic payload, and it left the mafias cornered and bankrupt.

This was no longer just a crime crackdown, this was also a war of total financial annihilation. The impact of this unprecedented assault on organized crime was immediate and irreversible. With thousands of mafia operatives behind bars, hundreds of high-profile criminals killed and billions of rupees in illegal wealth stripped away, the underworld's hold on UP was shattered.

Fear had changed sides.

For decades, mafia dons had dictated the rules of engagement – police officers feared political repercussions, witnesses feared testifying and the common people feared speaking against criminals. But now, the fear belonged to the mafias. There was nowhere left to run, no money left to buy protection, no power left to wield in the corridors of influence.

The state had spoken and its message was final: there would be no return, no resurgence, no second coming of organized crime in UP.

The law had finally caught up with them, and there was no escaping justice.

What had begun as a determined campaign against organized crime had now transformed into a historic benchmark for law enforcement in India.

The UP government and PHQ, through a combination of surgical operations, legal precision and relentless pursuit of justice, had achieved what once seemed impossible. They had systematically identified, dismantled and erased the state's most powerful mafia networks.

With every district, every police commissionerate mobilized, the crackdown expanded beyond conventional mafia operations, targeting a wide range of criminal networks that had been looting the state for years. New battlegrounds were drawn against the biggest and most organized mafias in the country: the land mafia that operated through open encroachments, property fraud and forced land grabs; the mining mafia that drained UP's natural resources, running illegal mining and smuggling operations with political backing; and the forest mafia, whose gangs cleared protected forests, turning nature into black-market riches. But the offensive didn't stop there. Drug gangs and liquor syndicates were chased down with the same force; their secret factories shut, their supply chains cut off. Even education had been corrupted. Fake degree scams, admissions fraud and exploitation inside academic institutions were exposed and rooted out. The cattle smuggling mafia, with its vast network of transporters, middlemen and cross-border operators, was taken apart piece by piece. For the first time, these powerful crime syndicates who had long believed they were untouchable were dragged into the open and made to pay. Their empires, built on fear and political connections, crumbled under one unshakable message: the state was no longer theirs to plunder.

The effect was immediate.

The eradication of these networks didn't just lower crime rates, it also transformed the very fabric of the state.

For the first time in decades, public confidence in the law was restored. Businesses, once fearful of mafia extortion, invested freely. Citizens, once afraid to speak up, walked without fear.

This was economic revival, social transformation and a statement to the world that UP was now a state governed by law.

The battle had been long, the war had been brutal and the sacrifices had been immense. But the result was undeniable. The mafias were finished. UP had been reclaimed.

The impact of UP's most ambitious crackdown on organized crime was not measured in arrests, encounters or confiscated assets. Its true success lay in the transformation of the state itself.

For years, crime and corruption had strangled the potential of UP, scaring away investors, stalling development and making lawlessness an accepted reality. That era was now over.

With the mafias' power dismantled, the streets were safer, law and order had been restored and crime rates had dropped to historic lows. The fear that once gripped the common man had been lifted, replaced by a renewed trust in governance and security forces.

The effects rippled far beyond the realm of law enforcement. Investor confidence surged, as businesses – both domestic and international – saw a transformed UP, no longer controlled by the hand of organized crime. What was once a state notorious for corruption and criminal–political nexus had now become a beacon of investment and economic revival.

The 'ease of doing business' index soared, with the government's aggressive reforms ensuring a smoother, more transparent bureaucratic framework. The legacy of red tape, extortion and backdoor dealings was being wiped out, making UP an emerging economic powerhouse in India.

The most significant victory of this campaign wasn't in crime control or economic growth, it was in the dismantling of a long-standing narrative that law enforcement in UP was selective, biased and politically motivated.

From the very beginning, critics, Opposition leaders, media analysts, social activists and NGOs had targeted the police force, accusing them of religious and political bias in their crackdown. Every operation, every encounter and every arrest was scrutinized, questioned and politicized.

Yet the facts stood in stark contrast to the accusations.

The list of criminals killed, arrested and prosecuted under Prashant Kumar's leadership cut across every divide – caste, creed, religion and political affiliation. Mob bosses who had once thrived under political protection, regardless of which party they aligned with, found themselves equally hunted by the law. There were no exceptions, no safe havens, no protected territories.

The police force, battered by criticism, responded in the only way they knew how – with action.

Every encounter, every crackdown, every case pursued was a resounding answer to those who doubted the integrity of this campaign. The rule of law had replaced the rule of crime and justice had been delivered without prejudice.

There was still work to be done – no battle against crime was ever truly over. New threats would emerge, new criminals would attempt to rise, and the war on lawlessness would remain ongoing. But with this historic offensive, UP had set a precedent that would be studied, analysed and remembered. This was the story of a state that refused to surrender to crime, a police force that refused to be intimidated, and a government that refused to let fear dictate policy.

The march towards progress had begun, and there was no turning back as UP evolved from a state once crippled by lawlessness and limited opportunities into a thriving business powerhouse.

With the mafias crushed, their financial empires obliterated and their influence buried in legal oblivion, UP stood at a crossroads. Would the state merely celebrate its hard-fought victory over crime, or would it seize this moment to rewrite its destiny?

The answer came in the form of an economic revolution.

Freed from the shackles of organized crime, the state became fertile ground for investment industry, and infrastructure. The fear that once kept investors at bay had been replaced by unshakable confidence. Corporates that once dismissed UP as hostile territory now saw it as the next big frontier. Entrepreneurs who once factored in 'protection costs' as an unavoidable business expense now found themselves dealing with a government that protected them, not extorted them.

This was not just about economic policy, it was also about the triumph of governance over anarchy.

The transformation was swift, undeniable and staggering. UP, which had languished under the weight of corruption and crime, surged past West Bengal to become the third-largest state in terms of operational companies – a feat unthinkable just a few years prior. A total of 145,009 active companies now called UP home, edging past West Bengal and standing only behind Maharashtra and Delhi.

The state's industrial revolution wasn't built on empty rhetoric. In just eighteen months, UP added nearly 30,000 new companies, a rate of business expansion second only to Maharashtra.[40] The change was so profound that even long-time critics of the administration had to acknowledge the shift.

This wasn't just an increase in numbers. It was the dawn of a new era – one where UP was no longer a mere political giant but an economic powerhouse, a magnet for investment and the heart of India's industrial resurgence.

The numbers were a direct result of sweeping reforms that synchronized law enforcement with economic policymaking. Under the Business Reform Action Plan (BRAP), UP implemented 186 of the 187 policy recommendations prescribed by the central government. The changes touched every aspect of industry – labour laws, land administration, commercial dispute resolution and construction permits.

At the heart of this transformation was Nivesh Mitra, the state's single-window clearance system, which slashed bureaucratic red tape and made business registrations seamless. Over 2.2 lakh applications for No Objection Certificates (NOCs) had been processed, with a staggering 94 per cent resolved, signalling the state's commitment to efficiency.

What once required months of navigating corrupt networks and kickbacks could now be achieved with a few clicks. The era of 'babu culture' and backdoor deals had been erased, replaced by digital governance and transparency.

Investor confidence was at an all-time high as the momentum didn't go unnoticed. When UP hosted the Global Investors Summit in 2023, the response was overwhelming, with investment proposals crossing ₹40 lakh crore – a sum that, if fully realized, would transform India's largest state forever. More importantly, ₹10 lakh crore worth of investments had already been materialized, with projects breaking ground at a record pace. The industries flocking to UP weren't limited to traditional manufacturing. Consumer electronics, IT, defence production and high-tech startups began to see UP as fertile ground.

The message was clear. This was no longer a crime-ridden badland. This was India's new land of opportunity.

What made this economic transformation possible was the iron-fisted law enforcement that ensured criminals no longer held businesses hostage. With crime no longer a barrier, UP's workforce, one of the largest in India, was finally able to work and innovate without the looming threat of extortion, creating a business-friendly environment that fuelled growth and investment.

Foreign investors, once wary of setting up operations in the state due to its volatile crime history, now saw one that prioritized security, economic incentives and infrastructure development.

For the first time, law and order were no longer a challenge but a competitive advantage. The transformation of UP wasn't merely about numbers, rankings or reforms – it was about reclaiming the state's future. A place once dictated by fear was now driven by ambition.

Where mafia dons once controlled entire cities, today, multinational corporations were setting up factories. Where extortion money once fuelled political campaigns, today, legitimate business investments were pouring in. Where fear silenced people, today, economic optimism was the loudest voice. This was the new UP – a state where crime had been hunted down, justice had been served and economic prosperity had become the new order of the day.

The purge of organized crime had been brutal, decisive and absolute. But the true victory lay not just in the fall of the mafias, it lay also in the rise of a new UP, one built on the foundations of law, order and limitless economic potential.

And this was only the beginning.

6
Justice Delivered

They weren't just donning khaki. They were shouldering the mandate of 240 million lives.

In the heartland of India, the UP Police – the world's largest civilian police force – was undergoing a quiet but profound transformation. Under the steady, unflinching leadership of Prashant Kumar, a new chapter was being written in law enforcement. Not with fanfare, but with fierce resolve. Not through slogans, but through results.

A vision took root: 'Safety and Respect for All'. This was a solemn promise, one that echoed through dusty chowkis and high-tech control rooms alike. With zero tolerance for crime and criminals, and a mission to weave peace and harmony through the thread of law, this was transformation sweeping across the state like a tide.

Armed with technology, compassion and resolve, the UP Police embraced a new era of citizen-friendly, smart policing – where modernization met accountability and law met humanity.

Since 2017, a silent but sweeping transformation has redefined the very idea of law enforcement in India's most populous state. Behind this turnaround was a man who believed in steel-clad discipline wrapped in silent conviction – Prashant Kumar. Under his watch, law and order was not just enforced, it was also restored, recalibrated and reimagined.

The shift was systemic. With the establishment of police commissionerates in seven of the state's biggest cities, the tempo of policing changed quickly. Complaints were no longer mere entries in registers. They became calls to action. Public grievances were heard. Crime was chased, not just recorded.

And the results? The state, long known for its volatile fault lines, witnessed a marked decline in large-scale communal and caste-based violence, an achievement many once thought impossible.

Through years where India braved some of its most sensitive moments, UP witnessed an unprecedented calm. Ganesh Chaturthi, Eid, Diwali, Muharram, Holi, Chehlum, Chhath Puja, Barawafat, Shravan Shivratri – every festival that once carried the scent of tension now flowed in celebration. Even mammoth gatherings like the Magh Mela, Ayodhya Deepotsav and Kumbh, once nightmares for the law-and-order machinery, were managed with near-military precision and a civilian heart.

Then came 22 January 2024 – etched forever in Indian history. The day Lord Shri Ram was consecrated at the newly built Ram Mandir in Ayodhya. A moment of divine emotion for millions. A potential flashpoint for disruption. But the UP Police had already done their math. Under Prashant Kumar's calibrated planning, the Pran Pratishtha ceremony unfolded without a single untoward incident. What followed was even more telling – a tidal wave of devotees that continues to surge through Ayodhya, flowing in disciplined, spiritual synchrony, guided by invisible lines of police mastery.

This capacity for meticulous crowd management and pre-emptive peacekeeping would soon be tested on an even grander scale.

The success didn't stop at religious events. Global Investors Summit 2023, G-20 meetings, IPL matches, World Cup cricket, T20 internationals – events that drew the eyes of the world – were policed with such ease that disruption seemed not just unlikely, but impossible.

Behind the scenes, the police were not just managing people, they were also managing sound. Over 1.09 lakh loudspeakers were removed, another 1.65 lakh adjusted – all under a campaign of compliance, not coercion, with the cooperation of citizens and clerics alike. Noise levels dipped. Harmony soared.

And when democracy called, the police responded – not as enforcers but as guardians. From panchayat to Parliament, elections were held over seven years in an environment of peace, fairness and trust. Not a single booth was shaken. Not a single vote was stolen under the shadow of violence.

This wasn't just a shift in policing. It was a recalibration – from fear to faith, from chaos to calm. And Prashant Kumar was at the helm of it all – not chasing headlines, just quietly rewriting the story of a state once synonymous with strife.

Prashant Kumar knew that crime doesn't just wear a mask – it wears a crown. And to break that legacy, he went after the mafias. From September 2019 to January 2025, the state launched an unrelenting offensive against sixty-eight mafia kingpins and their sprawling networks. Their files were opened, their crimes revisited and their arrogance dismantled – in courtrooms, on roads and through bulldozers.

- Thirty-one mafias and seventy-four accomplices convicted in seventy-three airtight cases

- Two sentenced to death
- Nineteen killed in police operations
- 617 arrests made
- 113 gangs officially recognized and prosecuted

Weapons were seized. Firearms licenses revoked. Bail cancelled. Eviction notices pasted on once-untouchable properties. Every loophole once exploited by dons was now being used to bury them.

And then came the most devastating blow – the seizure and demolition of illegally acquired property worth over ₹4,076 crore. Palatial bungalows, commercial complexes, farmlands, warehouses – all swallowed by the state in one swift sweep of justice.

This wasn't just policing. It was reclamation – of streets, of power, of public faith. And at the centre of this relentless storm stood Prashant Kumar – a man who never flinched but made sure that criminals across UP slept with one eye open.

In a state once ruled by fear, even the dead weren't spared.

The new chapter in UP's war on crime wasn't just about arresting gangsters or demolishing hideouts – it was about reclaiming the soul of the state, rupee by rupee, acre by acre. Under the steadfast command of Prashant Kumar, the UP Police began to rewrite history by targeting what was once considered untouchable: the criminal economy itself.

Beyond the staggering scale of previous crackdowns, where mafia strongholds were bulldozed and underground empires crumbled, came a bold move – the identification and confiscation of benami properties. These were the faceless assets that had kept the underworld alive long after its faces had been jailed or killed.

And this time, the state didn't stop at freezing accounts or seizing properties – it went a step further. The ownership of these illegal assets was formally vested into the name of the

UP government. One of the most symbolic moments came in Prayagraj, where over ₹50 crore worth of benami property belonging to the late mafia don Atiq Ahmed was snatched from the shadows and transferred into the state's hands in a poetic justice etched in bricks and mortar.

On land once owned and lorded over by a gangster rose something unimaginable: housing for the poor. In the heart of Prayagraj, two modest towers – built from the ruins of crime – stood ready to house the very people who had once cowered under its legacy.

On a quiet Friday morning, the keys to these homes were handed over to the poor, the marginalized, the forgotten. Chosen through a transparent lottery, the new residents included the elderly, the differently abled, Dalits, tribals and Other Backward Classes (OBCs).

Arvind Chauhan, vice-chairman of the Prayagraj Development Authority, told the media, 'This was the land where Atiq ran his empire. Today, it runs on justice.'[41]

Once the nerve centre of Atiq Ahmed's criminal empire, the land had changed hands – not through sale or negotiation, but through the assertion of the law. What was once a fortress of fear had been reclaimed by the state. Bulldozers rolled in where extortionists once roamed, and in place of intimidation now stood a renewed sense of order.[42] Justice, not muscle, now defined the soil.

Each flat, priced at ₹6 lakh, came equipped with basic modern comforts: a bedroom, a hall, a kitchen, bathroom, balcony, electricity, sewerage and even parking. The beneficiaries would pay only ₹3.5 lakh. The rest was covered by the central and state governments – ₹1.5 lakh and ₹1 lakh, respectively.

This wasn't just a housing project, it was a statement as well – that the State doesn't forget, that justice can be a set of keys, a new address and the smile of a mother who finally has a place to call home.

In Prashant Kumar's interpretation, 'It was more than an administrative act. It was a public reclamation of stolen dignity.' Across the state, the police's drive to convert ill-gotten gains into public wealth gathered unprecedented momentum. What began with isolated actions soon snowballed into a statewide movement, where wealth once weaponized against society was now repurposed to uplift it.

The result was not just moral victory, it was also financial transformation. An extraordinary revenue surge followed, directly tied to Prashant Kumar's unrelenting campaign to ensure that no criminal legacy, not even one buried in bricks or bank accounts, would outlive the reach of justice.

But Prashant wasn't merely content with toppling empires.

He wanted closure. He wanted convictions.

That's how Operation Conviction was born – not as a policy, but as a mission. A war cry wrapped in silence. A final, unforgiving pursuit of justice that didn't rest at arrests. It aimed higher: at verdicts.

At the heart of this sweeping campaign was a radical overhaul of UP's criminal justice ecosystem. For too long, arrests had been celebrated while convictions lagged, buried under paperwork, adjournments and forgotten witnesses. Prashant Kumar decided to change the script.

He envisioned an unbreakable bridge between investigation and prosecution – a seamless relay from the moment of arrest to the clang of a prison gate.

And so, the state launched a digital brain – the Investigation, Prosecution and Conviction (IPC) Portal – a real-time tracker of justice.

From remote chowkis to the DG's command room, the system left no room for delay, oversight or excuse. District officers updated progress daily. Senior officers monitored it with clinical precision. The message was unambiguous: no case will fall through, no criminal will slip away.

To reinforce this machinery, a Prosecution Cell was created. It was led by seasoned officers, supported by ground-level coordination units and armed with a single motto: Justice, Delivered.

Each district was ordered to pick twenty of the most heinous cases in categories determined by the state, such as rape, murder, dacoity, illegal conversions, cow slaughter and fast-track them to conclusion. The goal: conviction within thirty days of charges being framed.

The results were seismic. Between July 2023 and February 2025:

- 74,059 individuals were convicted.
- 54 were sentenced to death.
- 6,664 were sentenced to life imprisonment.
- 1,167 were handed over twenty-year terms.
- 4,098 were jailed for ten to nineteen years.
- 6,141 were sentenced between five and nine years.
- 55,935 received shorter yet decisive sentences.[43]

Each judgment was a brick laid in the foundation of a justice system reborn. The operation's velocity was staggering – an average of 150 convictions per day.

To ensure quality didn't suffer in speed, a standardized crime-wise checklist was rolled out by DGP (Prosecution) Dipesh Juneja – ensuring forensic, digital and testimonial procedures aligned with India's new criminal code. Even the Allahabad High Court acknowledged its impact.

Meanwhile, the state's forensic infrastructure exploded – growing from four labs to twelve, with real-time fingerprint analysis through the National Automated Fingerprint Identification System (NAFIS), aiding in the resolution of over 75,000 cases.

In September 2024 alone, over 50,000 convictions were clocked across more than 36,000 cases. The operation's digital backbone even bagged a SKOCH Award for excellence in policing and governance.

This was justice as strategy, justice as architecture and, above all, justice with teeth. Operation Conviction redefined what a state can do when led by intent and powered by innovation. It turned a broken promise into a constitutional roar. And Prashant Kumar, calm and focused, never claimed credit. He simply ensured that the wheels of justice turned faster than ever before.

The age of impunity was over.

Even as the judicial machinery roared to life, another warfront was being fortified – one that demanded precision forces and strategic muscle. For a state as vast, diverse and volatile as UP, conventional policing was no longer enough. What it needed was surgical firepower.

Under Prashant Kumar's leadership, the state reimagined its operational backbone, giving birth to specialized forces tailored to tackle modern-day threats – from narcotics and terrorism to natural disasters and digital crime.

The Anti-Narcotics Task Force (ANTF) was first out of the gate, slicing through the dark web of drug syndicates that preyed on UP's youth. Armed with intelligence, coordination and field-ready agility, the ANTF struck at hideouts, cross-border networks and supply chains like a scalpel.

The Anti-Terrorism Squad (ATS) was then deployed with expanded infrastructure across sensitive districts – Prayagraj, Bahraich, Ayodhya, Gautam Buddha Nagar, Shravasti, Lucknow and Jhansi. These weren't just anti-terror hubs, they were also early warning systems. Surveillance, cyber intelligence and tactical strike units worked as one, neutralizing threats before they could grow legs.

The STF in Ayodhya added another layer of surgical capability – targeting organized crime with speed, stealth and unforgiving precision.

Meanwhile, UP's Special Security Force (SSF) was carved out in 2021 to shield the state's most critical assets – airports, high-risk court complexes and government installations. With 5,037 posts sanctioned and eighty-seven top command roles created, the SSF stood guard not just with guns, but with purpose.

In tandem, the state bolstered its State Disaster Response Force (SDRF) – tripling its capacity to six fully operational companies. Earthquakes, floods, building collapses – no crisis went unanswered.

Then came the heart of the human shield: Mission Shakti.

A war against fear. A revolution of resolve. A state-wide campaign to make women and children not just safe, but fearless.

Then came the real test. How to translate law and order into lasting security for the most vulnerable. For Prashant Kumar, that meant Mission Shakti.

As head of the UP Police, he launched Anti-Romeo Squads across the state, patrolling over one crore locations, interacting with more than four crore people, and taking legal action against more than 32,000 offenders, while issuing 1.4 crore warnings.

Designed to reclaim public spaces for women, the initiative sparked debate. If it was praised by some for dramatically reducing harassment, it was also criticized by others for overreach, moral policing and instances of privacy encroachment.

Despite the backlash, Kumar defended the squads, reinforcing their mandate to issue warnings first and prosecute repeat offenders in a stance that kept the programme alive through multiple phases.

Prashant Kumar didn't stop at enforcement. He personally directed the deployment of 20,000 female beat officers, who met 2.7 lakh survivors, hearing their stories, offering counsel and restoring faith in the system. Under his stewardship, Mission Shakti 4.0 registered 3.9 lakh complaints – resolving more than 3.8 lakh. Each case became a measure of his belief: policing must be visible, accessible and accountable.

When Mission Shakti 5.0 was rolled out on Navratri 2024, Kumar engineered a multi-pronged offensive: Operation Garud targeted cybercrime, Majnu confronted public harassment, Bachpan rescued missing children, and Shield and Destroy struck illicit dens. These operations weren't bureaucratic mandates. They were tactical campaigns he personally championed, with precision, urgency and measurable results.

This was not just crime-fighting. It was confidence-building. Prashant Kumar faced opposition; critics questioned the squadrons' methods, but he stood firm. By maintaining a legal-first approach, he ensured the mission survived scrutiny and took root. For him, Mission Shakti became more than policing; it was a personal mission to prove that law enforcement can be both firm and fair, unshakeable yet humane.

Additional Director General Padmaja Chauhan received national recognition for her leadership in expanding the role of women beat constables and launching targeted drives against illegal activities affecting women's safety.

UP was acknowledged for having the highest number of women police personnel in India, reflecting the state's commitment to gender-inclusive policing.

Mission Shakti 5.0 stands as a testament to the state's unwavering dedication to creating a safe, empowering and inclusive environment for women and children. Through strategic operations, infrastructural developments and community engagement, the initiative has set a benchmark for holistic governance and proactive policing.

Each mission, each raid, each rescue was a promise kept. The khaki no longer just chased crime, it also anticipated, intercepted and annihilated it. And in the middle of it all stood Prashant Kumar – watching, guiding, correcting, commanding – not as a figurehead but as a man who turned a police force into a public shield. He had redefined what it meant to govern with resolve, lead with compassion and protect with might.

What began as a quiet churn in 2017 had, by 2025, erupted into a full-blown transformation of law enforcement in India's most complex state. This was no longer a story about policing. It was about power held to account. It was about fear being uprooted. It was about citizens learning to live without looking over their shoulders.

In every corner of UP, there now echoed a different kind of siren. Not one of alarm but of assurance.

Children walked to school without fear. Women raised their voices without shame. Officers stood as shields. For the first time in decades, people believed in justice.

Prashant believed that a khaki uniform could still inspire confidence. That laws could still speak louder than lathis. That a force built on discipline and driven by empathy could rewrite the future of India's most populous state. Under his watch, the UP Police redefined what it meant to enforce the law. And in doing so, they turned the tide – not just against crime but against cynicism.

This belief was a blueprint for a better state, a better system, a better tomorrow. The revolution had no drumrolls – only resolve and results.

PART 2
Organizing the Greatest Mela on Earth

7
Faith, Flow and the Force

It began as a sacred ritual but soon became a global phenomenon. Over forty-five winter days, from 13 January to 26 February 2025, the city of Prayagraj witnessed a gathering so vast, so relentless and so awe-inspiring that it defied modern comprehension. An estimated 66 crore people – nearly half the population of India – descended upon the banks of the Ganga, Yamuna and the mythical Saraswati, transforming the Maha Kumbh Mela into what many now call the largest human congregation in recorded history. But to fully grasp the weight of that statement, one must place it beside other legendary gatherings – religious pilgrimages, political rallies and global movements. Only then can the staggering scale, ambition and spiritual gravitas of Maha Kumbh 2025 be truly understood.

Over forty-five days, the Maha Kumbh Mela 2025 became a living, breathing superorganism, pulsing with the footsteps of over half-a-billion pilgrims. Unlike India's general elections, which unfold in phases, the Kumbh gathered this ocean of humanity in one place, beneath the same sky, at the same time.

On its most sacred day – Mauni Amavasya, 29 January – an estimated 8 to 10 crore pilgrims took the holy dip, making it possibly the busiest single day in human history. No other spiritual or civic gathering has witnessed such intensity within such a narrow window of time.

And it wasn't just the count – it was also the density and the choreography. Spread across a labyrinthine 4,000 hectares, the Kumbh was partitioned into twenty-five self-contained sectors, each functioning like a city within a city. On any given day, between 15 to 17.5 million people flowed through the grounds – an ebb and tide of faith unlike anything the world has ever managed to orchestrate. For forty-five days straight, Prayagraj carried the weight of humanity's most sacred longing – and didn't buckle.

Even accounting for repeat bathers and returning locals, a conservative estimate of 40 crore unique attendees still places the 2025 Maha Kumbh in a league of its own. This wasn't a congregation – it was civilization convened. To call it the largest human gathering in history isn't hyperbole, it's an acknowledgement of statistical fact, logistical mastery and cultural gravity. Against the backdrop of the world's most iconic events, the comparison becomes strikingly one-sided.

Previous Kumbh Melas – once the gold standard of large-scale pilgrimages – seem modest in retrospect. The 2013 edition attracted 12 crore people over fifty-five days. By 2019, that figure doubled to 25 crore. Yet the 2025 Maha Kumbh obliterated records. It was 5.5 times larger than the 2013 Mela and more than twice the size of the 2019 Ardh Kumbh.[44] With superior transport, digital outreach and a surge in global spiritual curiosity, the Kumbh didn't expand – it evolved.

What about global religious events? By 2012, the annual Hajj pilgrimage drew a staggering 3.16 million pilgrims to Mecca, the highest figure on record at the time, and even on its holiest day at Arafat, nearly 2 million came together in prayer and reflection.[45] The Maha Kumbh welcomed that many people before breakfast every day. While the Hajj excels in density and precision, the Kumbh's sprawling scale and daily rhythm are of an entirely different dimension.

Even the most emotional flashpoints in human history pale in comparison to the scale of the Kumbh. Ayatollah Khomeini's funeral in 1989 drew as many as 17 million mourners in a single, chaotic day; Fidel Castro's triumphant entry into Havana saw a million line the streets; Pope John Paul II's mass in Manila gathered 5 million and the 2003 anti-Iraq War protests spanned 600 cities with an estimated 15 million people. But none matched the single-day peak of the Kumbh's Mauni Amavasya, when close to 10 crore pilgrims bathed in the icy waters of faith – an intensity sustained not for a moment but for six uninterrupted weeks, and without breaking down.

In every measurable way – volume, consistency, planning and spiritual significance – Maha Kumbh 2025 didn't stand apart, it stood alone. If it was a miracle of faith, it was equally a masterclass in statecraft and strategy. At the centre of this miracle stood the UP Police, whose job was not merely to maintain order but to anticipate chaos and prevent it from ever arriving.

More than 37,000 police personnel were deployed across the event, including 1,378 women officers dedicated specifically to the safety and dignity of female devotees.[46] Specialized units like the Rapid Action Force (RAF), PAC and National Disaster Response Force (NDRF) stood ready to tackle any escalation – natural or man-made.

But the real strength of the system lay not in its numbers, but in its layers. While boots on the ground maintained physical order, a quieter, more clinical battle was being fought in the background. The force's surveillance and intelligence wing quietly ran a parallel mission – integrating AI-generated data with human inputs to flag and neutralize threats, including potential terrorist activity. Regular sweeps by the Bomb Detection and Disposal Squad ensured that not a single suspicious object turned into a calamity. This constant background vigilance, largely invisible to the public, became the unseen scaffolding of the entire operation. When the final sacred bath took place on 26 February, as the Maha Kumbh culminated with the Maha Shivratri *snan*, Prashant Kumar stood before the press – not as a triumphant officer but as a man who had weathered the unimaginable andkept the system from falling.

'We have presented an unprecedented model of crowd management, security and techniques,' he said, in a composed voice that belied the storm he had walked through. 'We made use of world-class technologies and AI for crowd management and surveillance.'

This wasn't a statement of pride, it was a summary of survival. Over 15 to 17.5 million pilgrims every day, and a staggering 80 million on Mauni Amavasya alone.[47] No global event, no religious gathering, no festival – not even the Hajj – came close. And yet the city endured. The rituals continued. The system held.

Prashant Kumar was quick to credit Chief Minister Yogi Adityanath's vision for the scale and ambition behind the preparations. But the execution, the moment-to-moment calibration, the real-time decision-making was the UP Police's burden. And it was under Prashant's command that the 37,000 personnel, the 2,700 AI-enabled cameras, the drones, the mobile app and the layers of analogue wisdom came together as one organism.[48]

It wasn't perfect. But it was, in every sense of the word, unprecedented.

By the end of it all, standing on the banks of a city that had hosted the world, Prashant Kumar didn't speak in metaphors. He spoke in numbers because that was the language this Kumbh had forced everyone to learn.

'More than 65 crore devotees took a holy dip in Prayagraj,' he said on the final day, as Maha Shivratri brought the Kumbh to a close.

The official figure would later settle at 66 crore, but in that moment, his number came from the nerve centre – the Integrated Command and Control Centre (ICCC) – which had tracked the movement of bodies and belief with real-time precision. It was a staggering number, a figure that dwarfed every global comparison. The Hajj's 2–3 million, Brazil's Carnival, the Ardh Kumbh of 2019 – no event came remotely close.

And yet it wasn't just about quantity. It was about how, despite the surge, the system adapted. 'Each day,' Prashant noted, 'the crowd exceeded what we'd anticipated. But the systems held – because they had to.' It was a subtle acknowledgement: the plan had evolved in real time, as millions beyond prediction flowed in.

If faith was the heartbeat of the Kumbh, then technology was its nervous system – quiet, precise and indispensable. And no one understood that better than Prashant Kumar.

At the heart of this massive operation was a digital nervous system, pulsing 24/7 with intelligence, instinct and innovation. Over 2,700 surveillance cameras – including 328 powered by AI – streamed crowd density and behaviour metrics to the ICCC, turning the control room into a live dashboard of faith in motion.[49] Above, Garuda Rakshak drones swept the skies, their offline, satellite-tracked systems immune to network failures. On the ground, officers synced in real time via the Maha Kumbh Mela 2025 Police App, geotagging incidents, flagging bottlenecks and coordinating responses from ghat to highway with zero delay.

This wasn't innovation for the sake of spectacle. It was technology repurposed for survival – a hard-learned evolution from earlier Kumbh editions where blind spots, network collapse and human fatigue had nearly undone the best-laid plans. This time, the tools worked. The alerts triggered. The cameras predicted. The app connected.

'Technology wasn't just our support system,' Prashant later said. 'It was our second skin.'

While the crowd saw prayers, hymns and sacred baths, those in uniform saw something else too: possibility of sabotage. In the background of this grand spiritual confluence, danger was watching.

'Lajar Masih had planned a major terrorist attack during the Maha Kumbh,' Prashant Kumar revealed on 6 March in a chilling post-event briefing. 'His links to the ISI were established.'

Masih wasn't just a rogue element, he was part of a cross-border plan involving arms and narcotics smuggling using drones, a new frontier of threat. He was arrested by the UP Police's STF in Kaushambi weeks before his plan could take shape among the vulnerable millions at the Kumbh.

Prashant Kumar spoke of it without theatrics. But the subtext was unmistakable: a catastrophe had been averted by layers of vigilance.

The seven-tier security grid – already a logistical marvel – was also a strategic firewall. Under Prashant's directive, sensitive zones and key chokepoints were under constant surveillance. The Bomb Detection and Disposal Squads worked in silent rotations.

Every entry point was scrutinized, not just for traffic but also for intent.

This was counter-terrorism at devotional scale. And it happened quietly, away from the chants and conches, because of a system that had learned to look where the eye couldn't.

The morning of 29 January left behind more than flowers and wet footprints. It left behind questions.

The Mauni Amavasya stampede, which occurred around 1–2 a.m., became the darkest hour of the Maha Kumbh. At least thirty people died, possibly more – some reports placed the toll as high as seventy-nine.[50] A crush of pilgrims, a breach in crowd control, a moment of panic, and the world's largest gathering was suddenly staring at its most public failure.

Prashant Kumar, by then the face of the Kumbh's policing, didn't dodge the questions. But he didn't offer easy answers either.

'The commission's investigation will bring out the truth,' he told *Navbharat Times* a few days later. 'We acted swiftly to manage the situation and ensure the festival continued.'

He refused to cite a final death toll, citing the ongoing judicial probe, and instead pointed to the response: over fifty ambulances dispatched within minutes, creation of a green corridor for medical teams and the fact that by 8 a.m., over 30 million devotees had bathed without further disruption.

It was a difficult balancing act – honouring the dead, restoring order and not letting panic derail faith. But critics were vocal. Videos circulated of police allegedly using sticks to rouse sleeping pilgrims, possibly worsening the stampede. Some questioned whether the urgency to restore the flow of the festival had overtaken the need to pause and reassess.

Prashant Kumar didn't lash out or rebut headlines. He simply held his ground.'The system responded,' he said. And then he let the data, the recovery and the rest of the Kumbh tell the story.

As the festival moved towards its final snan on Maha Shivratri, the memory of the Mauni Amavasya stampede still hung in the air. The system, frayed but intact, had to prove itself one last time. 'We are making comprehensive arrangements for traffic control, crowd management and ensuring a smooth experience for devotees, especially during the last bath,' Prashant told reporters on 22 February.

He said it not as reassurance but as obligation. Alongside Chief Secretary Manoj Kumar Singh, Prashant Kumar reviewed every corridor, checkpoint and ghat, focusing on regulated movement, parking expansions across 1,800 hectares, and the ten recalibrated traffic schemes designed after the chaos of late January. The learned scars of Mauni Amavasya had birthed Operation Eleven, a blueprint that was now the backbone of their final-phase planning: extra barricades, a surge in boots on the ground and rehearsed response patterns for every possible scenario.

And yet even as physical flows were controlled, another threat loomed – the invisible kind.

On 19 February, Prashant shifted his focus to a new battlefield: cyberspace.

'A robust cyber monitoring plan ensured Maha Kumbh's security,' he said, 'and strict action was taken against over 101 accounts in ten cases for misinformation.'

In a digital world where panic spreads faster than people, the UP Police had adapted. First information reports were lodged against users sharing fake videos, including one particularly viral clip showing a stampede that was later traced back to an accident in Pakistan. Troll accounts on Instagram and Telegram were tracked for selling images of women bathing at the ghats, and notices were issued to Meta, demanding swift cooperation.

Faith, Flow and the Force

It was a reminder that modern policing isn't just boots and barricades – it is algorithms, takedowns and fighting for dignity in places where the uniform had no visibility. Here, too, Prashant Kumar's approach was clear: predict, prevent and preserve the sanctity of the event, both on the ground and across the web.

When asked what made the Kumbh possible – not just functional, but humane – he didn't point to weapons, numbers or even technology.

'Uttar Pradesh Police won everyone's hearts with their behaviour, not weapons,' he said on 26 February, as the last ritual bath brought the Kumbh to its final moment of stillness.

It wasn't an empty sentiment. Over 1,378 women officers had been deployed specifically for the safety of female pilgrims – a quiet but powerful statement in an event where vulnerability moved barefoot. Community policing, too, was more than a buzzword. Local youth volunteers, trained and mobilized by the police, became both eyes and voices, helping guide crowds, flag concerns and share verified updates.

It was a human-first model of policing, grounded in the belief that order doesn't require aggression, it requires presence. This stood in quiet contrast to scattered reports online of theft and rude behaviour, which had cast brief shadows. But the larger story was one of restraint, grace and a visible attempt at public trust-building in the most unforgiving of environments.

And Prashant Kumar didn't claim all credit. In his final press briefing, he stepped aside to make room for others.

'The cooperation from various agencies helped us perform in an unprecedented way,' he acknowledged. 'The Maha Kumbh concluded without any major tragedy.'

It was a moment of institutional humility. The NDRF, SDRF, RAF, PAC, Central Reserve Police Force (CRPF) – all were part of the great machinery that had carried the Kumbh across seven weeks and an incredibly high number of footfalls. The ICCC became a physical symbol of synergy, a war room where lines blurred between uniform, rank and agency. And though the Mauni Amavasya stampede would remain a mark of sorrow, Prashant Kumar's focus was also clear: the absence of a larger disaster, in a setting where even one spark could have turned sacred ground into catastrophe.

If the Maha Kumbh 2025 was a miracle of faith, its success was equally a masterclass in statecraft and strategy. At the centre of this miracle stood the UP Police, whose job was not just to maintain order but to anticipate chaos and prevent it from ever arriving.

The event's operational footprint was staggering: 4,000 hectares of floodplain divided into ten zones, twenty-five sectors, fifty-six police stations and 155 police posts.[51] It functioned like a temporary nation, with its own geography, its own crises and a population that swelled to the size of a small continent every single day. This was no longer just a religious gathering, it was also an exercise in governing the impossible.

To handle this tidal wave of humanity, the UP government, under Chief Minister Yogi Adityanath, deployed a seven-tier security architecture – meticulously structured from the city's outskirts to the sacred heart of the Triveni Sangam. It wasn't just about crowd barriers or personnel deployment. What distinguished this Kumbh from the rest was the seamless integration of layered intelligence with cutting-edge digital surveillance, where conventional policing met technological foresight.

While the Kumbh's beating heart was faith and its nervous system was security, what kept it upright – its skeleton, scaffolding – was something else entirely: money. Cold, hard, unapologetic money. For all the chanting and chillums, Maha Kumbh 2025 was also a financial blockbuster, pulled off with the precision of a megaproject and the pressure of a general election.

By the end of March, the numbers began rolling in, and even the sceptics blinked. The UP government, under Chief Minister Yogi Adityanath, had pulled out all stops. Budget estimates vary depending on which department you ask or which babu you corner, but the consensus sat somewhere between ₹6,382 crore and ₹7,500 crore – an amount that would make a medium-sized country raise its eyebrows.

The state's own contribution was close to ₹5,600 crore, released in phases across three fiscal years. The centre added a ₹2,100 crore boost, nudging the grand total closer to the ₹7,500 crore mark. All this to build a temporary spiritual city that housed more people per square metre than some of India's most congested towns.

And this wasn't ornamental spending. This was nuts-and-bolts, bricks-and-barricades, sweat-and-sanitizer money. Around ₹4,000 crore alone was poured into roads, bridges, power lines and drainage grids that stretched across the 4,000-hectare floodplain like arteries. Where faith needed movement, the government laid down smooth roads.[52]

The logistics budget read like a sci-fi fantasy, with expenditure on 40,000 police personnel, 150,000 toilets, 10,000 sweepers, 7,000 buses, 550 intra-city shuttles and 549 individual projects approved and completed under the chief minister's watch.

For perspective, the 2013 Maha Kumbh cost ₹1,300 crore. In 2019, the cost jumped to ₹4,200 crore. By 2025, it had leapfrogged into a different economic orbit – but so had the expectations. You can't host 66 crore pilgrims with last decade's playbook.

And here's the twist – not only was the spending big, the returns were divine too.

According to estimates from nodal officer Vijay Anand and minister Nand Gopal Gupta Nandi, the state expected direct revenue of over ₹25,000 crore. That included ₹18,000 crore through GST – powered by a booming hospitality and retail ecosystem – and ₹7,000 crore from tent rentals, stall fees and on-ground services. Even the skies chipped in: helicopter rides at ₹5,000 a spin earned ₹157 crore in just forty-five days.[53]

The centre didn't do too badly either. Reports pegged its take at an additional ₹23,000 crore, including ₹5,000 crore in income tax alone. That brought the projected government earnings to ₹48,000 crore.[54]

To put it mildly, the Kumbh wasn't just sacred, it was also scalable. And it proved a point that economists love to make and godmen rarely admit: organized faith, when done right, can outperform most industries.

Much of this success came down to orchestration. Yes, there were dozens of departments at work – urban development, transport, health, tourism. But what stitched them together was a climate of confidence, the kind that only comes when people feel safe, systems work and the machinery runs without a hiccup.

Over the past few years, under Prashant's stewardship, UP's law and order landscape had undergone a tectonic shift. Crime graphs dipped. Investor confidence rose. The idea of UP as a place where things could happen – safely, swiftly and at scale – began to take root. The Kumbh became a mirror to that transformation.

It wasn't just his force, of course. But ask anyone who managed a tent city, a transport corridor or a temporary hospital during the Kumbh, and they'll tell you, when the spine is strong, everything else can stand taller. Prashant Kumar brought that spine by helping create an UP where the impossible began to feel operational.

The numbers were astonishing, yes. But the real story was of how a state stitched together belief and bureaucracy, devotion and data, incense and infrastructure and made it all work, made it all pay.

Scale alone doesn't make it to the history books. Execution helps. And what unfolded on the ground in Prayagraj over those forty-five days was nothing short of a logistical ballet, choreographed with precision and backed by unrelenting vigilance.

To keep the arterial flow of humanity from collapsing into chaos, the UP Police engineered separate entry and exit routes across all major bathing ghats. Pontoon bridges, like temporary veins, ferried the masses over the river's shifting tides, while barricades regulated directionality, especially during the surge of peak bathing days. Holding areas acted like breathing spaces – zones designed to absorb sudden surges, pause the tide and allow for a controlled redirection of flow before it became dangerous.

On the streets, a different choreography was underway. Parking zones were expanded dramatically – from 1,200 to 1,800 hectares. Ten separate traffic schemes were rolled out, including road closures, one-way systems and buffer areas to absorb overflow.[55] On 29 January, as Mauni Amavasya drew an ocean of humanity, vehicle congestion spilled over into Madhya Pradesh, yet the system only bent, it did not break.

In response to that day's tragedy, police rolled out Operation Eleven for the next major bathing day, Basant Panchami. A tactical masterpiece, it introduced heightened one-way controls, additional barricades and a surge deployment of forces: two RAF companies, three PAC units and fifty-six quick response teams. Mounted police – 181 officers on horseback – patrolled key chokepoints, using their elevated vantage and presence to quietly steer human waves.

The police also leaned on the community itself. Through a subtle but smart use of community policing, local youth volunteers were trained and mobilized to assist in managing flow, flag suspicious activity and even act as digital evangelists, pushing updates and advisories through social media. It was policing not just of people, but with people.

At the heart of this massive operation were men like Senior Superintendent of Police (SSP) Rajesh Kumar Dwivedi and DGP Prashant Kumar, whose command and clarity under pressure became the bedrock of the Kumbh's survival and success. On all six *shahi snan* (royal bath) days, crowd management was tested like never before. The events of all major snan days, which naturally drew the largest surges of devotees, were monitored from multiple war rooms across the city. But for the first time in the history of the Kumbh, the principal command centre was set up inside the chief minister's official residence. Yogi Adityanath himself sat at the helm, overseeing real-time updates, tracking critical developments and directing top-level coordination. At his side, always, was Prashant Kumar – guiding the police apparatus, issuing swift instructions and ready to respond the moment anything veered off-script. It was this layered vigilance that perhaps made the difference. In what can only be described as a statistical miracle, not a single case of theft, snatching, molestation, rape, physical violence, robbery or rioting was reported during the entire span of the Mela – an extraordinary feat for an event of this scale, where such crimes are otherwise routine.

In the midst of high-stakes operations and constant vigilance, it was often the quietest efforts that touched the deepest chords. Among the unsung heroes was the team behind the digital Khoya Paaya Kendra, launched ahead of the event on 1 December. Using platforms like X and Facebook, they worked round the clock to reunite lost pilgrims, particularly children and the elderly – a heart-warming fusion of technology and compassion that redefined public service.

Despite the overwhelming numbers, the results were staggering. An average of 1.5 to 1.75 crore people bathed daily, and even on days that saw peaks of 5 to 8 crore, the system held. Roads were strained, rituals paused, but the order never crumbled. It was policing that went beyond baton and whistle – into anticipation, empathy and architectural vision.

Prashant later described it as 'history in the making'. He wasn't wrong. No country, no force, no festival had ever endured such scale and emerged with such dignity intact. And if the world was watching, it now had its template for crowd control in the age of human deluge.

Yet the obstacles kept stacking. Traffic collapsed. Highways choked. A twenty-five km jam stretched all the way into Madhya Pradesh. Rail services halted. Prayagraj gasped under its own weight. On social media, videos of stranded families, missing children and unattended elderly began surfacing. And then, the voices of doubt arose: Was the state unprepared? Had the police overpromised? Where was the leadership?

Prashant Kumar didn't flinch. He didn't vanish into silence. In every media interaction, he chose transparency over denial, accountability over spin. He called the event a test of endurance, not perfection and made it clear that managing an ocean of people was not about eliminating all failure – but about ensuring the failure didn't become fatal for the system.

Still, the criticisms stung. Opposition leaders accused the state of vanity planning – preparing for 100 crore when they couldn't handle 40 crore. Volunteers spoke of exhaustion, overstretched forces and technology that sometimes misread human instinct. And through it all, Prashant kept moving – corridor to corridor, control room to ground, making calls that would make or break the rest of the Kumbh.

Because the Kumbh wasn't just a spectacle anymore. It was now a pressure cooker. And leading it meant feeling the heat, taking the blame and still showing up.

As the sacred chants of Basant Panchami echoed across the ghats on 10 February, and millions prepared for the auspicious snan, not everyone came to wash away sins. Some came to collect them – systematically, silently and one pocket at a time.

A twelve-member gang of thieves, blending effortlessly into the sea of saffron and sweat, had found the perfect cover: distracted pilgrims, unattended bags and the illusion of anonymity in a crowd of millions. They worked fast, professionally – chains were unclasped mid-prayer, wallets vanished during ablutions, mobile phones were slipped out of wet cloth bags. Among their many victims was a woman from Varanasi, who lost her ₹2 lakh gold chain somewhere between faith and foolish trust.

But what the gang hadn't accounted for was that this Kumbh was wired differently. This was not the 1980s where a clever disguise and a quick step could see you disappear into the masses. This time, the crowd had eyes – 2,700 of them. Cameras, drones and, most dangerously for them, plainclothes officers from all fifty-six police stations were embedded within the Mela's 4,000-hectare sprawl.

The police, by now fluent in the psychology of petty crime, didn't chase shadows. They launched a sting operation, cross-referenced complaints with facial recognition data, followed movement trails captured on CCTV and, finally, closed in near Sector 18, less than forty-eight hours after the thefts peaked. When the arrests came, they came quiet but clean – stolen goods worth ₹15 lakh were recovered, and the gang was booked under theft and organized crime laws.

In the end, it wasn't the drones, barricades or even the numbers that defined Maha Kumbh 2025. It was the people in the uniform – the ones who stood waist-deep in water for hours, who skipped meals to hold the line, who guided pilgrims with folded hands and calm eyes. It was the constable who found a lost child minutes before a surge, the woman officer who held an old man's hand through the crowd because he reminded her of her father, the volunteer who gave his only jacket to a shivering devotee before going back into the fog.

At the centre of this sprawling choreography stood one man – DGP Prashant Kumar – as a presence: tireless, composed and everywhere. He didn't just direct a security grid, he held together a beating, breathing ecosystem of belief. The city, under his watch, endured, transformed and rose.

As Maha Shivratri's final chants faded into silence and the last pilgrim stepped away from the Sangam, the Kumbh left behind more than wet footprints and numbers. It left behind stories – quiet, powerful, human stories of courage, of missteps, of redemption. And those are what we turn to next. Because behind the world's biggest gathering were moments no satellite could capture.

8
Poetry of Chaos

By the time the chants had settled into muscle memory and the Ganga's flow had become part of everyone's daily rhythm, the Kumbh had evolved into more than just a congregation. It had become a world of its own, full of logic that defied common sense, stories that belonged in fables and characters that seemed to have wandered out of a novel. If the first chapter of this great gathering was written in blueprints, battalions and barricades, this one was all about the unpredictable human theatre that unfolded in between. And no matter how tight the planning, you couldn't spreadsheet the chaos of the Indian soul.

On most days, Abhey Singh – once an engineer, now a self-declared spiritual guide known widely as 'IIT Baba' – held court on a dusty mat near the riverbank, delivering sermons on science, self-realization and salvation with the zeal of a TED speaker and the wardrobe of a sadhu. In a mela teeming with mystics and godmen, he was one of many curiosities. That is, until 20 January, when IIT Baba, the crowd and a curious quantity of ganja turned a snan morning into a small-scale spiritual crisis.

The trigger? A disagreement with a fellow ascetic – some say it was over space, others say it was ego, still others claim it was about nothing at all, which somehow made it worse. What mattered was the result: Baba declared he would end his life on the spot.

Theatrics followed. He yelled, threatened, gestured wildly. Other sadhus glared. Devotees stared. Someone live-streamed. And soon, the ghat wasn't so much spiritual as it was surreal.

The police arrived expecting perhaps a protest or a lost pilgrim. Instead, they found a wildly agitated man, shouting incoherently, and, most curiously, carrying under 10 gram of ganja in a side pouch.[56] There was no lathi-charge, no dragged drama. Just calm professionalism. Singh was detained for public nuisance and gently processed under the Narcotic Drugs and Psychotropic Substances Act. The matter ended not with divine redemption but a court date and a few bewildered laughs.

For the officers on duty, it was a sharp reminder: Not all threats come with a crowd surge or a terror plan. Some come wrapped in saffron, armed with a cult following and a soft corner for cannabis.

Chaos found more modern clothes too.

By mid-February, the battleground shifted from the ghats to the screen. The Kumbh's grandeur became bait for an entirely different kind of mischief – one that brewed in chat groups, screen grabs and algorithmic malice. A wave of fake videos, misleading posts and digitally altered images flooded social media. One especially viral clip claimed a bridge collapse had occurred at the Kumbh. It hadn't. The footage was old and from Pakistan – but

Poetry of Chaos

by the time fact-checkers responded, the damage was done. Panic had already reached phones in five states.

Worse was what followed – accounts using the Kumbh's name to share illicit imagery. Women bathing at the ghats had been photographed without consent and their images were now being sold online.

The UP Police's cyber cell responded like a digital strike team. Ten FIRs were filed. Over 100 accounts were flagged and shut. Arrests followed in Kanpur and Delhi. The charges ranged from defamation to incitement to obscenity – a buffet of digital-age crimes. Meta was looped in. Telegram got a knock. Servers were traced. Devices seized.

'A robust cyber monitoring plan ensured Maha Kumbh's security,' DGP Prashant Kumar said later. In other words, the police weren't just watching the crowd, they were also patrolling the cloud. Because in today's India, where narrative is half the battle, misinformation could be more corrosive than violence.

It wasn't just data that boiled over at the Kumbh. Ego did too – and in spectacular fashion.

It began, as such things often do, with a tent and some trampled pride. Near Sector 10, two rival akharas disagreed over territory – who could pitch where, how big and how loud. And with Naga sadhus, disputes aren't discussed over chai. They're shouted out loud while brandishing tridents.

By 15 February, the tension had exploded into a proper showdown. Sticks were raised. Tridents clashed. Pilgrims fled for cover. Five people were injured, including a poor man who was just waiting for jalebi and found himself dodging the clash.

The cavalry arrived – literally. Mounted police trotted in first, parting the chaos like medieval knights. Then came the RAF in full gear, forming human walls, separating the akharas with practised restraint. Seven sadhus were arrested. Their makeshift weapons – mostly ceremonial but still sharp – were confiscated. This skirmish was a potential flashpoint. Akhara rivalries run deep – some spanning generations and centuries. One spark and you've got a turf war with religious overtones and media attention. The police didn't just stop a fight, they may have stopped a symbolic war from spilling out of context and control. Officers were later instructed on cultural protocol – how to de-escalate a holy man without causing offense, how to stand firm without disrespecting tradition. Because here, brute force wasn't an option. Only wisdom was.

What could've become a national embarrassment was quietly reduced to an anecdote. But as the Kumbh would keep proving, peace was about understanding what truly makes people combust.

Just when it felt like things had settled – tridents holstered, tempers cooled, ash-smeared egos tucked into corners – the Kumbh reminded everyone that the real unpredictability didn't always come from the sadhus or the sky. Sometimes, it came from the road.

On the morning of 25 January, long before the sun painted the ghats in gold, chaos was already brewing 15 km away on the Prayagraj–Mirzapur highway. One tractor, three injured and a thousand stranded. That's all it took to send a ripple of disruption through the pilgrimage routes, like a hiccup in an otherwise fine-tuned orchestra.

Poetry of Chaos

The tractor itself was a miracle of imbalance – groaning under the weight of too many passengers and too few brakes. Pilgrims from Madhya Pradesh had piled on like it was Noah's Ark. The driver, likely someone who thought lane discipline was a myth and physics was negotiable, took a curve too fast. The vehicle tipped, flipped and collapsed sideways.

Three were hurt. Thankfully, none critically. But the wreckage sat stubbornly across the highway and, suddenly, a key artery was blocked. Thousands of pilgrims found themselves in halted buses, under a rising sun and rising blood pressure.

The response was swift, if a little dusty. Traffic police, aided by NDRF teams, cleared the wreck, rushed the injured to safety and slapped temporary diversions into place like tourniquets on a wounded limb. The driver was arrested. The tractor owner was fined. And vehicle checkposts, once routine, were now alert, unforgiving and ready for round two.

This accident was a lesson. In the world of mega events, it only takes one wheel out of place to tilt the whole system. And the Kumbh didn't forgive repeated mistakes.

Sometimes, the real danger came not with noise but with silence. She was nine. Alone. Frightened. Separated from her parents during the Maghi Purnima snan on 5 February – a day when the city felt like it was built from bodies and sound. She was taken to the lost and found centre in Sector 3, one of the safer corners in the floodplain. Volunteers offered warm food, kind words and digital assistance to track down her family.

Then, a man appeared.

He claimed to be her uncle. Knew her name. Spoke gently. Smiled. But something felt off. A volunteer noticed the way the girl stepped back when he moved closer. How she didn't reach out to him. How his eyes darted too much.

The volunteer didn't argue. He simply acted. A quick alert. A silent nod. Within minutes, the man was stopped as he tried to lead the girl away. Questioned. Prodded. His story unravelled like wet paper. And then the confession came – he had planned to traffic her out of Prayagraj before the system caught up.

He was arrested on the spot – booked under POCSO and human trafficking laws.

The girl? Reunited with her parents within the hour. The Khoya Paaya Kendra had worked. The man had tried to manipulate it; he failed.

It didn't make national headlines. But it did make everyone around the case go quiet for a long time. Because amid the grandeur and bhajans, sometimes the most dangerous figure wasn't the one holding a weapon but the one holding a little girl's hand with a lie on his lips.

One child was saved. How many weren't?

Cases didn't make national headlines, but it stayed with everyone who heard about it. Because in a crowd of 60 crore, you don't just guard roads and rivers. You guard people's children. You guard the spaces between safety and trust.

And as the Kumbh rolled on, its chants rising, its rituals deepening, the stories kept coming. Some absurd, some heroic, some quietly heartbreaking. But all of them part of the same massive, miraculous mess called the Maha Kumbh.

In a crowd this vast, every soul brings its own story – some saved from danger, others chasing opportunity. For every child rescued from vanishing, there was someone clawing their way back into visibility. And for a few, the river wasn't just holy, it was also a second chance.

If faith can move mountains, it can apparently float boats too – 130 of them, to be exact, all bearing the signature swagger of Pintu Mahara, boatman, accidental tycoon and perhaps the most unexpected economic success story of the Maha Kumbh 2025.

Born in Arail, on the sleepy banks of Prayagraj, Pintu wasn't exactly headed for sainthood. With twenty-one criminal cases to his name – including murder, extortion and enough small-time notoriety to keep a police file permanently warm – he might have been the last person one would peg as the future poster boy of spiritual commerce. But then came Ganga Maiyya and, with her, 66 crore people.

Sensing an opportunity the way some men sense a miracle, Pintu did what any shrewd businessman with a colourful past and a sharp nose for risk would do – he mortgaged everything. His mother's gold. Family land. A few debts no one wants to talk about. The goal? To double his fleet from 60 to 130 wooden boats. Each one cost about ₹80,000, and each one, by the end of the forty-five-day mela, had earned back ₹23 lakh.

That's right – Pintu Mahara, ex-con and river whisperer, cleared ₹30 crore in a month and a half, ferrying pilgrims, sadhus and VVIPs across the Ganga like a man possessed. His daily take? Around ₹50,000 to ₹52,000 per boat, every single day. Not bad for someone who, not too long ago, was dodging arrest warrants instead of offering life jackets.

His mother, Shuklavati Devi, called it a blessing. 'Ganga Maiyya has returned everything we lost after my husband's death,' she said, tearfully. It's hard to argue with her. Some worship the river. Others, like Pintu, build an empire on it.

Next up? The family plans to upgrade to motorboats for the next Kumbh. And maybe, just maybe, Pintu's rap sheet will finally make way for a business license.

If Pintu Mahara was the face of Kumbh's boatman gold rush, then the entire Nishad community was its silent engine. Thousands of rowers turned accidental entrepreneurs, whose oars sliced not just through water, but through years of poverty, generational debt and near-invisibility.

According to Pappu Lal Nishad, president of the Prayagraj Navik Association, more than 13,000 boatmen, operating around 4,500 oar boats, ferried an estimated 1.5 crore devotees across the Sangam. Many earned between ₹8–9 lakh each over just forty-five days.[57] For perspective, that's the kind of income most of them hadn't seen in entire decades.

The ripple effects were deeply personal. Sanjeet Kumar Nishad didn't hesitate. He used the earnings to fund his daughters' weddings in one go. Balwant Nishad, who had lived in a kutcha house for thirty years, finally built a proper home, threw in a new boat and probably earned lifelong bragging rights in the process. But perhaps the best indicator of this financial frenzy was the price of a boat ride. What was once a humble ₹6,000 journey for ten people from Arail Ghat was now being auctioned off, informally, of course, for as much as ₹30,000 during peak days.

Apparently, if your devotion couldn't wait, your wallet had to be full.

From sunburnt shoulders to millionaire mindsets, the Nishads' journey wasn't just about ferrying pilgrims – it was also about rowing out of poverty with the style of a startup. Some called it karma, others, divine timing. The Nishads just called it a good season. And for once, everyone agreed.

The Kumbh was never just about profit margins or divine return on investment. It was about the mad, the marvellous and the mildly unexplainable. For every spreadsheet-worthy statistic, there was a story that made you blink twice and say, 'Wait, what?'

There were monkey mobs that vanished mid-Mela, a billionaire widow dipped into the Sangam like a shy schoolteacher, tech sadhus had WiFi dongles tucked into their *kamandal*s.

Even after the tragic stampede on Mauni Amavasya, when for a few dark hours fear threatened to drown out faith, the Kumbh refused to crumble. It bounced back on the backs of its ordinary people doing extraordinary things – with no hashtags, no media and definitely no PR agencies.

Like the local boys who formed human chains to help elders cross the swirling crowds or the shopkeepers who gave away biscuits and water, even though they had spent weeks counting profits like accountants on sugar. And then there was Anil – barely sixteen, lanky, barefoot – who carried an injured woman on his back to the nearest makeshift clinic. No interviews. No Instagram reels. Just a small act of strength that went viral anyway. The Internet, in an uncharacteristic moment of wholesomeness, called him 'Sangam's Silent Hero'. And for once, nobody argued.

As the camps began to fold and the temporary city faded into memory, one story lingered like ghee in the air. A few die-hard devotees refused to leave even after the last aarti, last snan and last plate of overpriced jalebi. Their reason? 'We saw visions in the Ganga... of Krishna, maybe Shiva.' The authorities tried logic. The devotees offered faith. Eventually, both sides agreed on that ancient Indian compromise: peaceful disagreement. And the tents came down slowly, like a curtain on the world's longest, strangest stage play.

The Kumbh was never just about numbers, not even the mighty, record-breaking 66 crore. It was about a boatman who became a millionaire, a boy who carried a stranger like a hero, a woman who handed out sanitary pads with a smile and a sadhu who sang at midnight to an invisible, moonlit audience. It was about a chai seller who funded his son's college dreams one cup at a time, an auto driver who started speaking English because he ferried more foreigners than locals and a woman from Silicon Valley who dipped into the Ganga like she was slipping into her past life.

These were the heartbeat stories. The small, absurd, luminous moments that made the Kumbh feel less like a crowd and more like a carnival of humanity. They made you laugh, tear up and sometimes just shake your head and say, 'Only in India, boss.'

Because the stories just didn't stop coming.

Just when you thought the last miracle had been dunked, another one floated in. Some came with money. Others with faith. And at least one arrived on a bicycle.

Swami Vishwanath, fifty years old and bearded like a Himalayan rockstar, pedalled 1,200 km from Rishikesh on a bicycle held together by faith, flags and duct tape. With nothing but a water bottle and a tiny Shiva idol in his front basket, he rolled into Prayagraj like a spiritual Tour de France champion, just in time for the first shahi snan. 'Har Har Mahadev!' he yelled. Someone offered him tea. He accepted. Because even saints need a break.

Then came Mohan Lal's bullock – possibly the Kumbh's first viral bovine. Known for lowing in perfect bhajan rhythm, the beast drew bigger crowds than some pop-up gurus. 'He's blessed,' said Mohan, while pocketing ₹10,000 in donations. The bullock, for his part, mooed modestly and refused all interviews.

But the undisputed Instagram icon of the mela was Baba Selfieanand – the Digital Naga. Armed with a smartphone on a selfie stick and an uncanny ability to find flattering light at any hour, he documented his entire Kumbh yatra online. Photos with pilgrims. Snaps with VVIPs. A blurry selfie with Chris Martin from Coldplay (allegedly). *'Selfie bhi tapasya hai, beta,'* he told a reporter once. With 50,000 followers and counting, who's arguing?

Somewhere between sunrise snans and midnight bhajans, between missing monkeys and unexpected millionaires, the Kumbh reminded the world that faith may be eternal, but India always finds a way to make it unforgettable.

Amid this chaos and charm, one man kept shuttling silently between the spectacle and the state, between a makeshift command centre in Prayagraj and his main office 200 km away in Lucknow. As UP's police chief, Prashant Kumar wasn't just overseeing the Kumbh. He was juggling farmer protests, political rallies, law-and-order flashpoints and enough paperwork to choke a bureaucrat. And yet he kept showing up – often without warning, sometimes before sunrise, always alert. No fuss, no caravan of sirens. Just presence. And while the Kumbh unfolded like an epic with a million moving parts, he became the one constant in the background. Always moving, rarely seen, but somehow, always there.

The Maha Kumbh 2025 didn't need a red carpet – it had the river. And yet from Bollywood icons to billionaire board members, familiar faces quietly stepped into the sacred waters. No VIP barricades. No entourages. Just reverence.

Anupam Kher came earlier, visibly moved. 'Life became successful by taking a bath in the Ganga,' he said, praising the calm among chaos.[58] Vicky Kaushal echoed the feeling: 'I was waiting for this moment.'[59] Kabir Khan offered the deepest cut: 'This is not about Hindu or Muslim. This is about being Indian.'[60] Simple. Powerful. Unscripted.

Others, like Katrina Kaif and Adah Sharma, said little, but their silent presence did the talking. Remo D'Souza smiled through soaked selfies. Milind Soman walked barefoot and posted about life's vastness. Some brought cameras, others brought quiet.

And then there were those who said nothing at all. Laurene Powell Jobs, widow of Steve Jobs, visited in a sari. Chris Martin of Coldplay came with Dakota Johnson, stayed low-key and left without a word. The river, of course, kept their secrets.

Even Gautam Adani's family was spotted offering prayers on 21 January – no press, no quotes, just folded hands.

At the Kumbh, fame didn't matter. Faith did.

Celebrities weren't the only foreigners to drift into the festival's gravity. A band of yoga-obsessed Americans, led by a cheerful long-bearded expat called Swami Dave, pitched their ashram-in-a-tent somewhere between Sector 12 and musical anarchy. Their fusion of chanting, guitars and the occasional 'Om My God' rendition turned heads – and even drew a few Naga sadhus, who nodded along in what can only be described as spiritual curiosity. Locals dubbed it 'Sangam Woodstock'. No one disagreed.

And then came Makar Sankranti, when the skies above Prayagraj turned into a playground of flying colours and flying slogans. One particularly ambitious kite – shaped like a glowing 'Om' – soared too high, tangled itself around a police drone and caused the year's most peaceful face-off between faith and surveillance. The rescue effort, captured on dozens of phones, ended with applause, laughter and at least one new WhatsApp group titled Om vs AI.

That was the thing about the Kumbh. It wasn't just a mela. Or a pilgrimage. Or even an operation in crowd management. It was a full-blown, forty-five-day theatre of life. A living museum of the Indian soul – strange, hilarious, moving, impossible to define. In this ocean of 66 crore, stories surfaced like little ripples – some loud, some quiet, all unforgettable. From millionaire chaiwallahs and barefoot cyclists to selfie saints and bullocks who could carry a tune, every anecdote added a stitch to the Kumbh's massive quilt.

Because when the tents are folded, the lights are dimmed and the Ganga flows on like she always has, what remains isn't just data or drone footage. What remains are names, Raju with his chappal counter. Kamla Devi who brought her tractor and her faith. The boy who carried an old woman through a stampede.

They didn't plan the Kumbh. But they made it unforgettable. And now, as the spotlight fades from the ghats and returns to boardrooms, police files and ordinary lives, the question quietly turns: who was the man balancing this tidal wave from behind the scenes?

Before it even began, the UP government had promised the greenest Kumbh ever. And they meant business. 1.5 lakh bio-toilets, drones spraying herbal disinfectants and 10,000 sanitation workers in a spiritual-swashbuckling dance with hygiene. But mid-mela, *E. Coli* levels spiked near the Sangam. Environmentalists cried foul. The state countered with real-time water quality dashboards. The truth, like the river, was probably somewhere in the middle – flowing, murky and subject to divine interpretation.

If ecology stumbled, tech sprinted. Artificial intelligence didn't just count crowds – it redirected them, predicted surges and helped reunite over 1.2 lakh lost pilgrims. Facial recognition at the Khoya Paaya Kendra became the most generous use of machine learning in recent memory. Meanwhile, a virtual Kumbh experience let half-a-million global devotees 'bathe' online, raising ₹10 crore for sanitation. Faith met the metaverse, and no one even got their feet wet.

Rumours swirled that Coldplay's Chris Martin recorded a post-dip acoustic track with local sadhus. Whether fact or fiction, the Internet ran with it. Because who doesn't want a Grammy-winning song at the Sangam?

Meanwhile, the Kinnar Akhara made a glorious return – over 500 strong, garlanded in marigolds, claiming space not just in the snan but in the story. The kinnars' camps drew crowds, admirers and the occasional frown – but the mood was mostly celebratory. And then came the stats: 50 crore puris served in forty-five days.

That's over a million per day. One vendor near Sector 5 claimed to have fried 50,000 in a single shift. The record went viral. So did the cholesterol jokes.

But not all echoes were edible or elegant. Prayagraj's roads remained jammed long after the final aarti. A trucker posted, 'Still stuck three days after Maha Shivratri. Kumbh is eternal.' ₹500 crore was sanctioned for emergency road repairs. And one sadhu flatly refused to leave, insisting he had been divinely appointed to guard the Sangam forever. He lasted till 10 March, before either hunger or boredom won.

The world was watching. UNESCO, which had already declared the Kumbh an intangible cultural heritage, sent observers to study 2025's staggering scale. The NRIs donated ₹500 crore, and one California-based group pledged ₹50 crore to build a permanent Kumbh museum in Prayagraj. The Ganga wasn't just sacred, it was now syndicated.

These ripples – bio-toilets and drones, virtual snans and puri records – may not have made front-page news, but they were the soul of the story. Small, strange, unforgettable.

Because the Kumbh doesn't end when the crowd leaves. It lingers – in echoes, in memory, in the silence after the conch.

The Maha Kumbh Mela 2025 was a phenomenon. A human tide of 66 crore people converged over forty-five days on a city both blessed and burdened by its own significance. Every statistic, every scuffle, every whispered prayer, every logistical triumph and tremor – it all formed a mosaic of the modern Kumbh: part tradition, part tension, part transcendence.

In its vastness lay its wonder. In its vulnerabilities, its truths.

For Prashant Kumar, UP's top cop, the Kumbh wasn't just a security operation, it was a trial by fire and faith. Leadership under divine scrutiny. There were moments that bordered on the surreal: AI drones scanning crowds like digital deities, 1.2 lakh lost pilgrims reunited by facial recognition, a stampede that could have spiralled into catastrophe, calmed with precision and compassion. But there were critiques too – about jammed roads that refused to clear, about gaps in communication after crisis, about the small failures that sometimes slip through the largest plans.

Yet what lingered beyond the flowcharts and the fury was something far less measurable and far more profound.

A barefoot child from Bihar hopping towards the Sangam on crutches. A California trust pledging crores for a museum built on memory. A boatman with twenty-one criminal cases ferrying saints and celebrities with the same quiet reverence. Coldplay's Chris Martin sharing the same holy waters as the tea vendor who sold 10,000 cups in a single day. At the Kumbh, hierarchy dissolved. And everyone left a little altered.

This chapter on the Maha Kumbh could've ended with revenue charts and crowd control diagrams. But that would miss the point. The real legacy of this Kumbh lies not in its scale but in its contradictions. Sacred and profane. Order and chaos. Selfies and surrender. Sarcasm and sanctity. The scream of a megaphone and the hush of a prayer.

And perhaps that's where Prashant Kumar's success stands tallest. In the chaos of it all – things gone wrong, things gone right – he held the line. He had faith in people, in preparation that something this vast could be guided, if not fully tamed.

Even the Ganga pauses to acknowledge those who keep the current steady. As the last of the camps folded and the ghats began their slow return to silence, came the final act – one of recognition.

On 27 February, standing before a sea of uniformed men and women at the Ganga Mandapam, Chief Minister Yogi Adityanath addressed the very force that had guarded 66 crore souls over forty-five days. His words carried the weight of gratitude and the echo of validation: a special bonus of ₹10,000, the Maha Kumbh Seva Medal and seven days of phased leave for all 75,000 personnel who had served. Every constable, inspector and officer was acknowledged – not just as enforcer of law but as steward of a spiritual phenomenon.

'Our personnel were even pushed by people at times,' the chief minister said, 'but they displayed remarkable resilience and patience.'[61] He called the Kumbh the greatest spiritual gathering on earth and credited its smooth, secure conduct to the joint vision of Prime Minister Narendra Modi and the dedication of the security forces. The numbers spoke for themselves: 66.3 crore pilgrims, ₹3.5 lakh crore in economic activity and not a single day where safety took a back seat.

For Prashant Kumar, who had spent the Kumbh oscillating between urgency and unseen exhaustion, it wasn't just an official function. It was closure. A full-circle moment. His eyes scanned the uniformed crowd in silent solidarity. These were his men and women. These were the hands that had held the line when stampedes threatened, when misinformation erupted, when riverbanks turned into battlegrounds of belief. From drone surveillance to bullock traffic, from AI crowd tracking to child rescue missions – it had all come down to a force that chose calm over chaos.

The chief minister's voice rose again: 'Only those who participated in the Maha Kumbh can understand its scale and complexity. It is easy to sit far away and make negative comments.'[62]

But Prashant Kumar didn't need to say anything. He stood quietly at the edge of the gathering, the kind of man who doesn't claim credit, he carries it. He had seen the broken police lines of 2017, the sleeping barracks in Lucknow, the perception of UP as a land of mafias and riots. And now, here was a transformed force, globally hailed as 'Mitra Police' – friendly, firm, fearless.

Somewhere in that moment, surrounded by applause, fatigue and faces etched with sun and pride, he allowed himself to breathe a sigh of fulfilment.

The Maha Kumbh 2025 was lived, endured, protected. It had tested the limits of infrastructure, belief and endurance, and the police had passed not just with discipline but also with dignity.

From the first planning meeting to the last whispered prayer by the river, it had been their silent, steadfast mission.

And now, it was done.

The chants faded. The lights dimmed. The city exhaled.

Somewhere, just beyond the final conch, a man in uniform stood still, for one quiet moment, before walking back into the world that would soon need him again.

Because the Ganga keeps flowing.

And Prashant Kumar always knew – the Kumbh never truly ends.

PART 3
The Making of a Policeman

9
Roots of a Warrior

The journey to becoming one of India's most formidable police officers didn't begin with a uniform or a badge. It began in a modest household in Bihar, wrapped in the aroma of home-cooked food, the rhythm of the pages of textbooks turning and the quiet influence of a brilliant elder sibling.

When I asked Prashant Kumar what sparked his interest in the civil services, he didn't pause for effect or reach for a larger-than-life anecdote. He simply said, 'My brother.'

There was no drama in that sentence. Just honesty.

His elder brother, Susheel Kumar, was already in the civil services and was academically gifted – so gifted, in fact, that the family didn't need to look beyond their home for a role model. 'He was the inspiration right in front of me,' Prashant said.

Their household, nestled in Siwan, a small sub-divisional town in Bihar, revolved around books and simple, nourishing routines. His father was a schoolteacher, and Prashant, the youngest of four siblings, grew up in an environment where academic discipline was second nature. Some cousins stayed with them too, and the collective influence of elder siblings and relatives created an atmosphere where the only currency was academic excellence. There were no distractions. No fancy outings. Just studies, wholesome food and a quiet push to do well in life.

Up until Intermediate, he remained in his native town, attending the local school where his father taught. 'Till Class 10, I was quite bright,' he recalled. 'But somehow, between Class 10 and 12, I lost my tempo. Got a little distracted.'

Yet his fundamentals were solid. He tried for medicine – that golden ticket to respect and success in middle-class India – but it didn't work out. He remembers that phase as a blur of uncertainty. 'I was directionless,' he admitted.

It was then that his two brothers, already in Delhi, pulled him out of that fog. One of them, already a civil servant, brought him to the capital. 'I had done fairly well in my Intermediate exams – not the kind of marks students get today, where ninety is the new seventy – but decent enough,' he smiled.

Thanks to that, he secured admission in a college in Delhi University's North Campus. It was the start of a new chapter, but not an easy one.

'I came from a small town,' he told me. 'The moment I stepped into Delhi University, I was hit by a wall of complexes.'

He didn't have to explain. I've seen that story play out too many times – small-town brilliance crushed under the sneers of city kids who speak better English, wear better clothes and walk like they own the world. 'They used to taunt me,' he said quietly. 'Mock my language, my clothes, even the way I carried myself.'

The kid from Bihar wasn't polished enough for the capital's social clubs masquerading as classrooms. But what they didn't know was that behind that quiet, unsure boy was a stubborn resilience. A fuse had been lit.

Beneath the initial discomfort and alienation, there was something unshakeable in him – an instinctive belief in his own abilities. He didn't let the ridicule or the taunts from his peers define him. Instead, he turned inwards, focused on what he had always been taught: hard work, discipline and the quiet power of perseverance.

He began to study with single-minded determination. Each academic year became a stepping stone, a climb towards reclaiming his confidence. By the time he completed his graduation, he had managed to place himself among the top students – fourth in the university. Not quite the summit but close enough to know he could reach it. And then he was honoured with the gold medal for securing first position in MSc, Applied Geology (first class), from the University of Delhi in 1988.

It was during his post-graduation that he truly came into his own. The hesitation was gone, the self-doubt replaced by clarity. He topped the university that year – his first real academic triumph on a national platform. But even as he was pursuing his master's degree, another goal had begun to take shape: the civil services.

Delhi University in those days was a crucible of ambition. The hostel corridors, the canteens, even the tea stalls outside campus buzzed with the collective energy of hundreds of young minds preparing for Union Public Service Commission (UPSC). The air was thick with dreams of power and purpose. It was a time when the civil services weren't seen as a job. They were a mission. And in that environment, Prashant Kumar found his calling taking a more defined shape.

The atmosphere around him was academically rich as well as aspirational. Surrounded by like-minded peers – some equally focused, others more seasoned in their preparations – he sharpened his focus further. His days were filled with lectures and study sessions; his nights, with revisions and mock tests. The quiet boy from Bihar was no longer trying to fit in. He was beginning to stand out.

As he had mentioned earlier, it was his elder brother – already in the civil services – who had set the benchmark early on. But what struck me during our conversation was how deeply embedded that influence remained throughout his student years. His brother wasn't just a source of inspiration, he was also a constant presence, surrounded by a circle of batchmates and peers, all immersed in their own preparation for the civil services.

Naturally, that atmosphere rubbed off. The shift from ambition to action was organic – almost inevitable.

And so, with the same quiet determination that had carried him through Delhi University, Prashant began preparing in earnest. He cleared the civil services examination – a feat that in itself sets thousands apart from lakhs. But like so many others who cross that threshold, he was met with the unpredictable nature of service allocation.

The civil services offer choices, but those choices don't always align with outcomes. Very few get the exact posting they aim for; most accept what they're given and move forward. Prashant was assigned the IPS – not the more sought-after Indian Administrative Service (IAS) – but he wasn't disappointed. He accepted it with grace and clarity. It was a prestigious service and, more importantly, a place where he felt he could make a real difference.

Still, there was some pressure from the family – perhaps the kind that comes from well-meaning elders who dream a little more for you than you might for yourself. So he took one more shot, reappeared for the examination. The result didn't change. The IAS remained elusive.

But if anyone had doubted his ability to crack the civil services, they hadn't met Prashant Kumar. He never chased glamour. He chased goals. Cracking the UPSC wasn't just an ambition. It was a mission. And like every mission in his life, he approached it with single-minded focus. *Karna hai toh karna hai*, that was his mindset. With his elder brother Susheel Kumar already in the IAS, the expectations were high. But Prashant wasn't trying to match anyone; he was simply doing what he always did: cutting out distractions and locking into his objective. Whether it was preparing for one of the toughest exams in the country or chasing a fugitive years later, the method remained the same that I have to crack it. Losing is not an option. He didn't dwell on being assigned the IPS over the IAS. He accepted it with quiet dignity and moved on.

But this time, there were no second thoughts.

There was a smile in his voice when he said it. No bitterness. No 'what ifs'. Just contentment. He had made peace with it. More than that, he had embraced it. In 1991, he formally joined the IPS.

That's when the story of Prashant Kumar the police officer truly began.

Training began in the misty hills of Mussoorie, and later shifted to the sun-soaked campus of the Sardar Vallabhbhai Patel National Police Academy in Hyderabad. That was where the foundation was laid – the drills, the discipline, the ethics and the law. It's where the idealism of service first collided with the realities of policing.

Prashant was candid about his early days as a trainee. He didn't consider himself the brightest in the batch. He described himself – and a few others like him – as 'keen type professionals' – those who might not have dazzled in every assessment but were sharp, diligent and constantly evolving.

In the academy too, just like at Delhi University, it was the peer group that made all the difference. Surrounded by talented batchmates, spirited instructors and lifelong friends, he pushed himself harder and steadily climbed up the merit ladder. His academic scores improved and so did his confidence.

After passing out of the academy, he was allotted the Tamil Nadu cadre and posted as an SDPO – a sub-divisional police officer – in one of the state's districts. That was where his on-ground policing began, far away from the familiarity of the Hindi heartland, in a state with its own language, culture and complexities. Yet he adapted. The learning curve was steep, but it prepared him for the unpredictability of the job.

It was around this time that life took another decisive turn – one not marked by a police file or a posting order but by something far more personal.

His marriage to Dimple Verma, a serving IAS officer in UP, led him back to his home turf. On marital grounds, he was granted an inter-cadre transfer from Tamil Nadu to UP.

That's how his journey in UP began – not just as an officer but also as someone destined to become a central figure in its war against crime.

But even before Tamil Nadu, before the academy and before Delhi, there was a memory – one that stayed lodged deep in his consciousness. It was a moment from childhood, seared into the back of his mind like a silent vow.

We were talking about courage – not in the abstract, but in the real, often unspoken decisions that define a family, a generation. And then, without any buildup, Prashant took me back to 1971. He must have been barely six or seven years old when war broke out between India and Pakistan. Bangladesh hadn't yet been born; it was still East Pakistan, struggling for its freedom, and India had thrown its weight behind the Mukti Bahini.

With his family. Prashant Kumar is in his mother's lap.

Prashant Kumar as a child

Prashant Kumar and his sister as children

Prashant Kumar being appointed as the DGP

Prashant Kumar taking charge as the DGP from his predecessor

Prashant Kumar taking charge as the DGP

Prashant Kumar after taking charge as the DGP

Prashant Kumar at an official function with the CM Yogi Adityanath of UP

Prashant Kumar distributing food during COVID-19

Managing daily wage labourers at the UP–Delhi border during COVID-19

Prashant Kumar at Mahakumbh 2025

Prashant Kumar heading for inspection at Mahakumbh 2025

Prashant Kumar waiting to recieve CM Yogi Adityanath on the last day of Mahakumbh 2025

Prashant Kumar with the Chief Secretary of UP, Manoj Kumar Singh at Mahakumbh 2025

Prashant Kumar at the Ram Mandir, Ayodhya, before the Pran Pratishtha ceremony

Prashant Kumar recieving Prime Minister Narendra Modi

Prashant Kumar featured on the Wall of Fame at his college – Hansraj, Delhi

Prashant Kumar on his Kailash journey

Prashant Kumar taking a selfie with the DGP House in Lucknow in the background, although he never stayed there during his tenure as the DGP.

Prashant Kumar with Union Home Secretary A.K. Bhalla

Prashant Kumar with his wife Dimple on the left at a function

Prashant Kumar with his wife Dimple Verma, daughter Shivani and grand niece

Prashant Kumar at a reunion ceremony

Prashant Kumar; no private moments

Prashant Kumar, ADG (L&O) on duty

Prashant Kumar, ADG (L&O) handing a boy to his family at Bikru, Kanpur. The boy had been kidnapped and ransomed for Rs 5 crore. The boy was rescued without paying any ransom.

He remembered blackouts and sirens – long, wailing cries that fractured the silence of the night. He remembered neighbours talking in hushed voices about soldiers from Bihar being sent to the eastern front. The war was close, not just in geography but also in emotion. It entered homes, changed conversations, rewired imaginations.

What stayed with him most, though, weren't the sirens or the darkness. It was something his father said – something spoken with such calm finality that it struck him even as a child.

'I have three sons,' his father had said. 'I will send one or two to join the forces.'

Decades later, Prashant Kumar still carried the weight of those words. Not because it was a display of patriotism but because it was a rare glimpse into moral clarity, into selflessness, into the terrifying grace of choosing country over comfort.

He told me he often wondered if he could ever match that kind of courage. Whether, if faced with the same decision, he could ask the same of his own child. Could he send his daughter to war if the country demanded it?

There was no clear answer. But there didn't need to be. The point was never about answering the question. It was about understanding where his moral spine had come from. About the kind of household he had grown up in. And about the values that had quietly, steadily shaped him long before a badge ever sat on his chest.

That moment in 1971 didn't simply stay with him. It followed him into every decision he made, every oath he took. And perhaps, it still does.

As we spoke more about his early influences, the conversation drifted back to his father – this time, not during a war but in the ordinary, humdrum rhythms of everyday life. And yet it was this ordinariness that had left the deepest impression on him.

His father wasn't a man of grand speeches or visible power. He was a teacher. A simple, middle-class man who ran a large household with limited means and unshakable dignity. What stood out about him were his integrity and consistency. Day after day, year after year, he lived by a routine so disciplined it felt like a silent code.

And the children followed. Not out of fear but out of a quiet sense of duty. If he asked them to wake up early, they did. If he told them to read or help or stay on course, they tried their best. There was no chaos in that household – just a clear, steady rhythm that shaped each of them in its own way.

Prashant admits that he never thought of himself as exceptionally gifted academically. Especially in a family like his, where the bar was set impossibly high. His father's sense of uprightness was one yardstick; his elder brother – always topping exams – was another. There was little room for excuses or underachievement. You either rose to the occasion or you didn't. And Prashant did. Because, in a household like that, he had no choice.

Looking back, he credits these two pillars – his father's discipline and his brother's excellence – for everything he would later go on to achieve. They gave him a framework. Not just for studying or working hard but for living with purpose.

It wasn't that anyone in the family ever compared him to the others, at least not overtly. But the benchmark was always there, quietly looming in the background. It didn't need to be spoken aloud. In a house where excellence was the norm, falling short was not something you needed to be told – you simply felt it.

And yet there was one thing Prashant Kumar never lacked: quiet confidence. Not the chest-thumping kind but the deeper, more enduring belief that, given time, he would get there. Slowly, methodically, in his own way.

That's how he approached life even in Delhi University. He began as a backbencher – unsure, a little out of place. But over time, he found his rhythm, his own quiet way to rise. His elder brother had studied at the same university years earlier, and that legacy gave him a sense of familiarity. But more than anything, it was his mindset that shaped him. He wasn't trying to outshine anyone, just to hold his ground and grow, one step at a time.

He spoke about this phase without self-congratulation. 'You'd have to do a peer group analysis to get the full picture,' he told me, almost as if he didn't want to judge himself. 'I just know I progressed.' And perhaps that was enough.

For a boy from a small town in Bihar, stepping into the charged, often ruthless environment of Delhi University was more than just academic. It was personal. The classroom wasn't just a place to learn, it was also a space where you were judged – by your accent, your shoes, your confidence or lack of it.

He told me something I found especially telling. As a child back home, he had never felt any sense of inferiority. His family may not have had luxuries, but it was a happy, secure home. The basics were never missing – good food, support and a clear direction in life. There weren't many clothes, no flashy toys or birthday parties, but there was warmth. There was purpose.

That's where the focus remained: food and academics. Everything else could wait. And perhaps that's what gave him the quiet steel to keep going. He didn't arrive in Delhi to impress anyone. He came to make something of himself.

After joining the service, Prashant got married. In the initial phase, he and his wife were fortunate enough to receive postings that kept them in the same region. But that didn't last long. His first major promotion came in 1992, and with it, a posting to Varanasi – a city that, at the time, was a tinderbox of communal tensions.

It was not unfamiliar territory. During his training days, he had passed through Varanasi en route Sonebhadra for village attachment. A particular incident, as he recalled it, now seemed almost cinematic in hindsight – if not outright ironic.

He had just arrived at the Varanasi railway station with his group from Mussoorie, preparing to catch a bus to Sonebhadra. At the station, a fellow probationer, a female officer, casually mentioned that an SDM posted nearby was also from Bihar. 'Why don't we go and say hello?' she had suggested. 'She's from your home state.'

His response had been characteristically dismissive. 'What's the fun in meeting someone just because they're from Bihar?' he'd said. 'I can't meet everyone from my state.'

He chose to stay back at the office instead, uninterested in casual introductions or impromptu social calls. Coming from a background steeped in traditional values and the idea of arranged marriages, the thought of seeking out a woman he didn't know simply didn't occur to him.

What he didn't know then – what he couldn't have imagined – is that the woman he declined to meet that day would eventually become his wife. Fate had tapped him on the shoulder at a railway station in Varanasi, and he had politely shrugged it off.

But fate, as it turns out, has a long memory.

At the time of that earlier training visit, Varanasi was under curfew. Tensions gripped the streets, the city simmering with unease. Not much had changed when Prashant Kumar returned –

this time, not as a passing trainee, but as the SP (City). The situation was still volatile, the atmosphere thick with communal mistrust.

It was a tough posting, but one that proved transformative. Law and order was the foremost priority. Everything else came second. The city had its own pulse – ancient, restless, deeply layered. To police Varanasi was not just to respond to crime, it was also to understand its contradictions, its cultural friction and its history of religious sensitivities. Few cities in the world carry the weight that Varanasi does. Revered as one of the oldest living cities on the planet, Varanasi was a crucible.

'World saw India through Varanasi,' Prashant said once. And in many ways, the challenges mirrored that weight of symbolism. It wasn't just about religion. The city had long-standing labour issues, complex student dynamics – thanks to the presence of multiple universities – and a deep-rooted history of mafia operations that clashed often with state authority.

For a young officer still finding his feet, it was the kind of assignment that could either break you or shape you. In Prashant Kumar's case, it did the latter.

Back then, Chandauli was still part of the larger Varanasi district. The city, already vast in scale, was even more expansive in its jurisdiction and demands. Rich in culture, history and contradiction, Varanasi was a district that never truly slept – and neither did its police.

Every week brought a new festival, every festival a fresh challenge. For Prashant, the on-ground reality of policing began in the noise, movement and uncertainty of street-level duty. He often found himself staying the night in his office – there simply wasn't time to go home. There were processions that ran non-stop for twenty-four, even thirty-six hours. And he had to stay on top of every one of them – every crowd movement, every sensitive locality, every point of possible flare-up.

That's where the real cop in him began to take shape.

It was a baptism by fire. There was no script. Each day was a different battle – some won, some not. But each left him more seasoned, more ready.

And as if the cultural and communal dimensions weren't demanding enough, Varanasi was also navigating a politically turbulent phase. Alliances shifted, tempers flared and local dynamics changed overnight. Policing in such a climate required more than training – it needed instinct, quick judgment and nerves of steel.

Fortunately, he wasn't alone. He had a team that believed in the mission. Officers who didn't buckle under pressure. Together, they carried out two to three high-stakes operations in the heart of Varanasi – operations that were, in his words, 'unheard of at that time'.

They got the job done. And crucially, they got the backing they needed – from the senior brass, from the state, from the machinery that often looks the other way when things get complicated.

For Prashant, Varanasi wasn't just a posting. It was a proving ground.

After his eventful stint in Varanasi, Prashant Kumar sought a transfer, not for career advancement but for something far more personal. His daughter had just been born and wasn't keeping well. His wife was posted in Bareilly, and the young family needed to be together.

He moved to Bareilly, and for a while, life regained some balance.

Then came his first independent district command – Bhadohi, a newly carved-out district that had only recently been separated from Varanasi. He was the second SP of the district, a posting that held promise, visibility and pressure in equal measure.

At first, things went smoothly. But then came a case that would leave a lasting mark – not because of its scale but because of how it unravelled.

A labourer had died under suspicious circumstances in a carpet factory owned by a politically influential businessman. The incident should have been manageable but it wasn't. It escalated quickly – too quickly. The local unit fumbled the response. Communication was muddled. Rumours filled the vacuum. And before he could assert control, the situation spiralled into a full-blown law-and-order crisis.

Looking back, Prashant Kumar doesn't deflect responsibility. He doesn't pin the blame on others. He calls it what it was: a professional bungle. 'I wasn't mature enough then,' he said. 'I should have guided my team better.'

What made it worse was the web of divided loyalties around him. Some of the officers who briefed him were simultaneously passing on the same information to the factory owner – a man who had both powerful friends and deep rivalries. It became clear, much too late, that the ground beneath his feet was shifting. And then came the final blow.

He was unceremoniously removed from his post.

It was his first real professional ouster. And it hurt – not because of the politics around it but because his intent had never been wrong. He had tried to do the right thing. He simply hadn't yet learned how to control a narrative before it consumed him.

That moment became a turning point.

It was there, amid the humiliation and the self-doubt, that Prashant made a decision. Going forward, he would never depend entirely on second-hand reports. He would be on the ground himself. He would see, listen and decide based on firsthand intelligence. No more triangulated whispers. No more middlemen. If there was a crisis, he would be present at ground zero.

It was a lesson learnt the hard way. But it would shape the kind of officer he would become.

In hindsight, Prashant Kumar knew what should have been done. The factory owner – politically connected or not – should have been arrested. It would have sent the right message, cut through the noise and reasserted the authority of the law. That one decision, taken swiftly, might have diffused the entire crisis.

But inexperience got the better of instinct.

An inquiry followed. It stretched over five to six months, a slow-burning process that felt longer than it was. When the report finally came in, it cleared him of any wrongdoing. His intent had never been questioned. His decisions, however, had.

There were no penalties. No official censure. But the mental toll was heavy.

For someone who had always acted in good faith, the episode left scars professionally and personally. It was the kind of silent trauma no file could document. The kind that lingers long after the headlines fade.

And yet just when things seemed to drift into uncertainty, a lifeline appeared. He was posted as SP, Intelligence, at the headquarters. It wasn't a punishment posting. It was, in fact, a place where he would begin to heal and rebuild.

His new superior, an ADG, (Late) S.C. Chaubey, turned out to be one of the most competent officers he ever worked under: someone who combined professional excellence with human empathy. A rare blend in a system often too busy to pause for the person behind the post.

The ADG went on to serve in the CBI and later became the chief of the CRPF. But for Prashant Kumar, it wasn't his résumé that mattered. It was the way he stood by him during a vulnerable phase.

That posting gave him breathing space. And more importantly, it gave him direction again.

Nine months into his posting at the Intelligence headquarters, just when life had begun to settle into a rhythm again, the unexpected happened.

One evening, Prashant Kumar received transfer orders – he was being sent to a hill district. At the time, Uttarakhand was still part of UP. The district was remote, unfamiliar terrain. There had been no prior warning, no hint of movement. The orders had arrived out of the blue.

The next morning, he walked into his ADG's office, part confused, part concerned. His wife was posted in the same city, his daughter was still very young. The sudden relocation felt overwhelming. He explained all this, hoping for a reprieve.

What he got instead was clarity.

'I got you posted,' the ADG said, without any preamble. It was during governor's rule – there was no elected government in place – and he had personally requested the governor to give Prashant command of a district, one with real responsibility.

'This is the time for you to work as a team person,' the senior officer told him. 'You and your wife are both in service. You can't always be posted together. That's the reality.'

Then came the part that stung – but also stayed.

'You committed a blunder by asking for a transfer from Varanasi,' the ADG said.

He was from Varanasi himself. Somewhere, someone had whispered to him that Prashant Kumar had voluntarily sought that earlier transfer, citing family reasons. Whether that version was entirely accurate or not no longer mattered. What mattered was the perception it had created.

'If you want to grow professionally,' the ADG said, 'your professional commitment cannot be seen as negotiable, even though your family is important. People shouldn't think you're unwilling to take on a challenging posting.'

There was no anger in his voice – just truth. It wasn't a scolding. It was a lesson. One that would become foundational to Prashant's growth: that in uniformed service, the question isn't whether you want the challenge. The question is whether you're ready to rise when it comes for you.

And so, he packed his bags. Amid the seriousness of professional corrections and tough postings, there were moments that reminded Prashant that even in the uniformed services, life had its quirks.

During his time at Intelligence headquarters, there was a constable – one of the 'orderlies' assigned to carry files – who had taken it upon himself to offer unsolicited career advice. He was convinced that Prashant Kumar was wasting his time in Intelligence. According to him, this was not the kind of posting an officer like him deserved. 'Sir, you should be in the field,' he would say, often and with great sincerity. 'Some district where there's action, not this desk job.'

Prashant would laugh it off. 'What does it matter to you where I'm posted?' he would tease. 'Why are you losing sleep over my job description?' But the constable was relentless – and oddly prophetic.

One day, he leaned in with a sense of mystery and declared that 'charge' was coming. The expression made Prashant laugh even harder. 'Charge' was what non-gazetted officers got – an SHO, for instance, taking charge of a thana or a sub-inspector being posted as circle in-charge. It wasn't the term used for gazetted officers taking up full-fledged district commands.

But the constable stuck to his prediction. He had, he claimed, quietly read Prashant's palm. 'It's there,' he said, matter-of-factly. 'A new posting is coming soon.'

Finding it amusing, Prashant shared the incident with the DIG posted in the adjacent room. Even he couldn't make sense of the constable's sudden burst of clairvoyance.

And yet whether by coincidence or sheer timing, a few weeks later, the orders arrived. He was being posted to Pauri Garhwal. It was his next big command – and it would come with all the field action the constable had promised.

Years later, through multiple tough assignments and volatile districts, one piece of advice stayed with Prashant Kumar. It came back to him like muscle memory – his ADG's quiet reprimand about never giving the impression that he was dodging responsibility. It had become a kind of internal compass. Whenever he found himself walking into a difficult posting, he remembered those words.

And so, when the Pauri Garhwal order came, there was no time for hesitation – or even preparation.

In UP, transfer orders don't come with a grace period. Once they're out, the clock starts ticking. Everyone, from observers to local administrators, starts tracking your movement. Where has he reached? Why hasn't he reported yet? The pressure isn't subtle. It's bureaucratic muscle memory. And compliance is non-negotiable.

Prashant Kumar rushed to Pauri.

10
Red Dust and Silent Guns

The district, normally known for its calm and mountainous stillness, was in turmoil. A regional agitation had erupted, with demands for a separate state – a precursor to what would eventually become Uttarakhand. The protests had turned violent. Law and order had spiralled. One of his predecessors had already been suspended for failing to bring the situation under control.

Hill districts didn't usually need intensive policing. The terrain did most of the filtering. Rural law enforcement was often managed through the age-old revenue police system – a colonial legacy where local revenue officers played part-time custodians of peace. Formal police were largely restricted to motorable areas. But this was different. The unrest had spread and the old model had cracked. His time in Pauri was short but intense. He didn't have the luxury of easing into the terrain or understanding the politics in layers. The moment he settled in, another transfer order arrived.

He was being sent to Sonebhadra. If Pauri had been about political identity and agitation, Sonebhadra was about resource, power and insurgency – sometimes all rolled into one.

It bordered Bihar, Jharkhand and Madhya Pradesh. A district flush with mineral wealth – coal, limestone, bauxite. Big corporations like Hindalco had sprawling operations there. Several power generation units dotted the landscape. But alongside the riches ran a deep vein of poverty and discontent.

And then came the whispers.

In certain pockets of Sonebhadra, and the adjoining districts of Chandauli and Mirzapur, Naxal activity had begun surfacing. It wasn't an epidemic – not yet – but it was enough to make the air feel different. The ground was shifting beneath the administrative veneer.

The state had sent Prashant Kumar. Now it was time to see what he would do with it. By the time he joined Sonebhadra, the murmurs had begun to grow louder. Reports started trickling in – discreet at first but persistent. Naxal activities were on the rise. In the remote interiors of Sonebhadra, Mirzapur and parts of Chandauli, something was shifting. And like most such shifts, it wasn't ideological at the surface – it was economic.

At the heart of it was the *tendu patta* trade – tendu leaves, used for rolling bidis, were a prized commodity. But the industry thrived on a brutal truth: the relentless exploitation of rural labour.

In villages tucked deep inside the forests, men, women, even children, were forced to work for whatever paltry sums they were offered. There was no negotiation, no fallback. Poverty had removed the luxury of options. The system didn't just exploit – it trapped.

The irony ran deeper.

The people who toiled in these forests rarely owned anything. The land, the trees, the forest produce – they all belonged to others. Migrants from districts like Ballia, Jaunpur and Varanasi had settled here years ago, carving out vast estates and claiming control over large swathes of forest land. They had become the absentee landlords of the hills.

It was these powerful outsiders who held the rights over the tendu leaves, the timber, the forest bounty. And it was the locals – those whose ancestors had lived in these forests for generations – who worked the land, gathered the produce and earned just enough to stay alive.

A pittance for their labour. And silence.

This wasn't just a law-and-order problem. It was the kind of smouldering inequality that could easily spiral into violence – especially when whispers of revolution began to mingle with desperation.

For Prashant Kumar, it was clear: Sonebhadra was no ordinary district. And the unrest brewing in its shadow wouldn't be solved with conventional policing.

It didn't take long for the reality of Sonebhadra to hit him – not from files or intelligence reports but from the red dust of its forgotten villages.

On his first few visits to the interior, Prashant encountered a truth more damning than any criminal dossier: schools that existed only on paper, buildings that stood hollow with no teachers and entire stretches of the district where governance had simply never arrived.

There was no public infrastructure. No working transport. No hospitals. No support systems. If someone was unwell, they were carried on foot. If a police outpost was sanctioned, there was no one willing to man it. No constable wanted to be posted in these areas. 'What will we do there?' they would ask. 'There's not even a roof, sir.'

And they weren't exaggerating.

It wasn't just physical remoteness. It was institutional absence. The government, as an entity, had vanished beyond the tarred road.

That vacuum was being filled – quietly, strategically – by the Naxals. Their starting point was simple: the people of Sonebhadra have been abandoned. The Naxals pointed to the absentee state, to the exploitative forest owners, to the unchecked poverty. They told villagers, 'You've been left to rot while others get rich on your land.'

And for many, it was hard to argue with that logic. The insurgents weren't just wielding guns, they were seeding doubt. Positioning themselves as saviours in a land where the government looked like a rumour.

And the danger was real.

The situation on the ground was grim enough that even the police had begun hesitating. At certain outposts, no officer wanted to take charge. Entire stations stood empty. Roads disappeared into thickets. There were no jeeps, no infrastructure, nothing to hold on to. One didn't drive to these villages, one walked. For miles.

This was not a policing challenge. This was a vacuum of trust. And now, Prashant had to figure out how to fill it. Eventually, something had to give.

Prashant Kumar knew that no plan would work unless his men were willing to walk the hard miles – literally. So, he changed the approach. Instead of waiting for volunteers or issuing dry orders, he tried something simple and human.

He convinced them. 'You'll go into those areas, spend six months. Don't go in to make arrests, don't go in as commandos. Just observe. Study the terrain. See who's who. What's happening. Why it's happening. And once you complete your six-month term, that very day, write it down in the general diary, and return to the police lines.'

It was a practical promise. And it worked. One by one, the boys started going in. Quietly. No drama. Just boots on ground. And then came an incident that jolted the district.

A train derailed – an unexpected, loud event in a place known for its silences. While the Railways cited poor track maintenance, the narrative quickly shifted. Whispers began that it was sabotage. An early sign of Naxal presence made itself known.

There were no casualties. But there didn't need to be. The message had gone out. That's when Prashant Kumar knew the passive phase was over. He couldn't just receive reports anymore. He had to act. He shifted his focus to the Naxal front.

Until then, most of what came his way was hearsay – something had happened here, someone had disappeared there. But now, he was initiating action. Groundwork began. Informers were activated. Patterns emerged.

The first few arrests followed. Two or three suspects were picked up from the interiors. In their possession were primitive but telling weapons – muzzle-loading guns, the kind that had to be packed from the front. *Bharuwa bandook*, as they were known locally. Rudimentary, but functional.

It wasn't much. But it was a start.

The breakthrough arrests triggered something else entirely. For the boys on the ground, it felt like momentum – like a curtain had finally lifted. More weapons were discovered. Ammunition caches emerged from the underbrush. It was a catch big enough to shift morale. The unit was ecstatic. The adrenaline kicked in.

There was talk of launching a larger operation – some suspected that more arms and operatives were holed up nearby. The mood was unmistakable. This was the kind of mission every field unit waited for. They were ready. Some were already mapping out the next move, eyes gleaming with the unspoken thrill often tagged to what the world calls 'trigger-happy cops'.

But Prashant Kumar didn't give them the green light. Not yet. He said he wanted to go there himself. So he did.

He made the long journey to the interior, walked the same muddy trails his men had, stood in the same heat, the same suspicion-soaked silence of the forest edge. He spent hours interrogating the boys they had arrested – talking to them not just like a cop but also like someone trying to peel back layers. And what he found shook him. These weren't hardened insurgents. They weren't ideologues or career militants. They were just local boys – young, nervous, barely literate. They had been pulled in, drawn into something far bigger than them by forces they didn't fully understand.

They kept referring to a group they called 'toli wale'. *Toli wale aaye the...* Toli wale had come.' That's how they spoke of them – always as an external force. The 'toli' moved in groups, led by Naxal ideologues. They would descend on villages with carefully calibrated messaging – rhetoric tailored to the frustrations of the forgotten. 'Why are you working for these people?' they would ask. 'Does this government do anything for you? Do you have roads? Electricity? Water? Any dignity?' And in those villages, the answer was often a silent, resounding no.

The toli didn't need to fight. They just had to convince. The vacuum did the rest.

For Prashant Kumar, it was no longer just about restoring order. It was about understanding how easily discontent could be repackaged into rebellion. And how, sometimes, the enemy didn't look like a militant but like a desperate boy with no other option.

What struck Prashant most during those visits wasn't the presence of armed groups or the risk of ambush – it was the absence of everything else. Governance, dignity, basic human needs – none of it existed in those remote, hilly terrains. He saw it with his own eyes. There was no drinking water, just a small pond where the entire village would gather, often barefoot, carrying rusted containers. And when the summer hit and the pond dried up, people relied on the leaves from forest trees just to fill their stomachs. Not fruits. Leaves.

But the most searing image of all came from what the women had to endure. He saw it himself. Women owning just one sari. If they needed to bathe, they would wash the cloth and then hide behind trees, waiting for it to dry, clutching themselves, exposed and invisible at the same time. It wasn't just poverty – it was erasure. Entire communities were surviving in conditions so inhumane that even the government's radar didn't seem to reach them.

It was this reality, more than anything else, that convinced him to initiate regular patrolling of these neglected interiors. The intent wasn't just law enforcement – it was presence. A signal that someone was watching. That the state hadn't disappeared entirely.

But that presence provoked a response. Shortly after patrols began, the warning came – not as a threat but as a brutal, irreversible act. A local man, known only as Mr Jaiswal, was found murdered. He was a moneylender, someone who gave small loans to poor families in the area.

Whatever his methods might have been, he was known. He was local. And now he was gone. He hadn't just been killed – he had been beheaded. It was a message.

The beheading of Jaiswal was the beginning. That evening, the atmosphere turned electric with tension. Information began filtering in, piecemeal and hazy, but laced with urgency. There were whispers of a planned Naxal strike – an assault on potentially multiple police stations across the region. The threat felt imminent, credible and terrifyingly plausible.

In response to Prashant Kumar's repeated alarms and persistent escalation of the ground situation, the administration finally moved. For the first time in weeks, his unit received additional arms, ammunition and reinforcements. Not a flood of them but enough to brace for impact. Enough to say they weren't alone.

Up until then, those police stations had stood like abandoned fortresses – isolated, exposed and largely forgotten. Unlike urban precincts with walls, towers and backup, these rural outposts were easy targets. In fact, in districts like Sonebhadra, Chandauli and beyond, it had become disturbingly normal for Naxals to overrun police stations. Across UP, Bihar and Madhya Pradesh, such attacks had become a familiar part of the insurgency's playbook. Policemen were killed in their sleep, outposts looted, arms seized, radios destroyed – each incident feeding into a growing narrative: the state was losing its grip.

And now, it seemed, Sonebhadra's turn had come. Night was approaching fast. The patrols were in position. Lights dimmed. Every movement was calibrated. And somewhere out in the jungle, unseen and unheard, a different patrol – armed, trained and angry – was possibly making its way towards them.

With the threat hanging heavy over them, Prashant Kumar made the call. 'Let's go,' he said. 'We cannot let our boys die like this.' There was resistance. Someone pointed out what everyone was thinking – that this could very well be a trap. That the reported plan to attack the police station might be bait. A strategy designed to provoke panic and force the police to rush into the jungle, only to be ambushed en route or overwhelmed at the gate. It was classic guerrilla warfare logic: provoke, draw out, kill.

But Prashant stood firm. These men were there on his word, on his assurance that they only had to endure six months in those cut-off regions. That promise, however informal, was a contract. 'We can wait till morning, sure,' he said, 'but what if something happens tonight? What will we do then? Count bodies?' The room fell silent. The weight of that question sank in. A hurried strategy meeting followed. Everyone looked tense, but there was agreement. Prashant wasn't sending anyone into the unknown

he was leading them. A team was formed – one or two DSPs, several SHOs, and about thirty to forty officers, fully armed. By early evening, they moved, with Prashant Kumar at the front, eyes sharp, voice calm. The terrain was harsh, rising into a plateau where every step had to be calculated, every rustle in the trees monitored. The air felt dense with anticipation, and yes, fear. But with their ADG leading from the front, they pushed forward.

By the time they reached the station, nestled atop a hill, it was close to nine. And what they saw there wiped away all doubts about whether the risk had been worth it. The faces of the men posted at that remote outpost lit up at the very sight of them. Relief, joy and a kind of silent vindication passed between them – one that didn't need a single word spoken. They had been remembered. They had not been abandoned.

And sometimes, in the middle of a conflict zone, that is the only thing that matters.

Reaching the station without resistance felt like a quiet victory. There were no ambushes, no shadows in the trees, no sudden firefights – just a long, tense journey that ended in safety. And with that, something inside Prashant Kumar eased. The decision to act, to go that very night, had paid off, not just tactically but emotionally too. The team felt it. What could have been a night of bloodshed turned into something else entirely – a rare, unplanned celebration at the heart of a conflict zone.

They had a gala dinner right there in the police station courtyard. Someone made tea for everyone. Snacks followed. Deputy Superintendent of Police A.K. Ray – an old-school officer who had risen through the ranks from regional inspector (RI) – took charge of the regimental matters. Ray, who's no more today, had that unmistakable blend of toughness and warmth that only comes from years of living the field life. He arranged for basic rations, drawn from whatever local sources were available, plus the stock they had carried in case an overnight stay was needed. Firewood wasn't a problem – they were in the jungle. Drinking water had been arranged. They even carried a few tables and chairs to prop up some comfort amidst the dust.

It wasn't extravagant. But it felt grand.

The boys relaxed for the first time in days. Laughter returned. So did the unspoken bond that holds police units together in hostile environments. They had shown up for each other. They had survived the night.

But it wasn't just about the uniformed men.

Prashant Kumar made sure to meet the villagers as well. He and his officers greeted them with food, tea and gestures of goodwill. They listened to complaints, offered reassurances, promised not just protection but attention. And in those small exchanges – over leaf-plates and hesitant smiles – something shifted. Fear made way for familiarity. Suspicion softened into cautious trust. His men saw it too. They had come expecting bullets. Instead, they found warmth, respect and perhaps most importantly, a reaffirmation of the support they had from their senior officer.

For many of them, it was the first time they truly felt that the chain of command wasn't paperwork but presence.

Only after all this – after the food, the conversations and the reassurances – did Prashant make the long journey back to his office. And by then, the forest had changed. Not geographically but emotionally.

After returning from the field, Prashant Kumar knew the time for silence was over. He put everything he had observed and experienced into writing and sent a formal report to headquarters. He detailed the emerging Naxal activity, the visible signs, the past incidents that had gone unreported or dismissed and the intelligence his men had gathered. It wasn't alarmist – it was precise, fact-based and urgent.

But the response from above was cautious, almost sceptical.

Some at headquarters felt that the alarm was premature. 'The moment you join, you're reporting Naxal activity?' one senior officer had reportedly remarked. It wasn't meant as criticism, but it hinted at a familiar bureaucracy-induced suspicion – that sometimes field officers exaggerate early to trigger visibility or resources.

Prashant didn't argue. He simply insisted: verify it.

The state machinery, to its credit, did just that. Intelligence officers were dispatched from Varanasi, including the SP, Intelligence. What came back surprised even the sceptics.

The report they filed painted a disturbingly grim picture. It confirmed the presence of insurgent ideology in the region and, more worryingly, cited plans that included a possible attack on the SP residence. This wasn't field speculation anymore. It was validated, cross-checked intelligence. And it could no longer be brushed aside.

The gravity of the situation triggered an immediate response. Two ADG-level officers were brought in to assess the region, including his former superior, who knew the credibility Prashant Kumar brought to the table. He was asked to draw up a detailed map and an action plan. It was not reactive policing but structural fortification. How should the police stations be defended? Where could infrastructure be reinforced? Which outposts could be upgraded into full-fledged stations?

Prashant laid it out clearly. Certain chowkis had to be elevated to thanas. Strategic posts required perimeter defences, elevated platforms, additional manpower and secure communication lines. Everything – layout, deployment, reinforcement – was marked in his plan.

And to his relief, the ADGs didn't push back. The proposal was approved and forwarded to the state level. What followed next was a decisive shift. Funds began flowing in – real, tangible support from the state machinery.

What had begun as a single officer raising his hand against silence had now transformed into institutional momentum. The region was finally being taken seriously. And with it, so was Prashant Kumar.

With the state now taking notice, the momentum continued to build. Soon after, the Government of India stepped in, extending financial support through the Security-Related Expenditure (SRE) scheme. It was part of a twin-track policy: develop the region and simultaneously deal firmly with those who threatened its peace. It wasn't just about suppressing the insurgency, it was also about addressing the vacuum that had allowed it to thrive.

And slowly, the system began to move.

Alongside the tightening of security measures came a parallel effort to offer a way out to those who had been pulled into the Naxal orbit. Young boys – brainwashed and used as couriers, eyes or frontline foot soldiers – were now being offered rehabilitation. Those who surrendered were reabsorbed through various welfare schemes floated by the government. It wasn't always smooth, and it wasn't always enough, but the message had shifted: there was a door open for those who wanted to step away from the gun.

Yet the institutional gaps remained glaring.

At that time, there wasn't even a proper police line in place. The men operated from temporary camps, often just makeshift tents and asbestos sheds – hardly the infrastructure one expected in a conflict zone. Prashant decided that had to change. He needed land. He needed a base. And he knew exactly where to find it.

There was a patch of land, long earmarked for police use, but it had been encroached upon by a self-styled godman – a 'Baba' with considerable local influence and a devoted following He had built an ashram on the land, expanded it gradually and embedded himself into the fabric of the region, not just spiritually but politically as well. Challenging him was never going to be easy, but it was necessary.

Prashant Kumar moved decisively. Legal paperwork was reviewed, boundaries re-verified, notices issued. Resistance followed, as expected. The Baba used his influence, his followers, and his connections. But none of it worked. The law was on the side of the police, and for once, the police stood firm.

The encroachment was demolished. The land was reclaimed. And with it, the State's presence was reasserted. In place of tents and temporary posts, a functional police line was finally revived – brick by brick, post by post. It wasn't just a matter of infrastructure. It was a statement.

The jungle didn't belong to whispers anymore.

In the background of all this action, the political climate was shifting. President's rule came to an end. A new elected government was sworn in. And with that, a sense of administrative stability returned to the state machinery. For officers like Prashant

Kumar, this change made day-to-day policing a little smoother. Orders were clearer, coordination tighter, and responses faster. The ground-level chaos of dual command during governor's rule gave way to more structured governance.

His time in Sonebhadra became one of those rare postings that was both difficult and defining. It built his confidence, not just tactically but also personally. He had navigated insurgency, institutional apathy, poor infrastructure and political sensitivities, and emerged with a better understanding of how power functioned at every level – from the jungle to the Secretariat. Professionally, it had been enriching. Personally, it had changed him.

After nearly a year and a half – seventeen or eighteen months, to be precise – he received orders for a new district. But due to personal reasons, he couldn't join that posting. Instead, he was reassigned to Jaunpur, in eastern UP. Jaunpur was a different beast altogether.

It was among the biggest districts in the state, not in size alone but also in political complexity. With thirteen–fourteen MLAs and a few members of Legislative Council (MLCs) representing it, the district was politically hyperactive – every decision a potential landmine, every movement scrutinized. But what made Jaunpur truly distinct was its tradition of going against the tide. If the ruling party held power in Lucknow, Jaunpur would often be painted in the colours of the Opposition. That contrarian streak had become almost cultural.

To be posted as an SP of limited seniority in such a politically charged district was always risky. One misstep could turn into a full-blown confrontation. And yet Prashant Kumar managed. He treated it like a chessboard – careful, calm and deliberate. His tenure, though short, was largely stable. He handled law and order with restraint, avoided unnecessary conflicts and maintained peace across what many considered a pressure-cooker district.

But as is often the case in UP policing, merit wasn't always enough.

After a year or so, a confrontation with a powerful figure in the ruling dispensation derailed things. The disagreement wasn't over a headline-grabbing incident – it was more subtle, political, deeply rooted in influence and expectation. The local people did not oppose him. In fact, many supported his stand. But the person he clashed with – a senior political leader – had enough clout to override public sentiment.

And just like that, the file moved. Prashant Kumar was transferred out of Jaunpur. There were no protests. No dramatic fallout. Just the quiet efficiency of power doing what it does best – exert itself.

But even in that, he took no bitterness. It was just another page in a growing book of experiences. One that had taught him that sometimes, real policing was about surviving systems, and surviving them with one's integrity intact.

Jaunpur wasn't a district. It was a storm held together by silence. The kind of place where gangsters set the rules and police stations kept their heads low. Among the names that dominated the crime maps of the region, Gopal Singh had built a legacy of violence and fear.

He was just thirty, but already wanted in twenty-seven cases – murder, loot, dacoity, snatching. His reach extended across districts. His name was a warning. Summons meant nothing. Raids turned up empty. Even the mention of his whereabouts felt speculative.

Until one cold morning, just before dawn.

Based on specific intelligence, the police laid a quiet trap across the city. Multiple units were deployed at precise locations where Gopal was likely to pass through. At 4 a.m., a motorcycle carrying three men approached a checkpoint. When asked to stop, the riders turned sharply and fled. The chase began instantly. Gunshots followed. The encounter was brief but telling.

Gopal Singh was shot dead. His two companions managed to flee into the shadows. A country-made revolver called the *katta* and a large cache of live cartridges were recovered from his possession. It wasn't just a criminal who had been killed. It was a message that the landscape was shifting.

And that message travelled fast. It reached even those who had built their empires not just on crime, but on politics.

Dhananjay Singh had long occupied the grey space between the two. His name needed no introduction in Jaunpur. A former student leader turned MLA and MP, his ascent was backed not just by political ambition but by a string of serious criminal allegations – murder, extortion, abduction, and more. For years, he had operated with a kind of casual impunity that made the law look ornamental.

But this time, the arrest did not come with delays or negotiations. It was direct.

When Dhananjay Singh was produced in court, he arrived cloaked in a burqa. The man who once ruled entire neighbourhoods by presence alone now chose to conceal his identity – not from the police but from the people. A battery of lawyers walked beside him. His usual crowd of supporters stood at a distance, unsure of how to process what they were seeing.

There were no slogans. No show of power. Just a man shielding his face, surrounded by silence. For a place like Jaunpur, that moment was more than procedural. It was symbolic.

Two men who had once defined fear in their own ways – one brought down by bullets, the other by a quiet courtroom walk in disguise. No big declarations had been made. No spectacles had been staged. But everyone watching knew that something had changed in the district.

Prashant Kumar had completed a full year in Jaunpur. The political wind had shifted once again, and with it came a new posting. This time, he was transferred to the Crime Branch.

For many in the service, a posting to the Crime Branch was often whispered about as a 'shunting posting' – a place where officers were sent when the corridors of power wanted them benched without saying it out loud. But Prashant didn't see it that way. For him, every department within the police system was a learning opportunity, a fresh lens into the functioning of law enforcement. This was his first posting in Crime Branch, and he embraced it with the same seriousness he had brought to Sonebhadra, Varanasi and Jaunpur.

He stayed there for around seven to eight months. It was a quieter stint, yes, but never a wasted one.

Then, another change arrived. Though the ruling party in UP remained the same, the chief minister changed. And with a new chief minister came a ripple effect across the administrative machinery. It was during those early days of transition that Prashant received a call from the PHQ.

A senior officer on the line asked him a simple, loaded question: 'Where would you like to go?'

It was the kind of offer that could mean anything. An invitation, a test, a courtesy. But his response was immediate – and telling of the man he had become. 'I have no preference,' he said. 'I'm only here because my wife is posted here. But wherever the headquarters finds fit for me, I'll go.'

No lobbying. No pushing. Just a calm acceptance of duty, wherever it led. A few days later, in the final stretch of 1999, his next order came through. He was being posted as SSP Ghaziabad. A new millennium was on the horizon. And so was the next phase of his journey, as a senior leader in one of the most volatile, high-pressure districts of western UP.

PART 4
Significant Cases

11
The Furnace of the West

Until then, most of Prashant Kumar's policing career had played out in eastern UP – a terrain he had come to know intimately, with all its political volatility, cultural contradictions and district-level complexities. But now, the compass needle pointed west. And this wasn't just a change in geography. It was a change in texture.

Western UP had a different reputation altogether. Among officers, it was often referred to – half-jokingly, half-warningly – as the 'Wild West'. The name wasn't accidental. Land mafias, organized crime syndicates, political strongmen and gun culture were as common in the region as wheat fields and sugarcane. Ghaziabad, Meerut, Muzaffarnagar – these weren't just districts. They were battlegrounds where reputations were made and destroyed.

When the Ghaziabad posting order came through, fear gripped him for the first time in years. Not because he doubted his own ability but because he understood the stakes. This wasn't about just managing law and order. This was about entering a theatre where your every move was under the scanner – by criminals, politicians, the media, even your own seniors.

That night, as he tried to make peace with the posting, he discussed it with his wife. They had to attend a wedding, ironically, of the brother of a senior officer. The usual crowd, the smiling faces, the polite gossip. But his mind kept drifting back to the order. When they returned home, he turned to her again.

'What should I do?' he asked. 'I'm scared.'

She didn't laugh. She didn't brush it aside. She had served in western UP herself as an SDM, and she knew exactly what he was feeling. But instead of caution, she offered perspective.

'This is your real playground now,' she said. 'This is where your policing will be tested. If you survive here, people will see you as a competent officer. This is your Lords. Go hit a century.'

It was the clarity he needed. And with that, the decision was made. He would report for duty in Ghaziabad at the earliest.

Some friends suggested he arrive by flight – it was, after all, a high-profile district. 'Let them see your stature,' they said. 'Land like an officer who belongs.' He refused. 'I'll go by train,' he said. 'Let the arrival be humble. I'll let the work speak.'

The furnace was ready. And he was walking into it head held high.

At first, he didn't quite realize what he was walking into. Ghaziabad – yes, Prashant Kumar knew it had a reputation. But it hadn't quite sunk in him that this was considered a prized posting, the kind of place where careers could either take flight or explode in slow motion. So, he landed there, quietly, as SSP, Ghaziabad – armed more with instinct than ceremony.

The district was fierce. It kept everyone on their toes – criminals, cops, even the occasional senior officer who liked to micromanage from a safe distance. 'But what surprised me the most wasn't the crime charts or the late-night public control rooms (PCR) calls –

it was the team I inherited. Efficient, sharp, and surprisingly committed. I realized I'd walked in with the wrong impression. The setup here was primed. I just had to calibrate myself to its speed,' was his immediate deduction.

One of his first calls after taking charge was to meet the Divisional Commissioner, who, as per tradition, sat in Meerut. Still does. A very proper South Indian gentleman – courteous, cultured and the kind of dry that made the desert look emotional. Prashant Kumar was actually in Meerut to call on his IG and DIG, and thought he would check that courtesy box while he was at it.

The Commissioner greeted him with polite scepticism. 'So, where were you posted earlier?' he asked, tone neutral, eyes sharp.

'I rattled off a list of districts – some that had left bruises, some that hadn't. But somehow, I forgot to mention Jaunpur.'

He looked me up and down and said, 'I don't think you can handle Ghaziabad.'

Just like that. No warm-up.

'You don't have the exposure,' he added, not maliciously, just... clinically.

Prashant smiled and said, 'Sir, I'll try.'

'No, no,' he waved it off. 'You don't know how fast crime happens here.'

Now, that intrigued him. Not the crime but the speed of his judgment.

'Sir, I've just joined,' he said. 'Let me at least fail before you write me off.'

Something shifted in his expression. He stared for a beat, then asked, 'List out the places again. Where else have you served?'

He said, 'Jaunpur.'

He blinked. 'How long?'

'About a year.'

The commissioner stood up immediately and extended his hand with a smile that had been missing since Prashant Kumar had walked in. 'In that case, you'll do great here.'

The new SSP blinked this time. 'Sir, you just said I wasn't fit for this district.'

He chuckled. 'Well, I did a year in Jaunpur as DM. That place trains you for anything.'

And he wasn't wrong.

In UP, if you have done time in Jaunpur or Azamgarh and lived to tell the tale, you're basically certified to handle anything the state throws at you. Ghaziabad might have been the Wild West – but to a Jaunpur veteran, it was just another stage.

As it turned out, that handshake in Meerut marked the beginning of one of the most defining phases of his career.

His tenure in Ghaziabad would go on to stretch almost three years – an eternity by UP policing standards, where transfers often arrive faster than results. It was tough, chaotic, political and wildly unpredictable. But it was also deeply fulfilling. 'I had a great team, a solid command structure, and enough challenges to keep every instinct in me on high alert. Looking back, I'd say I did well – really well. And perhaps, for the first time, I also thoroughly enjoyed the ride.'

But he was already experienced enough not to mistake that for comfort. Because what followed wasn't just about law and order. It was a series of stories – some explosive, some emotional, some outright bizarre – that punctuated my time in Ghaziabad and left an imprint Prashant Kumar still carries.

So yes, the furnace was hot. But what came out of it? Well, let's just say... hold your horses.

What followed in Ghaziabad wasn't just good policing – it was a full-scale crackdown. The kind that reshapes the power dynamic of an entire region.

The Furnace of the West

The police team under the new SSP went after criminals, gangsters and mafia networks that had long operated with impunity. Over 150 separate police actions were carried out during his tenure – raids, chases, arrests and, in many cases, encounters. These weren't petty criminals; these were hardened, notorious figures who had terrorized not just Ghaziabad, but also Meerut, Delhi and the surrounding NCR belt.

Their method was textbook evasive: commit a crime in one district, then disappear into another – using inter-jurisdictional gaps like camouflage. They banked on poor coordination between districts. 'We broke that model. With the support of my DIG and IG – both stellar officers who backed every tough call I had to make – we began hunting them down, across city limits, across state lines, across the shadows.'

It wasn't just the UP Police that noticed. Even Delhi Police Commissioner Ajay Raj Sharma sent in words of appreciation. The coordination between Ghaziabad and Delhi became seamless. The wall criminals used to jump across – Prashant Kumar's boys turned that into a trap.

It was a watershed moment in the region's policing narrative. For too long, gangsters had treated the NCR as a playground – knowing full well the loopholes, the delays, the apathy. That era came to an end. 'Ask people in Ghaziabad even today, and many will tell you without hesitation – there was absolute peace in those years. Not just quiet, but peace with authority,' he told me. That wasn't luck. That was work. That was planning. That was resolve. And behind every headline, every raid, every funeral wreath laid on a gangster's body, there was a story.

'It wasn't just the encounters and crackdowns that defined my tenure in Ghaziabad – it was also the cases.' The kind that make national headlines. The kind that push districts into the spotlight of Delhi newsrooms and sometimes even the corridors of power.

Two cases, in particular, sent ripples far beyond the district borders.

One was the Nitish Katara case – a brutal, high-profile murder that combined elements of family honour, political muscle and sheer cold-bloodedness. The other involved the kidnapping and murder of an NRI – a case that shook public confidence and sent a clear message that no one, not even those flying in from abroad, was beyond reach of organized criminality.

Both cases were closely followed, not just by the state leadership, but by the Prime Minister's Office itself. 'Not that anyone from the PMO ever spoke to me directly – but I could sense the weight. My DG was constantly on the line. And back in those days, a call from the DG wasn't a gentle nudge – it was a thunderclap. Unlike today, where a WhatsApp message might casually land on an SP's phone, back then a direct call from the DG to an SP was rare. And when it did happen, 99 out of 100 times, it wasn't a pat on the back. It was a dressing-down, often loud enough for your entire staff room to go silent.'

'There was no real guidance in those moments – just pressure. The only guidance you had came from your immediate supervisory officers – your DIG, your IG – and if you were lucky, they were fair, intelligent and supportive. If you weren't, well... you were on your own. And you suffered. That was the culture of policing then. You learned by falling. You learned by absorbing the blows. And sometimes, if you held your ground, you walked away having cracked cases that were being followed all the way up to South Block.'

On the night of the incident, while his own family celebrated their Grihapravesh ceremony, Prashant Kumar was pulled back into duty. Near midnight, a call came directly from the Prime Minister's Office – the kind that freezes a household. An NRI had gone missing, and the PMO was monitoring every move.

By then, Prashant's team had already recovered the body from a canal cutting through the paddy fields of in present-day Uttarakhand (then known as Uttaranchal). What began as a routine missing persons complaint had quickly escalated into a murder investigation. And under the glare of the centre's attention, it was cracked just as swiftly.

It was the kind of high-stakes case that defined his early tenure in the region – quick action, precise coordination and a message sent loud and clear: this wouldn't be a cop who blinked under pressure.

Because that's what western UP had become in those years – a kind of lawless frontier where land feuds were settled at gunpoint, business rivalries ended in blood and gated colonies served more as bunkers than homes. It was in this simmering terrain, where the line between wealth and vulnerability had all but vanished, that another case reached Prashant Kumar's table – one that started with a missing man, a forged cheque and a silver motorbike, and ended with a confession so cold it haunted even hardened officers.

In September 2000, the Delhi skies were grey with late monsoon clouds when an expatriate industrialist vanished into thin air.

Ajit Kohli, sixty, urbane and wealthy, had made his fortune in London but returned to India to set up base in Delhi–NCR. He was the embodiment of the 'liberalized India' dream: a man of means, class and confidence. With a flourishing hardware export business in East Delhi's industrial belt and a second factory under construction in Greater Noida, Kohli split his time between his high-end Neel Padam Kunj apartment and business commitments. His wife and daughter still lived in London. Kohli, ever optimistic, believed in building a legacy in his homeland.

But on the morning of 15 September, something felt off. His driver arrived for duty at the usual time and found Kohli's car parked but the apartment locked. Hours passed. Kohli didn't make an appearance. Calls to his mobile went unanswered. By afternoon, the driver alerted Kapil, Kohli's trusted manager.

That evening, a call finally came. The voice on the other end claimed to be Kohli, asking Kapil to withdraw ₹6 lakh from the company account at Grindlays Bank. Two men would come to collect it with a signed cheque. Kapil complied.

A short while later, the same routine repeated – this time, another ₹4 lakh was withdrawn from Indian Bank, Ghaziabad. In total, ₹10 lakh changed hands that day – handed over to two unknown young men riding a flashy new silver Honda CBZ motorbike.

By the next morning, there was still no sign of Kohli. His apartment was still locked; there were no further calls, no trace. Panic set in. Kapil informed Kohli's wife, Pushpa, in London. She flew down the same night with their daughter, Priya, and drove straight from the airport to Ajit's Neel Padam Kunj apartment.

They broke the lock. Inside, the flat was untouched – immaculate, luxurious and hauntingly quiet – except for one chilling detail: on the centre table in the drawing room sat four empty glasses, a bottle of imported whiskey, finger snacks and soda bottles – evidence of a recent drinking session. But with whom?

Pushpa insisted on filing a report. Inspector Narendra Singh Sengar, then SHO at Indirapuram Police Station, registered a case under IPC 364A – kidnapping for ransom. The case quickly escalated to the top brass, and soon reached SSP Prashant Kumar. When he was first briefed on the Ajit Kohli disappearance, the evidence – or the lack of it – bothered him. There was no body. No ransom call. No demand. No motive on paper. What he had was a missing man, forged cheques and the uneasy sense that this wasn't a random act of violence but something far more calculated.

For a seasoned officer like Prashant Kumar, the mystery wasn't in what was visible but in what was being carefully concealed. He could sense the artifice. He personally spoke to the senior officers on ground – R.K. Chaturvedi, Ajay Sahdev and Inspector Sengar – and issued clear directions: Follow the money. Focus on people inside the circle. Don't get distracted by decoys.

Prashant's leadership style had always leaned on two pillars – speed and depth. A sensational case like this needed both. And it needed quietness. 'Don't leak it to the press yet' he had warned. 'We don't even know what we're dealing with.'

The search began. A multi-pronged special team was constituted under Circle Officer Ajay Sahdev, reporting to R.K. Chaturvedi. The team began mapping Kohli's contacts, movements and banking activity. They questioned club staff, neighbours, his personal aides and even analysed fingerprints from the drinking session.

Still no ransom calls came. No letters. No sightings.

But then came a sliver of hope. Kapil remembered the bike. He couldn't recall the full license number, but with a technician named Sunil, they pieced together the likely digits – DL 9SA 9920. That number cracked the case.

The bike belonged to a young man named Rohit Sethi, living in Krishna Enclave, Sadar Bazar. When police reached his house on 22 September, the silver CBZ was parked in the driveway. Rohit opened the door, and Kapil, who had accompanied the police, immediately recognized him as one of the men who had collected the cash.

Rohit was arrested on the spot. During interrogation, he confessed to everything. He had gone with a man named Raj Singh to collect the money. The plan, he claimed, was hatched by none other than Surendra Arora, Rohit's elder cousin and a fellow resident of Neel Padam Kunj, who also happened to be a friend of Kohli's.

Prashant Kumar, who was receiving real-time updates, ordered a swift takedown. 'Go in tonight. Hit all locations at once. Don't give them time to regroup.'

But the end was gruesome. Surendra Arora's house was raided that same night. Along with Arora, police arrested Raj Singh and Rohit's brother, Rohan Sethi, the other key player. During the raid, police found two suitcases full of counterfeit currency notes.[63] It was a sting of irony that a man who died over real money was ultimately betrayed for counterfeit cash.

Once in custody, Arora broke down. He confessed that Ajit Kohli had been murdered on the night of 15 or 16 September. The plan was never just about ransom. After taking the ₹10 lakh, the conspirators feared Kohli would go to the police. He knew them, after all.

So, they did what cold-blooded criminals do – they killed him. The body was never recovered. Prashant's reaction to the confession was not of triumph. It was of grim vindication. 'I had hoped we were wrong,' he told one of his juniors, 'but I knew we weren't.'

Behind the curtain were greed and desperation. Surendra Arora's life was a cautionary tale of ambition gone rotten. A family man from Roorkee with a wife, daughter and his own real estate business, he had drowned himself in debts and deceit. When his financial empire collapsed, he came to Delhi with borrowed confidence and a flashy lifestyle built on lies.

At Neel Padam Kunj, he rebranded himself as a property dealer and joined the elite club where Kohli was a member. He watched Kohli closely – the money, the solitude, the habits. And then he decided.

The kidnapping was staged with chilling precision. A fake call made from Kohli's phone. Cheques that were signed during captivity. A planned false drop at Barakhamba's Hans Plaza, never intended to be real. And a quiet, final act of murder in a world where trust had become currency, and currency a death sentence. For Prashant Kumar and his team, the Kohli case was not just another file. It was a reminder of how criminality often wears silk shirts and lives next door. A case where police had nothing – no body, no ransom call, no direct evidence except pressure and a gut feeling that something was wrong.

And yet they cracked it – with patient, methodical digging.

But the Ajit Kohli case was only a prelude. The region had barely caught its breath when it was rocked again – this time not by greed but by a chilling cocktail of power, honour and rage. If Kohli's murder revealed the dangers of misplaced trust, the next case would expose the savagery that unfolds when love crosses the red lines drawn by political families. It was the brutal killing of Nitish Katara – a young, promising man punished for loving a girl he shouldn't have loved. And once again, the weight of public outrage, media glare and institutional pressure would land on the same police machinery. The demand would be not just for resolution but also for redemption.

It began like so many real tragedies do – with a missing boy and a mother's growing fear.

Nitish Katara, a twenty-five-year-old MBA graduate, had travelled to Ghaziabad to attend a wedding. That much was known. He was bright, well-spoken, and – by all accounts – stood out in any crowd. But after that wedding night, he vanished. No word, no call, no return home. Someone – possibly a relative or a friend – reached out to the police station, saying Nitish hadn't come back, and could they check if there had been an accident or some trouble en route.

At that point, there was no panic. Just protocol. The Ghaziabad police, under SSP Prashant Kumar, initiated a quiet but thorough search. Hospitals were checked. Morgues, accident reports, road mishaps – nothing. No one matching Nitish's description had turned up anywhere. It was as if the boy had walked into the night and disappeared.

But there was one person who knew something was wrong from the very beginning – Neelam Katara, Nitish's mother. Hers wasn't concern; it was intuition, dread, a mother's sixth sense. She didn't believe in waiting passively for answers. She began pushing – hard – asking questions, demanding follow-ups, offering whatever details she could piece together.

During the course of the inquiry, a name surfaced – Bharti Yadav, daughter of D.P. Yadav, a politician whose reputation was as large as it was controversial. Nitish, it turned out, was romantically involved with Bharti. The two had known each other from college, and their relationship, though not hidden, had ruffled feathers in powerful circles.

That wedding Nitish had attended? Bharti was present too. And that detail changed everything.

Because D.P. Yadav wasn't just another political figure in western UP. He was what many called a Bahubali – a muscleman, a strongman, a name that carried weight in every corridor that mattered, from party offices to police stations. His political career had been controversial, with enough whispers and newsprint to suggest that his empire was built not just on votes but also on fear.

Some called him a mafia boss in a politician's clothing.

There was no direct evidence yet. But the moment Nitish's connection to Bharti Yadav came to light, and the fact that he disappeared immediately after attending an event she was at, the investigation shifted from a routine missing person's case to something far darker.

At that time, Prashant's wife, an IAS officer, was posted as the district magistrate in the neighbouring district. As the search for Nitish intensified and the phone calls from his increasingly desperate father – an officer serving in the railway ministry –became more frequent, the investigation remained stuck in a frustrating standstill. No leads. No eyewitnesses. Just a gnawing void.

Until a call came from across the district border.

Late one evening, Prashant Kumar's wife informed him that a body had been found in her district – badly burnt, left in an isolated area near a canal, hidden in the shadows of paddy fields. There were no initial clues to identify him, but something about the appearance the face, the posture, the clothes – suggested that the boy was from a well-to-do family.

'You may want to pass this information to the boy's family,' she told him.

The hunch was too strong to ignore. Prashant made a call to Neelam Katara, who had by now become a pillar of steel wrapped in maternal grief. He carefully explained the situation, trying to strike a balance between transparency and gentleness. 'Ma'am,' he said, 'we've found a body that may be relevant to our investigation. It's late, I understand, but if you're willing, we can go together to verify…'

What he hadn't fully realized then – but would soon enough – was that Neelam Katara was no ordinary woman. Her response was immediate: 'Yes. I'll come now.'

There was no hesitation. Just calm resolve.

Security was sent to escort her. When they reached the spot, Neelam stepped forward with remarkable composure, walked to the charred remains, and after only a few seconds, said, 'This is my son.'

Startled, Prashant asked her how she could be sure.

She pointed to Nitish's feet. 'His feet were unusually small for his height,' she said quietly. 'A mother never forgets.'

That moment, beneath the rural night sky, at a crime scene still echoing with the horror of what had been done, the truth surfaced.

Nitish Katara had not just gone missing. He had been murdered. Burnt. Discarded.

And now, there was no turning back.

The news spread with the force of a firestorm. First local media picked it up. Then state channels. And by the next morning, the national press was in overdrive. Prime-time anchors dissected the details. Headlines screamed murder. Fingers began pointing.

The Katara murder had officially become a national scandal, and the district police, led by Prashant Kumar, was squarely in the spotlight.

Once the identity of the body was confirmed, the case turned from tragedy to test – of both the police system and the criminal justice framework. The task ahead was clear: to build a watertight case that would not just expose the killers but survive the courtroom crucible, where every shred of evidence would be questioned and political pressure would lurk just outside the door.

The first priority was to establish scientific confirmation through DNA analysis – not common in routine cases at the time, and certainly not easily accessible in criminal investigations across most districts. The pressure was immense. Not only was this a case that had already captured national attention, but it involved names no local official wanted to be caught standing against.

Prashant Kumar knew that no room for error could be allowed. He decided to get the DNA matched through one of India's foremost experts in forensic science – Dr Lalji Singh, often referred to as the father of DNA fingerprinting in India. Though Singh hailed from Jaunpur, he was then based in Hyderabad, heading the Centre for DNA Fingerprinting and Diagnostics (CDFD). His integrity was unquestionable. His expertise unmatched.

'We deliberately didn't want any local lab or officer involved in the DNA process,' Prashant told me. 'There was too much pressure. Too many powerful names.'

Alongside the DNA work, a post-mortem examination was ordered at AIIMS, New Delhi – India's most prestigious medical institution. The intention was clear: eliminate any chance of tampering and let science speak louder than influence.

As the noose of evidence began tightening, D.P. Yadav, the towering political strongman whose name was now floating in every report and conversation, began publicly distancing himself. He ran from pillar to post, claiming the entire case was fabricated, a political conspiracy aimed at tarnishing him and his family. 'There is no evidence,' he thundered to cameras and microphones. 'We are being framed.'

And yet even in the chaos, the investigators kept their heads down. They knew the difference between noise and truth.

'There was no question that he was a man of clout,' Prashant admitted. 'But the system doesn't work on who you are. It works on what you've done. Or at least, it should.'

But in India, influence can quietly rewrite definitions, which made the next steps even more critical. No court would convict anyone, let alone politically connected individuals, without hard, verifiable evidence. That meant not only physical proof but also witnesses – people who had seen what had happened and had the courage to say it.

And just when it seemed like the silence would win, a crack appeared in the wall.

The police located a handful of witnesses – individuals who had seen Nitish being taken away from the wedding venue forcibly, shortly after Bharti Yadav had left. These were not hearsay accounts. They were firsthand observations, and they matched the timeline perfectly.

It was the first real break.

Now the case wasn't just about forensics and theories. It had a timeline, a location, an eyewitness account – and a motive.

What was once a murky disappearance was beginning to take the shape of a cold-blooded, premeditated murder, rooted in rage, power and the toxic obsession with family honour.

Then came another breakthrough – this time not from the forensics lab but from a wedding video.

As the investigation dug deeper, the police managed to retrieve footage from the wedding party where Nitish Katara was last seen alive. The video showed Nitish dancing with Bharti Yadav, her face clearly visible, their chemistry unmissable. Minutes later, the footage captured men – identified later as Vikas and Vishal Yadav, Bharti's brothers – intervening aggressively, confronting Nitish and leading him away from the venue.

It was a grainy window into the night the nation would come to know in chilling detail. And it corroborated the eyewitness accounts the police had just begun to gather. The motive – unspoken until then – suddenly had a face: a family unwilling to tolerate their daughter's relationship with a man they believed didn't fit their 'status'.

Even with the video and witnesses, the cornerstone of the case remained DNA. Public scrutiny had reached a fever pitch. The national media had turned Nitish's murder into a flashpoint debate on honour killings, political impunity and the broken nerves of the justice system. Every move the police made was being dissected, second-guessed.

And while the investigation team had full faith in Dr Lalji Singh, they also knew perception was everything in a case like this.

'We trusted Lalji Singh completely,' Prashant Kumar told me. 'But the noise was growing. The stakes were too high. We wanted to be one step ahead of any doubt.'

So instead of sending the samples to Lalji Singh's official lab in Hyderabad – where critics might later allege bias owing to his roots in Jaunpur – the team made a quiet, tactical move. The DNA samples were secretly flown to Kolkata, entrusted to an unrelated forensic lab, hand-delivered by a police officer on a commercial flight.

The result?

A conclusive match. The charred remains recovered from the sugarcane fields of Uttarakhand matched Neelam Katara's DNA. The identity of the victim was now beyond doubt. The young man who had vanished after dancing with Bharti Yadav at a wedding – the one whose body was found burnt and discarded like evidence – was indeed Nitish Katara.

With that, the first major hurdle was crossed. It was no longer a missing person's case. It was murder – premeditated, brutal, personal.

From that moment on, Nitish Katara was not just a name whispered in drawing rooms and college circles. It thundered across courtrooms, dominated television debates and pierced the conscience of an entire nation.

The real storm was just beginning.

12

Promotion, Protest and the Missing File

Once the identity of Nitish Katara had been confirmed and the timeline firmly established, the police turned their attention to building the case – a case that would need to withstand not only the rigour of the courtroom but also the formidable wall of privilege and political protection that now loomed ahead.

Heading the investigation on ground was a sharp additional SP named Ashok Kumar Raghav, whose persistence and attention to detail proved invaluable. Working under Prashant Kumar's leadership, he helped weave the narrative that would eventually convince the judiciary. Based on witness accounts, phone records, location analysis and the recovered video evidence, the investigators were able to directly link the crime to Vikas Yadav, the son of D.P. Yadav, and Vishal Yadav, his nephew.

Both were alleged to have forcibly abducted Nitish from the wedding venue, driven him across the state's borders, murdered him in cold blood and then attempted to burn the body to destroy evidence. What remained was a charred corpse and a trail of circumstantial and direct evidence.

But as often happens in high-profile cases, the suspects disappeared.

Vikas and Vishal Yadav went underground almost immediately after the police named them in connection with the murder. They stopped answering calls, their phones went dark, their legal teams activated. It became clear this was no ordinary manhunt. These weren't just fugitives – they were privileged fugitives, protected by layers of influence, connections and fear.

The Ghaziabad Police moved swiftly.

Bailable and non-bailable warrants were issued. Kurki proceedings – the attachment of properties belonging to the absconding accused – were initiated.

Kurki, a rarely used but powerful provision, allowed the police to petition the court to seize the immovable property of Vikas and Vishal Yadav until they surrendered. The idea was to apply pressure through law – through disruption of comfort, reputation and political face.

And yet they continued to evade arrest.

It would take years before the shadow of justice finally lengthened over them. Six years later, the image of police vehicles entering the compound of D.P. Yadav's house was etched into public memory. It wasn't just the culmination of an operation – it was the state knocking at the door of unchecked power.

And it all began with a mother who refused to believe her son had simply vanished. The kurki was executed with full legal force. Under court orders, the police entered the residence of D.P. Yadav and conducted a complete search-and-seize operation. Every room was inspected, every cabinet opened, every corner turned inside out. The accused – Vikas and Vishal – were not there, as expected. But the operation yielded clues and materials that helped tighten the case. It wasn't just about finding the boys anymore – it was about constructing an investigation so airtight that their eventual surrender or capture would be followed by immediate legal consequences, not procedural delays.

And then came the breakthrough.

Somewhere near Bhopal, the railway police – acting on coordinated alerts – intercepted a suspicious passenger. It was Vikas Yadav, finally within reach. There were protocols to follow. A court order was obtained and a team was dispatched to take him into custody and bring him back – from Bhopal to Delhi via Ghaziabad.

But this wasn't a quiet extraction. It was a media storm.

One news channel broadcast the entire journey live, without commercial breaks – a surreal mix of true crime, courtroom drama and primetime theatre. Viewers across the country watched in real time as the accused in one of India's most sensational murders was transported across state lines, handcuffed but not silenced, eyes darting as cameras followed his every movement.

The atmosphere was thick with tension. Rumours flew: Would there be retaliation? Would someone try to silence him? Would his father unleash chaos in the court?

No one knew what might unfold.

'Speculation was wild,' Prashant Kumar recalled. 'There was talk that the accused might do something drastic, or that there could be an attempt to disrupt the proceedings. Some feared an attack in the courtroom. Others thought D.P. Yadav might pull something unexpected.'

But the police remained unflinching.

'We were cautious, of course,' Prashant said, 'but unruffled. The case had reached a point where retreat was not even an option.'

Vikas Yadav was presented in court, and with the investigation nearly complete and a chain of evidence established, the team charge-sheeted him immediately.

The case was no longer a mystery or a political inconvenience – it was now a legal assault. The Katara investigation had evolved from whispers and shadows into a full-blown confrontation with power.

But what lay ahead would prove even tougher: the courtroom battles, the witness drama and the relentless, lonely war of a mother who had decided she wouldn't rest until justice had a face, a name and a punishment.

The road to conviction was long. It took nearly five years for the legal machinery to deliver its first clear judgment. And it wouldn't have happened – not in that timeline – without the unrelenting drive of one woman: Neelam Katara.

It was at her insistence, and with mounting concerns over influence and interference, that the trial was shifted from UP to Delhi. The fear was real. The reach of the Yadav family in western UP was far too deep, too entangled, too familiar with the corridors that could bend rules silently. The court, having reviewed the meticulous groundwork laid by the police, acknowledged the credibility of the investigation. It anticipated that any further proceedings in the state could risk being compromised by the accused's powerful connections. In Delhi, there was at least a chance to fight on neutral ground.

Each time there was a hearing, whether in the High Court or the Supreme Court, the police had to present the case file in full detail. The process was monitored with unusual intensity. Initially, courts insisted on reviewing every step: the investigation, the charge sheet, the witness statements, the forensic evidence. There were no shortcuts.

'We went to court for every hearing,' Prashant Kumar recalled. 'Every time, there were new arguments, new attempts to stall the process. But gradually, as we laid out the case, the judges began to see the truth emerge from the fog.'

Eventually, the charge sheet was accepted. The case moved into trial.

Vikas Yadav tried everything. He used his influence, his connections and at times pure intimidation – against witnesses, against the system and even within bureaucratic ranks. The threats were never overt but always present – through silence, through delay, through power plays that had long become familiar in India's elite criminal cases.

But the system, for once, held.

The investigation team never wavered. The evidence never collapsed. The witnesses – against all odds – stood firm. And Neelam Katara? She never missed a hearing, never took a break, never let grief outpace her resolve. She became a symbol of civilian courage, someone whose personal tragedy transformed into a national movement for justice.

The court was finally convinced.

Vikas Yadav was convicted for the abduction and murder of Nitish Katara. Later, Vishal Yadav too was brought under the same net of guilt.

The conviction was secured after many years. Prashant Kumar, by then serving as DIG on deputation, heard the news with quiet satisfaction. For him, and for the Ghaziabad Police, it was a matter of honour – of doing the job right, without compromise. The case was a testament to what the system could achieve when men on the ground refused to look away.

But the story didn't end there.

If the investigation belonged to the police, the justice that followed belonged to Neelam Katara – the mother who wouldn't let go.

There are moments in India's judicial history when justice feels like a hard-earned miracle – when it is not delivered from the dais of the court but extracted from a system built to resist the weak and bend to the powerful. The Nitish Katara murder case was one such moment. But if there is one person responsible for turning that moment into a movement, it is Neelam Katar – a mother who refused to mourn quietly and instead chose to battle publicly, stubbornly and with a kind of grace that courts, politicians and the nation could neither ignore nor undermine.

From the very beginning, Neelam Katara knew she wasn't just fighting for her son, she was fighting against a machinery designed to protect men like Vikas and Vishal Yadav. Men who were sons and nephews of a powerful political strongman – D.P. Yadav, a name that carried the weight of guns, goons and government in western UP.

She didn't wait for things to unfold. She took action.

Sensing that influence would seep into every part of the local investigation and prosecution, Neelam moved the courts to shift the trial from Ghaziabad to Delhi. It was a rare request at the time – often considered an admission of no confidence in the local judiciary or state apparatus. But the Delhi High Court agreed. The case moved, and so did the national spotlight.

What followed was a masterclass in citizen perseverance.

For over a decade, Neelam Katara pursued the case across every tier of the judiciary – from the sessions court in Delhi to the High Court to the Supreme Court. She filed RTIs, kept track of every date, every hearing, every technicality. She challenged every delay, fought every adjournment and exposed every attempt – subtle or blatant – to water down the prosecution.

The Yadav family tried every trick. Witnesses were intimidated.

Bharti Yadav, the key link between the victim and the accused, went missing for four years, conveniently 'studying in London' during crucial phases of the trial.

The pressure was immense. The case became personal. 'I didn't want my district's record to be tainted under my watch,' Prashant Kumar later said. 'It wasn't about ego. It was about sending a message – that Ghaziabad wouldn't fall.'

But the message, in this case, came a little late. Before the police could intercept, the ransom was paid. The victim was released. And the accused vanished.

It stung. It wasn't a procedural failure – it was a psychological blow. For a district that had made headlines for cracking down on mafias, this felt like a dent in the armour. And the media made sure it wasn't forgotten.

Worse, this wasn't the first time in recent weeks. Another kidnapping had preceded it – this one of a *lekhpaal*, a revenue official. The lekhpaals in Ghaziabad were known for their rough edges and powerful, often feared families. The idea that someone would dare abduct one was seen as a direct provocation.

That case, fortunately, had ended differently. The police had rescued the lekhpaal in time. But it showed that the kidnapping racket was becoming bolder, and the network behind it was spreading faster than expected. The sarpanch, meanwhile, had gone underground.

Months later, word came that he had surfaced in Saharanpur, in connection with yet another kidnapping. The police wasted no time. He was arrested, brought under Ghaziabad Police remand and was to be transported for interrogation. This was the moment they had waited for – the man who had embarrassed the force was finally in custody.

And then, in a moment that would haunt everyone involved, he escaped. Somewhere between transit and interrogation, he snatched the weapon of one of the officers and fled. It was a staggering breach of protocol – and a nightmare for the force. The news broke before the panic settled. A high-profile kidnapper had escaped custody. The same man they had failed to stop before ransom was paid.

Senior officers were furious. The backlash was immediate and brutal. But instead of retreating into silence or excuses, Prashant Kumar made a promise – to his team and to the brass. 'We will get him back. Dead or alive. And this time, there will be no mistake.' The manhunt resumed.

His location was narrowed down. Surveillance teams tracked movements. A search operation was launched and soon a locality was surrounded. There was no press briefing, no public drama. Just boots on ground. Nerves held tight. And then, as feared, shots were fired – from the other side.

The police retaliated. The encounter was brief but decisive. The sarpanch was killed. The file on the Pilkhuwa kidnapping was finally closed – with one last, deafening shot.

It wasn't a clean story. It wasn't even the kind that made for easy praise. But it reminded everyone that even in the toughest of tenures, some chapters don't begin with glory but earn their closure through grit.

Looking back, that period in Ghaziabad was not just about one case or a few encounters. It was a time when law enforcement reasserted itself against some of the most dreaded criminals who had long believed they were beyond the reach of the system. The police cracked several heinous crimes during that time, many of which, I believe, the people of that region still remember. The stories live on – in police files, in press clippings and, most importantly, in public memory. Anyone who wishes to verify them need only go back to the records or speak to those who lived through those years.

When she did appear, she turned hostile, claiming she never had a romantic relationship with Nitish, despite photographic and eyewitness evidence to the contrary.

But Neelam Katara was undaunted.

She didn't scream on news channels. She didn't incite mobs. She simply showed up. Every time. Everywhere. For thirteen years straight.

And slowly, the system began to yield.

In 2008, both Vikas and Vishal Yadav were convicted by a Delhi sessions court and sentenced to life imprisonment. In 2014, the Delhi High Court upheld the conviction. And in 2016, the Supreme Court, too, found no reason to doubt the verdict – declaring it a case of 'honour killing' motivated by caste and social status.

Still, Neelam Katara had hoped for more.

She wanted the court to pronounce capital punishment, not just life imprisonment. For her, the brutality of the crime – the abduction, the torture, the burning of her son's body – deserved the severest penalty the law could offer. But the courts held back. However, in 2015, the Delhi High Court had given them twenty-five-year sentences without remission – an unusual but significant legal precedent.

Yet in that moment, Neelam didn't collapse.

She stood outside the court, composed, and said, 'Even if they are released after twenty-five years, I will still be here. I will still fight. For my son. And for others.'[64]

She never asked for sympathy. She demanded only justice.

Over time, Neelam Katara became a national figure, often invited to panels on legal reform, women's rights and justice for victims' families. Her presence carried weight because she had endured. Without political clout. Without financial leverage. Without institutional backing.

Just one mother. Against everything.

In a country where cases involving powerful men often evaporate into silence, the Nitish Katara case endured because a grieving mother did not flinch. Her son's killers were brought to justice not just by investigation and court orders but also by a personal war fought in silence, in courtrooms and in the public eye for over a decade.

Neelam Katara didn't win everything. But what she won, she won for all of us.

Not every case in Ghaziabad ended with a headline-making encounter or a clean courtroom closure. Some left behind the bitter aftertaste of near failure, tempered only by the sheer tenacity of a team that refused to let go.

One such case began with a peculiar disappearance – a businessman from the trading community, abducted from Pilkhuwa, a town that today falls in Hapur district. In those days, it was under the Ghaziabad Police's jurisdiction. Kidnapping for ransom wasn't unheard of in western UP, but during Prashant Kumar's tenure as SSP, Ghaziabad had remained untouched by such high-profile extortion cases. This one shattered that streak.

The victim was well-known, respected in business circles. His sudden disappearance sparked concern, and then panic. It didn't take long for investigators to zero in on a familiar name, someone who had long terrorized parts of Haryana with his ransom operations: a notorious sarpanch, known for targeting wealthy individuals, collecting the money and releasing the victims once his demands were met.

This time, the same modus operandi was playing out in Ghaziabad.

Promotion, Protest and the Missing File

Criminals who once carried the aura of invincibility were either behind bars or on the run. It was a wave of policing that brought a sense of control back to a district once gripped by fear. The work done by the Ghaziabad Police became a model of success, and there was widespread appreciation for the ruling dispensation for backing such tough action against crime.

Of course, he was still very junior then – hardly in a position to grasp the macro impact or long-term political implications. But the facts are there in the public domain and open to anyone who wants to judge what that phase truly meant.

And this was only the beginning. There were more fires to walk through, more battles to wage and more stories waiting to be told.

For all the grit and resolve that Ghaziabad had demanded, Prashant Kumar knew one truth better than most – nothing in police service was ever permanent. With each new government came a silent wave of reshuffles. Legacies, no matter how *hard-earned*, could be dissolved with the stroke of a transfer order. And that's exactly what happened after the 2002 Assembly elections. A new chief minister took charge in Lucknow, and with him came a predictable change in the power structure across the state. Ghaziabad, too, fell under its sweep.

Prashant Kumar was moved out and posted back to the Intelligence department in Lucknow. It wasn't unexpected. His colleagues took it in stride, some even with faint amusement. 'You've had your innings,' one of them said. 'Now it's time to cool your heels at the headquarters.' The subtext was clear. The regime had changed, and so had the list of favoured officers.

Whatever goodwill he had earned in Ghaziabad had now been filed away, replaced by political arithmetic.

He didn't complain. He had been in the service long enough to know that some seasons were for action and others for waiting. But just three months into this quieter phase, something shifted. The message came, as such things often did in those days, not directly, but through the internal channels of hierarchy. His head of department, who had become both a conduit and a buffer, called him in with a note of formality. 'You're to meet the principal secretary to the chief minister,' he said.

It took Prashant by surprise. This wasn't protocol. Principal secretaries didn't summon mid-ranking officers without reason, and there had been no prior signal, no request, no political backchannel preparing the ground. He had no idea what the meeting was about, but he knew one thing: this wasn't going to be routine.

The next day, Prashant Kumar went to meet the principal secretary. It was a formal setting, but the tone was unexpectedly warm. 'How are you?' the senior officer asked. 'I'm fine, sir,' Prashant replied, still unsure of the purpose behind the meeting. And then, without preamble, the officer delivered the news. 'The chief minister has decided to post you back on field.'

Prashant was caught off guard. He had barely settled into his role in Intelligence. After three intense years in Ghaziabad, this was meant to be a brief interlude, a moment to regroup, to be with family, especially since his wife had just taken up a new posting in Lucknow. The idea of returning to a turbulent district so soon was not only unexpected, it also felt premature. But he didn't argue. He simply nodded, choosing his words carefully. 'Whatever you say, sir.'

There was a brief silence before the principal secretary leaned forward. 'You've already handled bigger districts,' he said. 'But this is different. You're being sent to a very sensitive posting. In the past fifteen days alone, there have been three separate incidents of mass killings. People have been butchered in the dead of night. The situation has completely spiralled out of control.'

That changed the tone of the conversation. This wasn't just another transfer – it was a fire assignment, a call to contain something rapidly unravelling. And then came the final line. 'The chief minister believes only you can go there and get things under control.'

The posting was to Faizabad – now known as Ayodhya.

At that point in time, Faizabad was more than just another district on the administrative map. It sat on a historical fault line, a place of profound religious significance and painful political memory. The disputed site of Ram Janmabhoomi fell within its jurisdiction. Though the area around the site was heavily fortified and under constant surveillance, the district itself was on edge – boiling with tension, fraying under the weight of mistrust and pierced by sudden, brutal violence that the local police had failed to anticipate or contain.

And so, he went.

The order came, and within days, Prashant Kumar was in Faizabad. The district was still reeling from the shock of three back-to-back mass killings, all within a fortnight. The air was thick with fear, and public confidence in the police machinery had all but collapsed. His immediate challenge was clear: stop the bloodshed, reassert control and signal that the state had returned.

He wasted no time. Within fifteen days of his arrival, the main accused, the man believed to be behind the string of targeted killings, was tracked and killed. It was a swift, high-stakes operation, but it sent the right message. The violence, which had gripped the district in a state of paralysis, stopped. No more bodies in the dead of night. No more blood in the dust.

From that point on, he stayed in Faizabad for exactly one year. And in that year, not a single incident of mass violence took place. His approach was old-school – deceptively simple, but brutally effective. He reinstated traditional policing methods, especially night patrolling, which had eroded over the years due to apathy and fatigue. He ramped up visibility, made the streets active after dark and focused on deterrence through presence. In towns like Faizabad, where fear often crept in through the shadows, a patrolling jeep's headlights at 2 a.m. could do what no press conference could. One of Kumar's batchmates happened to be the SSP of the district at the time – a coincidence that proved not just helpful but also critical. The understanding between them was instinctive, the coordination seamless. In a landscape where hierarchy could often slow things down, this camaraderie made swift, decisive policing possible.

At that time, Faizabad was still a sleepy town. Despite being the epicentre of one of India's most polarizing religious and political conflicts, it saw little movement. The site of the Babri Masjid demolition was sealed off, protected and largely silent. No political yatras. No flag marches. The silence was not peace – it was stasis.

But during his tenure, that changed.

The Archaeological Survey of India (ASI) began a full-scale excavation at the disputed site. While a smaller excavation had taken place earlier, this was different – a major, court-sanctioned effort launched under intense public and political scrutiny. The site wasn't just disputed, it was also combustible. And Prashant Kumar was now the SSP of a district sitting atop that fuse.

The security plan was airtight, drafted with surgical precision. It involved multiple components: paramilitary personnel, civil police and intelligence units, all operating in coordinated three-shift rotations. Every inch of the site was under surveillance.

Promotion, Protest and the Missing File

Every movement – whether of a machine, a worker or a rumour – was logged, analysed and responded to in real time. Even the slightest disturbance at the site – a stone moved, a trench dug an inch too deep – could explode into national headlines.

And yet nothing happened.

Because it was one of those rare moments in high-risk policing where proactive planning and disciplined execution held the line – quietly, invisibly.

The divisional commissioner held overall charge of the security operations at the site, acting as custodian under the direct supervision of the Supreme Court. That chain of command ensured that everything – from the excavation timeline to the deployment of forces – was closely monitored. Every month, there was a formal review of the security plan, attended by senior officers across departments. On paper, the coordination was robust. But on the ground, the cracks were visible.

One of the most glaring issues was the living condition of the jawans stationed at the site. The summer months were unforgiving – blistering heat baking through makeshift *machans* and poorly assembled watchtowers that passed off as sentry posts. These structures were neither safe nor sustainable. The duty was intense, the schedules relentless and the fatigue visible.

Then came the incident that brought everything to a boil.

During one of the summer rotations, a jawan fell from one of the watchtowers – an accident that could have been prevented. The fall triggered outrage. Fellow policemen, already exhausted and frustrated, protested what they saw as neglect by the administration. The news spread quickly and demanded a response. A high-level inquiry was ordered, led by the ADG of the PAC.

In retrospect, Prashant Kumar saw the incident with unflinching honesty.

'It was a mistake,' he would later say. 'And whatever happened, happened because of our failure. These jawans were guarding one of the most sensitive and politically volatile places in the country. The least they deserved was a dignified environment to live and work in.'

That incident became a quiet turning point. While the broader security framework remained intact, there was a renewed focus on the human element of policing – the condition of the barracks, the water supply, the food, the rest schedules. It didn't undo the accident, but it did realign priorities.

Because in a place like Ayodhya, where the cost of a single mistake could ripple across the nation, the uniform wasn't enough. The men inside it had to be protected too.

In one of the security review meetings during his tenure, Prashant Kumar raised a scenario that, at the time, felt more like a worst-case hypothetical than an imminent threat. 'We should be prepared for any eventuality,' he said. 'What if someone comes by car, rams into the outer periphery and then lobs grenades or uses rocket launchers to target the temporary structure?'

The room had gone quiet. The suggestion was seen as extreme – perhaps too far removed from the conventional models of protest or disruption the force had dealt with until then. But he had seen enough during his years in volatile districts to know that terror didn't always arrive in the expected form.

'Surprisingly, my foresight was not well appreciated at the time,' he later recalled. 'It was taken lightly, as if I was imagining too much.'

And yet not long after he left Faizabad, that exact scenario played out.

Terrorists arrived in a car, rammed it into the outer security cordon and launched a sudden, coordinated assault. They lobbed grenades and opened fire indiscriminately, mirroring the very threat Prashant had warned about. But this time, the forces stationed at the site were ready. There was swift retaliation. Every one of the attackers was killed before they could reach the heart of the disputed structure.

It was a vindication he never wished to have.

Because while the system had eventually responded with efficiency and strength, it had taken a brush with catastrophe to realize that good policing doesn't always wait for proof – it prepares for possibility.

Around the same period, another incident shook the nation – one that didn't originate from Faizabad but reverberated across every police line in the country. It was the terrorist attack on Indian Parliament in December 2001. Though Prashant Kumar was posted in Ghaziabad at the time, far from the capital's epicentre of power, he was the first officer in his zone to get wind of the incident.

It wasn't just the shock. It was the complete unfamiliarity of it. Ghaziabad had its share of serious crime. But a full-scale terror strike on the Indian Parliament which was arguably the most fortified building in the country was something else entirely. No officer in the region had dealt with anything of that nature. The very idea of such an attack had seemed implausible until that moment. And when it happened, it shook the entire force.

What followed was a wave of phone calls, alerts and rapid intelligence sharing. Protocols across districts were tightened. The ripple effect of a Delhi-based attack spread fast, reminding every senior officer that terror was no longer a distant reality. It could arrive unannounced. Anywhere.

But there was a lighter side to that moment too – an inside-joke of sorts that seasoned officers often shared. 'Besides keeping our seniors updated on our own districts,' Prashant Kumar would later say with a quiet smile, 'we'd also pass on breaking news from other states... not our jurisdiction, not our headache. But still, we'd be the first to share. Not exactly badmouthing – but yes, let's just say, gossip in uniform.'

It was one of those rare instances where the gravity of the moment was matched by the everyday culture of policing, where serious crime met dry wit and even the most hardened officers found ways to humanize the uniform.

When Prashant Kumar rang up his DIG that day, the senior officer picked up the call with the usual mix of expectation and routine.

'*Batao, tumhaare cases mein kya ho raha hai* (Tell me, what is happening with your cases?)' he asked, expecting the usual district-level updates. But Prashant cut straight to it. '*Sir, pehle Delhi mein kya hua yeh toh dekhiye* (Sir, you please see what is happening in Delhi first)!'

There was a pause. A slight chuckle. For a moment, the DIG thought he was joking. After all, it wasn't every day that a district SSP opened a call with breaking news from the national capital. But the tone shifted quickly. The attack on Parliament was real. And it had already begun spiralling into one of the most serious national security incidents in recent memory.

What made the moment even more striking was that personnel from the PAC were actually present at the scene of the attack.

Some of them, according to word that filtered back, had fired back at the terrorists. While the official version of events would eventually be recorded in post-incident reports and command logs, the reality on the ground was often faster than bureaucracy.

'One of our jawans came to me later and said, "Sir, *unko toh humne hi maara tha.*"' Prashant didn't dismiss it. He listened.

He knew better than to rely on unverified claims, but if the PAC jawans had indeed played an active role, their contribution needed to be documented. Heroism, especially in real time, often got buried under layers of paperwork, with credit distributed selectively. He advised the jawan, and others from the unit who had been at the site, to submit their statements in writing – clear, honest accounts of what had happened.

He then took the additional step of alerting the DIG, PAC, asking him to follow up so that any credit due to the PAC could be put on record. 'Whatever happened in the *likhaparhi* (documentation) – I wouldn't know,' he would later say. 'I wasn't there. But if our men did something that mattered, it shouldn't disappear into silence.' In the end, it wasn't about glory. It was about recognition for the men who had stood their ground, in what was, at the time, one of the gravest attacks on Indian democracy.

13
Transfers, Turmoil and a Prayer at Kailash

The calm that followed the Ayodhya excavation didn't last long. In September 2003, the government fell. Mulayam Singh Yadav returned to power. And with that came the inevitable reshuffle. Names shuffled, loyalties tested and placements reconsidered. Behind the scenes, a particular lobby close to the powers that be had already begun working the strings, trying to influence decisions about who should be posted where.

Prashant Kumar's name came up early in those deliberations. Some insiders believed that districts like Barabanki or Saharanpur weren't ideal for him. The unspoken message was clear: he wasn't 'one of them'. The lobby wanted him somewhere else. Somewhere less visible, less volatile, less important. But the decision from the top overrode those whispers. Prashant was sent to Barabanki.

It wasn't a posting he wanted. In fact, as per protocol, he had communicated his preference to the chief minister. Officers are often asked where they would like to be placed, and Prashant had made it clear that Barabanki didn't feel right. Not for personal reasons, but because he sensed that in the prevailing political climate, it would be difficult to function with the clarity and autonomy he valued. But when the posting order came, there was no room for debate.

'A government order is a government order,' he said quietly.

And he reported for duty.

Barabanki, on the surface, seemed quieter than his previous postings. But it was politically layered. The ruling party was grappling with internal tensions, and factions within the system operated with their own agendas. Yet despite his initial reluctance and despite the very lobby that didn't want him there, Prashant took charge and ran the district on his terms. No appeasement. No compromises. In a state often defined by push and pull, he stood straight. By the time he completed twenty months in Barabanki, he had turned an unwanted assignment into one of his most stable and impactful stints.

But the lobby hadn't forgotten even though the CM was noticing his good work.

When it was time for the next transfer after twenty months, the same group resurfaced. This time, the order was for Saharanpur. And once again, Prashant refused. Not out of defiance, but from a sense of déjà vu. He knew the same people who wanted him out of Barabanki were now trying to corner him again. But, once more, the system issued its command. And once more, he obeyed.

If they thought Saharanpur would wear him down, they hadn't paid attention to what he had just done in Barabanki.

The district came with its own complexities. 'All the important guys from the ruling dispensation were already there,' he would later say. 'And they weren't just influential. They practically ran the district like it was part of their extended backyard.' That came with expectations, of obedience, of deference, of looking the other way. Prashant Kumar offered none.

At one point, a senior party functionary stormed into the chief minister's office and declared, 'Your SSP has abused me! We won't allow such an officer to run our district. He must be removed immediately.' The charge was loud, but hollow.

The CM called Prashant in and began to question him. Prashant listened patiently. Then, with calm resolve, he replied, 'Sir, if I may remind you … I had told you I didn't want to go to Saharanpur. But you had insisted I take the posting and follow instructions.'

There was no arrogance in his voice but just the quiet confidence of a man with nothing to hide.

'You knew my family was in Lucknow at the time,' he added. 'I was due for promotion. But you still decided this was where I needed to be. And now, here I am.'

The chief minister didn't miss a beat. 'Then why,' he shot back, 'is such a senior politician from the district complaining against you?'

Prashant didn't flinch. 'Because' he replied, 'he wants every posting in the district to go through him. Every station, every officer – his list, his word.'

There was a brief pause. Then came the pivot.

The chief minister, a seasoned player of political chess, leaned back and reassessed. The outrage gave way to calculation. He had seen enough officers to know when one was bluffing – and Prashant Kumar wasn't. The chief minister made an about-turn in real time.

'Nothing doing,' he said flatly. 'You stay. Do what you think is right.'

Just like that, the fire turned into approval.

A few months passed, and the same politician was back in Lucknow with the same complaint against the same officer. Once again, he approached the chief minister, hoping for a transfer order to be pulled out like a rabbit from a hat. But the latter, now fully aware of the dynamics at play, waved him off with seasoned nonchalance.

'Don't worry,' he told the politician. 'He's about to be promoted.'

Prashant was in his office in Saharanpur when his phone rang. The caller ID flashed a name he hadn't expected – a political aide from a camp he knew too well, though not fondly. The voice on the other end was already glowing.

'Sir, *badhai ho!*' the man beamed. 'Congratulations!'

'What for?' Prashant's tone was dry.

'Sir, you're about to be promoted as DIG,' the man said, dropping the bomb with theatrical precision.

Prashant Kumar, mildly amused, responded, 'That's news to me. Last I checked, that was still a while away.'

'No, no, sir,' the man insisted, now lowering his voice as if delivering a classified briefing. 'The chief minister himself just said so. I'm speaking to you straight after walking out of his residence. It's done, sir.'

The flattery was unmistakable. So was the attempt to get ahead of the curve, perhaps in the hope of future goodwill. But Prashant had heard too many such whispers to place stock in any. He thanked the man, hung up and got back to work. If a promotion was indeed coming, it would come on paper, not through politicians with borrowed grins and half-truths.

Prashant smiled. 'Well then,' he said dryly, 'if the chief minister himself said so … then there's no confusion. It's definitely happening.'

Chief Minister Mulayam Singh Yadav was a shrewd politician – sharp as a tack and impossible to second-guess. Unfortunately, he is no more. But in that chapter of UP's ever-shifting political theatre, he played his part with remarkable clarity.

It took about five months, and Prashant Kumar was promoted and transferred out of Saharanpur. But what stood out wasn't the transfer – it was the fact that the chief minister never once buckled under pressure. Despite repeated lobbying, visits and whispers from within his own ranks, he let Prashant Kumar run the district his way. There was no micromanagement, no veiled threats. Just a silent understanding.

'I think he trusted me,' Prashant would later say. 'That I wouldn't do anything wrong, wouldn't mislead him.'

It was an unlikely rapport. The chief minister had a reputation – people often said he came under pressure, that he was quick to act on complaints and political nudges. But with Prashant, things were different. Whenever the minister asked for details – about an incident, a case or a brewing controversy – he was given the unvarnished version. And he appreciated that.

One such moment came around a by-election. The chief minister sought feedback. His party workers had painted an upbeat picture. Prashant Kumar didn't. He offered a ground-level report – the kind that didn't please anyone but happened to be true.

When the results came in, they confirmed what Prashant had said. The Samajwadi Party had lost the seat.

Ironically, the same local leaders who had earlier lobbied for his removal came crawling back to explain the defeat. The chief minister, never one to miss a cue, turned the tables.

'He didn't mince words,' Prashant recalled. 'He told them – "It wasn't the administration that failed. It was you. Maybe you didn't work hard enough. Maybe you assumed too much. But don't blame the officer. He gave me the correct picture, and I respected that."'

Sometimes, the truth doesn't just survive pressure, it also earns respect for standing alone.

By the time the promotion came through and Prashant was elevated to DIG, the fatigue had begun to show – not in performance but in patience. He had been through enough field postings, trouble spots and political tug-of-war assignments to last a full career. And now, all he wanted was a breather. A posting that didn't feel like a test or a trap.

But the system had other ideas.

Prashant Kumar was posted to Vindhyachal, a far-off range, one that felt less like a promotion and more like an exile. He voiced his protest – not in anger but in calm, pointed terms. 'Everyone else gets adjusted according to convenience,' he said. 'Everyone knows my wife is posted in Lucknow. And for the record, I never asked for a range posting.'

So, he didn't go.

A few days later, it was 26 January. After the ceremonial parade, he walked up to the DGP and made his position clear. 'It's very difficult for me to take up another field posting right now,' he said. 'Please find someone else.'

To the surprise of many, a substitute was posted. But the reaction from the system was swift and cold. Prashant Kumar was kept waiting, left without a posting. It was the establishment's way of making its displeasure known. 'How dare he refuse?' That was the unspoken sentiment.

It was around then that he began seriously considering deputation. He had seen the pattern too many times – every time there was a difficult district or an explosive situation, his name

Transfers, Turmoil and a Prayer at Kailash

appeared first. But when it came to seniority-based postings or desirable assignments, he was nowhere in the picture.

While the wait continued, another opportunity surfaced.

A recruitment scheme for the recruitment of constables in the UP Police was in motion, and he was selected to oversee the process. It was a sensitive, high-stakes assignment – exactly the kind that required integrity, precision and a refusal to bow to pressure.

The DG called him in. 'You'll do the recruitment,' he said. Prashant agreed, but with a disclaimer. 'Fine, I'll do it,' he said.

'But I'll stick to the existing policy of the government. Don't ask me to favour anyone.'

The DG didn't take it kindly.*Aap bahut bolte hain*,' ('You talk too much,') he muttered. Prashant smiled and said nothing. He had spoken his piece. Now, he would simply go and do the job. As always, by the book. Prashant Kumar conducted the recruitment drive exactly the way he said he would – honestly, transparently and without bending. At that time, the process was decentralized, handled at the range level. Unlike today, where everything is routed through centralized mechanisms in Lucknow, back then, the local officer bore the full weight of responsibility and scrutiny.

He supervised the entire process. In the end, around 370 candidates were selected, and every name on that final list had been earned, not arranged. There were no backdoor entries, no whispers in sealed envelopes, no favours granted or promised. He didn't allow any interference. Whatever pressure came his way – and plenty did – it stopped at his desk.

Once again, he had proven that clean work could still be done. But clean work didn't mean peace.

During the recruitment process, he found himself back in Faizabad as DIG (Range). The location had changed. The job hadn't. He was being sent where the terrain was hot and trust thin.

And then, just before the Vidhan Sabha elections in 2007 came another posting – DIG, Saharanpur Range. A politically sensitive belt, chronically unpredictable during polls and not exactly on anyone's wish list.

But the pattern by now was clear. When there was turbulence, they sent Prashant. He didn't chase these postings. They chased him.

Before the recruitment had begun, the chief minister had only one instruction for Prashant Kumar. In his signature, no-nonsense style, he said: *'Thik thak se recruitment karna.'* ('Make sure the recruitment is done properly.')

Now, Prashant being Prashant, took that to mean exactly what it sounded like – do it properly, fairly, within the rules. And that's precisely what he did.

But later, it would emerge, what the chief minister had meant by 'thik thak' wasn't quite what Prashant had heard. In political dialect, 'thik thak' had a different subtext. It loosely translated to 'take care of our people'. Specifically, the core vote bank – long considered the spine of the ruling party's electoral calculus.

Prashant Kumar had never been fluent in political dialects. He only spoke the language of the rulebook. So, while he might have nodded at the chief minister's instruction, what followed was a recruitment drive that made no exceptions, offered no favours and triggered no bias.

The result? His good conduct reportedly upset the very man who had picked him for the job. But the chief ministerr – sharp as ever – did nothing about it. Perhaps he was mildly irritated. Perhaps he admired the audacity. Either way, he let Prashant be. Because even in politics, there's grudging respect for the man who follows the brief too well.

Transfers, Turmoil and a Prayer at Kailash

The Vidhan Sabha elections happened then, and just like that, the ruling party was voted out. A new chief minister took oath, and the first signs of change came – as they usually did – with a list of fresh transfers.

As expected, Prashant Kumar was removed from Saharanpur. At that very moment, he happened to be on Chardham Yatra, somewhere between devotion and much-needed detachment, when his phone rang. It was the DG, sounding uncharacteristically alarmed.

'Where are you?' he asked. 'Why are you missing?'

Prashant replied, calm as ever: 'Sir, I'm on leave. It was sanctioned. I'm on Chardham Yatra.'

The DG wasn't impressed. 'Forget the yatra. Come back immediately and join.'

Prashant asked, reasonably, 'But join where, sir?'

'You're being posted as DIG, Meerut Range,' came the reply.

Now that was a surprise, but for once, a pleasant one. He reported to Meerut. But peace, predictably, was short-lived. Almost as soon as he took charge, a massive controversy erupted – a committee was formed to inquire into all previous police recruitments, including the 370 selections he had supervised during his last assignment.

There was no scandal, no allegation of malpractice, but the entire process was suddenly up for scrutiny. As if clean work needed revalidation after every change of guard. Prashant's response was brief and predictable: 'Fine. Let them inquire.'

He had nothing to hide. So, he continued with the job at hand. He stayed in Meerut for barely three-and-a-half months before a fresh twist surfaced. There was a disagreement with a senior officer at headquarters – not in the range but higher up the chain. The kind of disagreement that didn't require raised voices, just a refusal to comply with an 'adjustment' someone was hoping for.

Word later trickled down that the officer had wanted someone else posted in Meerut, and Prashant hadn't obliged. The result? Another transfer. This time, he was sent to Prayagraj – then still called Allahabad – as DIG (Establishment).

The location changed. The tempo didn't.

Then the recruitment scandal exploded in full view. A state-wide controversy that dragged in officers across the spectrum, triggered inquiries, and eventually led to the suspension of twelve or thirteen IPS officers. Major lapses were reported in several districts where recruitments had taken place, and the press – never known to underplay a headline – went into overdrive. Every other day, newspapers carried stories suggesting that wholesale arrests might follow. One popular phrase began to appear in print with unsettling frequency: '*Sab jail chale jayenge.*' ('Everyone will go to jail.')

At home, tension was palpable. Prashant Kumar never discussed these matters with his father, never shared the pressure or the innuendos that swirled around his name because, unlike others, he had nothing to hide. But that didn't stop his father from worrying.

He was alive at the time, a proud, upright man who had spent his life as a teacher. And even though no direct allegation had been made against his son, the constant media chatter wore him down. At night, when he believed his son was asleep, he would quietly walk over, peep into the room, watch him in silence – just to reassure himself. Then, not knowing where else to go, he would speak to Prashant's staff.

'*Unhone kuchh galat toh nahi kiya na?*' ('He has done nothing wrong?') he would ask.

The staff, loyal and aware of the facts, would try to console him.

'*Babuji, aap pareshan mat hoiye… Sir ne kuchh galat nahi kiya hai. Kuchh nahi hoga unko.*' ('Babuji, please don't worry … Sir hasn't done anything wrong. Nothing will happen to him.')

But it wasn't that simple. He would still press them, voice low and worried.

'*Kahin jail toh nahi chala jayega?*' ('He won't end up in jail, right?')

He had seen the headlines, heard the whispers. For a man who had raised his children on values of discipline and honesty, the idea that even a shadow of suspicion might fall on one of them was almost unbearable.

And that, more than anything else, was what disturbed Prashant: not the inquiries, not the politics, but the fact that his father had to carry that anxiety, even for a moment.

When the recruitment inquiry finally concluded, Prashant Kumar's file was the only one that received a clean chit from the government. There were other boards whose selections weren't scrapped, but those didn't get formal clearance either. His was the only recruitment officially approved and closed by the government – a quiet stamp of vindication in the middle of swirling uncertainty.

And while the headlines had moved on, the impact of that clearance was felt most at home.

For his father, who had lived through those months of anxiety, reading speculative headlines, whispering quiet worries to his son's staff, that one official closure meant everything. It restored not just peace of mind but reaffirmed a lifelong belief. His son would never do anything wrong.

'You can't imagine,' Prashant later said, 'what that moment meant for him. For the first time, his trust in me had been proven right in the eyes of the system.'

There was, of course, no deliberate wrongdoing in the process – no mala fide intent, no procedural subversion. But recruitment, by its very nature, is a massive operation. Minor errors – technical or clerical – are always possible. What mattered was that nothing in his conduct had ever suggested bias, manipulation or personal gain. And fortunately, the inquiry committee, despite reviewing every file under a magnifying lens, acknowledged that.

In fact, even the Allahabad High Court later restored the selection of all the candidates on his recruitment list – yet another layer of validation, both legal and moral.

So, when that final clearance came through, it was a restoration of dignity – for him, and even more so, for the man who had stood by him without ever asking for an explanation.

That phase – when the recruitment inquiry was underway – was, in many ways, the toughest stretch of Prashant Kumar's career. Not because of the professional scrutiny; he could handle that. But because he had to watch his parents go through the emotional toll of it all. Seeing them anxious, helpless, quietly checking if he was alright – it left a deeper mark than any departmental note ever could.

He had, in fact, already applied for central deputation back when he was serving as DIG, Ayodhya. The application had gone through the proper channels. The posting had come through too – in one of the central police organizations. But the state government refused to relieve him. The inquiry was still on, and he was being kept back, unofficially shackled to a controversy he had nothing to do with.

To make matters worse, there was a bureaucratic catch.

In that era – as is still true today – an officer couldn't be promoted to IG unless he had completed a central deputation at

Transfers, Turmoil and a Prayer at Kailash

DIG rank. So, Prashant found himself stuck in a cruel deadlock. The inquiry prevented his release, and the lack of central posting blocked his promotion. It was a double whammy – a perfect storm of bad timing, institutional hesitation and political silence. Once the inquiry wrapped up and he was officially cleared, he made his case again: 'Now that the report is out, relieve me.' But no one had the courage to walk up to the chief minister and say it out loud. The file stayed where it was. So did he.

And then, almost incidentally, came the turning point.

While the inquiry reports were still being reviewed, someone at the higher levels noticed that Prashant Kumar was still handling the establishment matters of constables and sub-inspectors. Given his prior involvement with recruitment, the optics weren't ideal. A conflict of interest, they said. And just like that, a decision was made.

He was posted to Lucknow as DIG, Intelligence. For him, it was an unexpected relief, not only because it offered distance from the controversy but also because his family was based in Lucknow. It felt like, for the first time in years, his professional and personal priorities had aligned.

And with that, the long wait finally ended. The clearance came through, and he was posted to the Central Industrial Security Force (CISF) as DIG. A chapter had closed. Once the inquiry was over and the clean chit had arrived, Prashant Kumar expected the machinery to move quickly. He had earned his clearance, waited long enough and now simply wanted to join his central deputation posting with the CISF. But even then, the file didn't budge.

He began making the rounds – gently reminding, firmly requesting. 'The inquiry is over. I've been cleared. Why am I still not being relieved?' But no one had a straight answer.

Whispers floated around the corridors. 'The officers who were involved in recruitment shouldn't be allowed to leave the state cadre,' some said. It wasn't an official order, more of a vibe. No one confirmed it on paper, but the reluctance was unmistakable.

It was an odd logic. Those who were already cleared were being held back, just in case. Prashant, of course, argued back. 'If the inquiry is over and there's no wrongdoing, then what are you holding me for?' He wasn't just chasing a posting. He was chasing time with his family.

The plan had been simple. He would first go to Delhi on deputation, and after a few months, his wife would follow. That's how it usually worked in the paramilitary – Delhi postings rarely came immediately. Officers often had to serve a year or so elsewhere before being considered for headquarters. So they had chalked out a staggered move.

But, as with most bureaucratic planning, the script flipped.

While he remained stuck in administrative limbo, his wife's deputation came through, and she was relieved immediately. The very thing that seemed impossible for him had been done for her, with astonishing speed.

To add to the chaos, their daughter – still in second or third grade at the time – was in the middle of her final exams. But the posting orders had arrived, the release was granted and there was no point resisting. She left, and Prashant stayed behind.

Their well-laid plan had gone up in smoke. The system had decided to write its own.

It was the end of 2007 when, quite incidentally, Prashant Kumar got assigned to an advanced security liaison duty during one of the chief minister's visits. For months, he had been trying to get an audience with her – submitting requests, knocking on the right doors, waiting for the appointment that never came. In hindsight, perhaps he hadn't been approaching through the 'proper' channels. But he didn't give up.

Transfers, Turmoil and a Prayer at Kailash

He had made up his mind – if he ever got a chance to speak to her in person, he would politely place his case before her.

The opportunity finally came. As the chief minister arrived at the venue, Prashant Kumar was stationed at his designated spot. She looked at him, slightly surprised.

'*Aap yahaan hain… Sab thik hai?*' ('You're here … Everything alright?') she asked. He didn't waste the moment.

With utmost civility, he said, 'Ma'am, now that the inquiry is over and I've been cleared, may I request to be relieved so I can join my deputation?'

She nodded almost casually. '*Haan, haan… Kyun nahin?*' ('Yes, yes … Why not?') Just like that.

Top officers were around. They murmured among themselves, made a few calls. There seemed to be some movement. But when he returned, a new twist awaited. 'Your file is missing,' someone said. He was told to submit his application again. And so he did, not surprised, not upset, just mildly amused at the theatre of it all.

Eventually, the file was 'found'. The needful was done. In this way, the first phase of his career in the UP cadre came to a close. No drama. No fanfare. Just a quiet, bureaucratic curtain fall.

14

The Assignment After

By the time 2007 drew to a close, Prashant Kumar's career had already become a study in navigating chaos – not just the chaos of the streets alone but also the quieter, more punishing chaos of systemic instability. In just a few years, he had worn multiple hats across some of UP's most sensitive and volatile districts – moving from the crime-prone lanes of Barabanki, to the communally delicate terrain of Saharanpur, to the resource-rich but troubled triangle of Mirzapur, Sonebhadra and Bhadohi. His postings flickered by with dizzying speed – SSP here, DIG there, sometimes barely months apart.

In Saharanpur, a district that walked a tightrope between caste tension and communal flare-ups, he tried to hold the line during a particularly fractious political climate. In Mirzapur and Sonebhadra, he oversaw vast stretches of forested hinterland, where law enforcement often meant balancing a stick and a handshake with tribal populations and emerging Naxal whispers. At Meerut Range, he supervised policing across western UP's 'Wild-West' belt – Ghaziabad, Muzaffarnagar, Bulandshahr. These areas were infamous for a crime graph that could spike faster than a district file could reach the DGP's table. Lucknow, Prayagraj, Faizabad – no posting lasted long enough to build a cot in the officer's mess, but every transfer left a new story etched into his ledger.

Yet for all the challenging assignments he was entrusted with, Prashant Kumar never quite got a deal he would have chosen for himself. He was shifted often, posted out too frequently and although he was never accused of unprofessional or unethical conduct, he rarely got the chance to settle down and build long-term stability. Perhaps the government genuinely believed he was best suited for fire-fighting roles. Or maybe, like many officers who remain politically neutral, he lacked a powerful politician or financial lobby pushing his case through the system's many invisible channels. Perhaps opportunities had come his way too, tempting him to trade independence for influence, but he chose to stay away, unwilling to owe anyone, unwilling to pay any kind of price later. He preferred to be correct – self-righteous almost, if one were to see it unkindly – and while that uncompromising stand won him respect, it certainly took its toll in ways he rarely acknowledged.

His personal life bore much of the brunt. His only child, Shivani, grew up largely with her mother, except for a brief period when she stayed with her aunt and uncle. An otherwise shy, soft-spoken girl, Shivani once let slip a memory that captured more than any official record could. They would celebrate what she called 'fake birthdays'. Curious, I asked her what that meant. She explained, with a small smile, that her father's work never allowed him to be present on her actual birthday. So, they celebrated it whenever he could make it home, sometimes before the date, sometimes after – whatever worked. The ritual became normal, a small, bittersweet adaptation to a life dominated by duty.

It reminded me of what legend Sunil Gavaskar once wrote when some critics accused him of desertion for contemplating a short break from Indian cricket to Kerry Packer's World XI in the late 1970s. Gavaskar had pointed out how he had missed every family occasion, every holiday, to answer the call of duty for his country, and yet he never refused. Prashant Kumar, too, never refused – never once allowed personal convenience to override the demands of the uniform. And perhaps, like in Gavaskar's case, somewhere along the line, the establishment began taking that commitment for granted.

The bosses leaned harder. The system leaned harder. And Prashant Kumar – like so many others cut from that rare cloth – simply stood his ground. Without complaint. Because that was life.

And life, in UP, was about to test him again.

Even as Prashant Kumar crossed a major milestone in his career, having survived inquiries, investigations and endless political whirlwinds, he couldn't shake off a growing sense of restlessness. In a quiet, almost reluctant admission, he described it to me once as a mid-service crisis – that strange, difficult phase many officers encounter when they realize they have gathered enough seniority, enough field experience, but the future still feels uncertain, unstructured.

He had risen steadily, but rarely was he allowed to stay anywhere long enough to consolidate his work. In every regime change, he found himself thrown into fresh field postings while his wife remained posted in Lucknow. It wasn't an ideal situation by any measure, especially when tenures themselves had become painfully unstable. Field postings were being decided not necessarily by an officer's career graph, but by the immediate needs of political and administrative firefighting.

Prashant Kumar didn't express bitterness – just a clear-eyed understanding of how the system functioned. 'Nobody sees your profile,' he said once, 'that you've already handled bigger districts. Whether the posting is bigger or smaller, it's only about immediate suitability.' And in states like UP, suitability was often calculated by different metrics altogether – caste dynamics, political loyalty, perceived neutrality. Sometimes governments preferred to post someone seen as a 'neutral' officer during sensitive times, someone who could manage crises without leaning towards any camp. In that sense, perhaps, his very refusal to play political games made him useful and expendable at the same time.

He cited an example without much fuss. When Mayawati posted him to Faizabad after a spate of brutal killings, it wasn't because of routine shuffling. It was because they needed someone who could stabilize a dangerously volatile district without inflaming tensions further. He had done that, successfully. For almost a year, Faizabad remained under control. No major incident occurred under his watch.

But the political situation shifted again. Mulayam Singh Yadav returned to power. And almost immediately, Prashant found himself moved again – this time to Barabanki, a smaller, quieter district by all measures compared to Faizabad. It wasn't the stature of the posting that troubled him. It was the realization that in the bureaucratic churn, merit and performance were rarely the primary criteria. At best, they were occasional bonuses. At worst, they were inconvenient truths, best forgotten when political arithmetic demanded otherwise.

Because of these reasons, and after much deliberation, Prashant Kumar had finally applied for an assignment outside his parent cadre. It wasn't a decision taken lightly. Someone senior had advised him that if he wished to have a more rounded career, and if he ever hoped to be empanelled at higher levels in the Government of India, he needed to do a deputation outside UP, preferably at the DIG level. It was good advice, rooted in the quiet realities of bureaucratic ladder-climbing, and he decided to follow it.

Thus, in 2007, Prashant Kumar joined the CISF on deputation and was sent to Hyderabad, assigned to the Department of Atomic Energy. His personal wish had been different – he had hoped for a Delhi posting since his wife had already been transferred there – but, looking back, he considered it a fortunate turn. Hyderabad turned out to be an unexpected classroom.

In his assignment, he worked closely with India's critical energy infrastructure – units involved in nuclear production, fuel manufacturing and atomic energy development. It was a rare window into a different world, far removed from the crime scenes and communal flashpoints he had known in UP districts. More importantly, he developed an all-India perspective, working with IPS officers from different cadres, backgrounds and ways of thinking. Professionally, it was deeply enriching. Personally, it gave him a glimpse of a broader canvas, one that extended far beyond the political whirlpools of his home state.

It wasn't Delhi. It wasn't perfect. But it was precisely the kind of exposure he hadn't even realized he needed until he was living it.

After completing his Hyderabad stint, Prashant was transferred to the CISF headquarters in Delhi. It was a significant move, not just geographically but also professionally.

In 2008, the DG of CISF retired, and N.R. Das took over as the new DG.

There was no prior connection between Prashant Kumar and the new chief – they barely knew each other. But for reasons he could never fully explain, Das seemed to place considerable trust in him almost from the outset. Within a short time, Prashant was entrusted with one of the most sensitive roles in the force – that of DIG, Personnel, a position central to internal postings, promotions and career management across the CISF.

It turned out to be a pivotal phase in his career. Working directly under Das, he found not just a senior but also a mentor, someone who guided him steadily through the complex maze of central police administration. The experience would shape his understanding of organizational dynamics beyond district-level policing, teaching him how large forces are managed, balanced and kept cohesive.

During his three-and-a-half years at the headquarters, he also achieved another key milestone: he was empanelled for the rank of IG at the Centre – a prestigious step that opened up higher administrative roles. Mr Das wanted him to continue longer in the CISF, a rare endorsement for an officer on deputation. But bureaucratic realities intervened. After three-and-a-half years, there were no suitable vacancies available at the headquarters, and extension without a post wasn't possible.

It was time to move again.

Around this time, a new opportunity surfaced. Prashant Kumar was asked to meet Vijay Kumar, the then DG of CRPF. Vijay Kumar was looking for someone who matched Prashant's profile – a strong field officer with experience across volatile terrains and organizational management. It could have been a promising move.

But life outside uniform had its own demands. His daughter was approaching her tenth-grade board examinations, a crucial milestone in any Indian household. For once, Prashant Kumar decided that family had to take precedence. He needed to be present – not just in spirit but in person as well.

Fate, perhaps, cooperated. Around the same time, an opening came up in the Indo-Tibetan Border Police (ITBP). After mutual consultations between the DG of ITBP and the DG of CISF, he was laterally shifted to the ITBP – a move that allowed him to remain posted closer to Delhi while also continuing his central deputation.

At the ITBP, he stayed for three-and-a-half years, completing a full seven-year tenure across both forces, which was the typical entitlement for a central deputation. And once again, the assignment proved professionally enriching. He was given charge of provisioning, a critical role involving logistics, supplies and operational support for an elite force deployed along India's most challenging and inhospitable borders.

The posting took him to places few civilians ever see – Leh, Ladakh (then part of Jammu and Kashmir), the icy frontier zones where the ITBP stands as India's first line of defence. It broadened his understanding of how the Indian security apparatus functioned in extreme conditions and gave him a rare glimpse into the silent wars fought not with guns alone but also with endurance, isolation and resilience.

It wasn't the original plan. But in retrospect, it had turned out to be exactly what he needed.

As his seven-year central deputation neared its end, Prashant Kumar decided to make another investment in his professional growth. He applied for admission to the prestigious National Defence College (NDC) – a premier institution where senior officers from the Army, Navy and Air Force, along with select civilian officers from the IAS, IPS and other central services, underwent advanced training in national security, strategic planning and defence policy. The NDC wasn't just a hub for India's top minds; it also included select officers from friendly foreign countries as well as senior personnel from international defence forces and civil services, making it a truly global learning platform.

Nomination to the NDC wasn't automatic. It was competitive and selective, and making the cut was considered a mark of distinction in an officer's career. Prashant was among the fortunate few. He completed the intensive course, rubbing shoulders with senior officers who, in a few years' time, would occupy some of the most critical positions in India's security establishment.

At the end of the course, he made a conscious decision. He formally requested the Government of India to post him to a hard area, preferably in Jammu and Kashmir and the Northeast. He wasn't keen on returning to UP just yet. Deep down, he knew how the system worked. If he went back to his cadre, he risked slipping once again into a cycle of unstable postings, political push-and-pull and professional drift.

But fate, once again, played its own hand. Just as his request was under consideration, the political winds shifted. The United Progressive Alliance (UPA) government lost power in 2014, and the National Democratic Alliance (NDA) government came to power at the Centre. In the reshuffle that followed, it seemed the new regime preferred familiar faces – officers they trusted, officers with whom they had worked earlier. Fresh deputations were frozen, and Prashant's request was quietly denied.

The Assignment After

Having no other viable option, he returned to his home cadre, UP, at the end of 2015. A chapter had closed. Another, far more turbulent one, was about to begin.

When Prashant Kumar rejoined his home cadre at the end of 2015, he was posted as ADG, Security. It was a prestigious and sensitive assignment – he was responsible for overseeing the security of the chief minister, the governor and all VVIP movements across UP. It wasn't a desk job by any stretch. The responsibility involved meticulous planning, coordination with central agencies and, often, a balancing act between political sensitivities and ground realities.

After about ten months, he was transferred to a new role – ADG, PAC. Again, it was no less prestigious. The PAC, a formidable force with a history of managing law and order during the most volatile times in UP, came under his command. Thirty-three battalions spread across the state were now under his leadership.

This transition from Security to PAC happened during a critical juncture. UP was on the cusp of one of the most fiercely contested state elections in its recent history – the 2017 Vidhan Sabha elections. The political temperature was rising, rallies were being organized at a frenetic pace, and the country's top political figures, including Prime Minister Narendra Modi, were frequenting the state.

Although officially in charge of the PAC, Prashant was also given additional charge of Security when the then-ADG, Security, went on a long leave to the United States (US). It meant that, in effect, Prashant Kumar was now responsible for handling both the law-and-order arm and the VVIP security apparatus –

a rare double role that demanded near-constant coordination, planning, and personal presence on the ground.

Throughout the 2017 election season, he attended almost every major rally of the prime minister and other top dignitaries, ensuring seamless security arrangements amidst crowds that sometimes swelled into lakhs. It was a logistical nightmare on paper, but on the ground, it required experience, instinct and a lot of split-second decision-making. And that was something Prashant Kumar had in abundance.

During the final phase of the 2017 election campaign, the regular ADG, Security, returned from his leave and resumed charge. But by then, for six crucial phases of the election, Prashant had been the man on the ground, juggling security for the prime minister, VVIPs, rallies, and law and order across one of India's most volatile states.

Then came the change. The elections concluded. The regime changed. Yogi Adityanath became the chief minister of UP. With the political winds shifting, the administrative dominoes soon followed. Within a month or so, a decision was taken to change the DGP. The outgoing DGP – a seasoned officer – was shifted to command the PAC, which in itself spoke volumes about the strategic importance of the PAC within the state's security framework.

As part of the reshuffle, Prashant Kumar was moved to the post of ADG, Traffic.

In many ways, it was a quieter assignment compared to his previous stormy postings. But fate, as usual, had other plans.

Around the same time, Prashant had applied for the Kailash Mansarovar Yatra as a liaison officer (LO) – a prestigious and deeply spiritual mission. His profile ticked all the right boxes: experience with border deployments during his ITBP days, administrative seniority as ADG and a solid track record of handling both civilian and security groups under pressure.

He was selected.

The interview panel, it seemed, had taken note not just of his professional history but also the nuanced understanding of border terrains he carried. They felt that entrusting a group of around sixty pilgrims to his leadership would ensure they were in safe hands.

Thus, even as he continued to formally serve as ADG, Traffic, he was temporarily seconded to lead one of India's most iconic pilgrimages – a journey to the sacred heights of Kailash Mansarovar, where altitude, faith and diplomacy often intersected in complex ways. While Prashant Kumar was still on the China side of the Kailash Mansarovar Yatra, far away from the administrative whirlpool of UP, fate quietly moved another piece on his career chessboard.

On 4 July, while still traversing one of the most sacred terrains in the world, he was appointed ADG, Meerut Zone – one of the most prestigious and challenging field postings in the UP Police hierarchy. He wasn't even in the country when the decision came through. Perhaps, he mused later, there was a hint of divine intervention. Though not deeply religious by nature, he couldn't help but wonder if it was more than coincidence, especially given the sacredness of where he was when the news arrived.

His wife, on the other hand, was deeply spiritual. For years, she had encouraged – almost insisted – that they should one day undertake the Kailash Mansarovar Yatra together. She had nurtured a quiet dream of setting foot on those hallowed grounds. But in the end, it was he who made the journey, while she stayed back, managing life, work and their home. And it wasn't lost on him. Only because of her constant persuasion, her sacrifices and her unwavering belief had he applied for the Yatra in the first place. Perhaps, in some intangible way, this prestigious posting –

one that came during the holiest journey of his life – was as much hers as it was his.

Although the Kailash Mansarovar Yatra had been an unforgettable experience, it was by no means an easy journey. It was brutally tough – physically, mentally and emotionally. Left to his own devices, Prashant Kumar confessed, he might never have gone. But perhaps, it was his wife's prayers or maybe some unknown divine nudge, that had led him there – and to what would come next.

When he received the news of his posting to Meerut Zone as ADG, it was a genuine surprise. He had absolutely no inkling. In fact, historically, Meerut Zone had been commanded by officers of IG rank, not ADG. That had been the practice for years.

But the administrative landscape had shifted. Due to cadre management challenges – a growing imbalance between the number of senior officers (ADGs) and middle-rank officers (IGs and DIGs) – the government was compelled to recalibrate. There were now plenty of ADGs and not enough positions at the IG and DIG level to absorb them. As a result, a new decision was taken: ADGs would now be posted to zones.

Interestingly, even before Prashant Kumar had left for Kailash Mansarovar, there had been a shake-up in the police leadership. Zones were reshuffled, senior officers were transferred and a new ADG had already been appointed to Meerut Zone. That officer had barely settled in, completing only about one or one-and-a-half months in charge, when the next wave of changes hit. It was in this flux that Prashant's appointment materialized – a transition he had neither sought nor anticipated, but one that would prove pivotal in the years to come.

Coming back to those sacred days when Prashant Kumar was still in China, on the Tibetan side of the Yatra, the defining moment came after his darshan of Mount Kailash. He had the rare opportunity to take a dip in the sacred Mansarovar Lake, believed to be the very embodiment of purity across Hindu, Buddhist and Jain traditions.

The lake stretched out before him, an endless expanse of turquoise blue, framed by stark mountains and an overwhelming silence that made the heart tremble. For a moment, standing there, every hardship – the biting cold, the lack of oxygen, the treacherous climbs – seemed insignificant. He had made it.

As he descended after completing the ritual bath, he instinctively reached for his phone and called home. His mother was alive at that time, and he wanted her to hear the news firsthand.

By the grace of God, the Yatra – one of the most difficult spiritual journeys known to humankind – had been completed.

Kailash Mansarovar is no ordinary trek. At an altitude of nearly 15,000 to 19,000 feet, the Yatra is a test of both body and spirit. The thin air leaves lungs gasping. The unpredictable weather can swing from sunshine to snowstorm within minutes. Landslides are not uncommon. Altitude sickness is a persistent threat. Every pilgrim battles exhaustion, fear and sometimes even despair.

For LOs like him, arrangements were somewhat better. He was provided a pony, a porter and logistical support, all as part of his official duties. But for the hundreds of pilgrims making the arduous circuit on foot, it was sheer determination and *aastha* – faith – that carried them through.

And yet despite the hardships, the beauty of the place was otherworldly.

Prashant Kumar could still recall the moment vividly: standing at Yam Dwar (the 'Gateway to the God of Death'), the traditional starting point of the Kora, the 52 km *parikrama* around Mount Kailash.

As he journeyed further, the sheer magnificence of Mount Kailash revealed itself. A towering, solitary black peak, dusted with snow, rising starkly against a barren, almost alien landscape. There was nothing else like it – no mountain range, no noisy cluster of peaks. Just this one majestic, numbing, awe-inspiring mountain that seemed to pierce the sky itself.

'You are just speechless,' he later recalled. 'You are numbed by what you see. The mountain stands alone, rising out of the earth like something beyond human comprehension.' That black mountain – still, silent, massive – held not just the icy winds of Tibet but also centuries of human longing, faith and myths.

It was not just a pilgrimage. It was a reckoning.

Around the time Prashant Kumar called home to share the news that he had successfully completed the Kailash Mansarovar Yatra, he checked in about his family as well. 'How is Shivani?' he asked, his first instinct still rooted in home. He also told his wife to inform his mother, who had been anxiously waiting for any update from her son traveling in such extreme conditions.

That's when his wife broke another piece of news. 'You've been posted to Meerut Zone,' she said. 'And the DG has been calling repeatedly, asking when you will return.'

Caught off guard, standing thousands of kilometres away, across a border, halfway up a sacred mountain range, he knew there was no question of abandoning the Yatra midway. He told his wife calmly, 'If the DG calls again, please convey to him that it is not possible for me to leave the journey incomplete. Tell him that the moment I am back in India, I will call him directly.'

There was no bravado in his words, just a simple matter of commitment. Having come so far, at such physical and spiritual cost, he wasn't about to turn back now.

The Assignment After

The next day, after completing the Yatra, Prashant Kumar and his group re-entered Indian territory. At the border post, there was a small ITBP camp and, thankfully, a satellite phone.

From there, he immediately called his DG.

The DG's tone was sharp. 'Where are you? Your transfer orders were issued long ago. You're not in compliance.'

Prashant Kumar responded with his characteristic calm, without any defensiveness but with quiet clarity: 'Sir, I am here on government permission, at government cost. I am carrying out a responsibility assigned to me. It's not a personal vacation. Not everyone is blessed enough to come on this Yatra, to experience this once-in-a-lifetime, mesmerizing journey. Leaving it incomplete was never an option – not professionally and certainly not spiritually.'

He added, respectfully but firmly, 'I am now on my way back. The earliest I can report is 14 July.'

There was nothing more to say. The transfer order had been issued on 4 July, while Prashant Kumar was still deep into his Mansarovar journey. He finally reached Delhi on the afternoon of 14 July 2017.

Without wasting time, he called the DG and informed him about his arrival. He mentioned that he would need to travel to Lucknow to collect his belongings and formally hand over his previous charge.

The DG cut him short. 'Nothing doing,' he said bluntly. 'You don't need to come to Lucknow. Hand over charge at Meerut itself and take over immediately.'

There was no room for negotiation.

The famous Kanwar Yatra was about to begin – a massive annual pilgrimage that brought tens of thousands of Shiva devotees

(Kanwarias) marching across UP's western districts. Meerut Zone, as always, would be at the heart of the action.

The district was already on edge, simmering with underlying tensions that typically flared during such mass movements. To add to the urgency, his predecessor – a senior officer he personally respected – had already been appointed ADG, Law and Order, at the state level, and needed to assume his new responsibilities without delay.

There was no time to unpack. No ceremonial farewells.

Prashant Kumar would be stepping straight into the fire.

Meerut Zone was no easy assignment. It spanned eight or nine districts, many of them notoriously crime-prone.

In Prashant Kumar's mind, the original plan had been straightforward. By the time he returned from deputation, he would have been promoted to ADG. And traditionally, once officers reached the ADG rank, field postings were rare.

Ideally, he would have been stationed in Lucknow or given a strategic headquarters assignments, closer to family, away from the unpredictable turbulence of district law and order. But destiny had other plans. Instead of slipping into a comfortable seniority posting, he found himself once again back in the field – smack in the middle of the action.

Sometimes, no matter how carefully you plot your career graph, the universe simply hands you a new assignment. There was no point protesting. Having barely finished the long, spiritual trek of Kailash Mansarovar, he now cut short his return to Hapur and headed straight to Meerut.

By then, Yogi Adityanath had taken charge as the chief minister of UP – a leader with a sharp mind for law and order, and known for backing officers he trusted. Was Prashant Kumar being denied a Lucknow assignment because the new chief minister had already marked him for bigger battles ahead? Had the chief minister already sketched a future roadmap for his blue-eyed officer? No one said it out loud. But the signs were clear enough.

Luck was not denying him a quieter life. It was preparing him for something larger.

But if you asked Prashant Kumar, he would smile at the suggestion of being a 'blue-eyed boy'.

'No,' he would say, 'I never had any direct interaction with the chief minister.'

Yes, there were the expected formal meetings – occasional introductions where senior officers like the DGP and ADGs were brought in to meet the new chief minister. But beyond that, there was no special proximity. No private audience. No secret nods. What had brought him to Meerut Zone was not political networking. It was, simply, trust in his professional record.

Meerut was a challenge by any standard. Not just on the crime front but also because, in the new political climate, law and order had become a headline issue. Maintaining peace was no longer enough; Prashant Kumar also had to represent the government's point of view to the media, articulate it clearly, calmly, without overstepping – a delicate balancing act few managed well.

'I gave my heart and soul to that posting,' he would later reflect. 'I wasn't an interfering boss. But I did set clear targets for my boys and followed through.'

He built a team quietly, brick by brick – one task, one breakthrough at a time. The results spoke louder than any press release. The mafias, who once moved freely across the Wild West districts, began finding the air thicker, the roads narrower, the hiding places fewer.

Meerut Zone was no longer just a crime map. It was turning into a battlefront, one where the old rules no longer applied.

Some excellent operations unfolded during Prashant Kumar's tenure in Meerut. One of the most dramatic was a kidnapping rescue – a case that could have easily slipped into tragedy but ended instead in a rare triumph of precision policing.

It began like something out of a crime thriller. Dr Srikant Gaur, a cancer specialist, travelling home late one evening in an Ola cab, vanished. The cabbie, it turned out, was part of a larger plan – he, along with his accomplices, abducted the unsuspecting passenger and spirited him away.

But the demand they made wasn't typical. The kidnappers didn't reach out to the doctor's family for ransom. Instead, they contacted Ola directly, demanding a staggering ₹5 crore. The audacity of it stunned everyone, even seasoned officers who had seen enough of UP's underbelly.

But Prashant Kumar's team refused to let that become an excuse. Armed with pinpoint intelligence and working under extreme pressure, the police traced the movements of the kidnappers. Two encounters followed – risky, tense confrontations, the kind where one wrong move could have turned rescue into bloodshed. After thirteen nerve-wracking days, the operation culminated in success.

The doctor was safely rescued from captivity. Four kidnappers were arrested in Meerut, their plans unravelling under interrogation. At least five others – including the masterminds – managed to escape in the immediate aftermath. But the police had their scent. A state-wide manhunt was launched, and the message was clear: there would be no easy escape. For the public, this rescue was a statement – that even in the middle of a global pandemic, law and order wasn't negotiable. For Prashant Kumar and his team, it was a reminder: in Meerut, there was no room for compromise.

The Assignment After

Even as the police intensified their efforts on the ground, the kidnappers continued to play a dangerous game of cat and mouse. In a fresh twist, they made another call, this time directly to the doctor's hospital. Speaking to a nurse on duty, they demanded that the hospital authorities build pressure on Ola to meet their ransom demands. They insisted they didn't intend to harm the doctor – all they wanted, they claimed, was to 'teach the company a lesson'. It was a curious justification, but nobody was taking any chances. Behind the scenes, the gang kept changing their locations with calculated precision, weaving through rural hideouts and urban corners alike, staying just ahead of the tracking teams.

To further complicate the search and evade technical surveillance, they cleverly used the doctor's own mobile phone as their communication tool. They shot chilling video clips of the captive doctor, some designed to heighten the sense of urgency, and sent them alternately to Ola representatives and the doctor's anxious family. Each clip was a cruel reminder that time was slipping away – and so were the kidnappers.

As investigators dug deeper, an important piece of the puzzle fell into place. It emerged that two of the accused were siblings who had previously worked with Ola. Disgruntled over alleged non-payment of incentives and bonuses, they had nursed a simmering resentment against the company, which ultimately took this dangerous and criminal turn. While the rescue of the doctor was a major success, these two key conspirators managed to slip through the cracks in the immediate aftermath, triggering a fresh round of pursuit across neighbouring states. Their arrest, though inevitable, would take time. But what became clear beyond doubt was the chilling new face of criminality – young, bitter, tech-savvy and reckless enough to gamble with human lives to settle corporate grudges.

The confrontation unfolded in the shadowy lanes of Shatabdi Nagar, Meerut – a place where the urban and the lawless often overlapped. Acting on a crucial lead, Prashant Kumar's boys moved swiftly, closing in near a railway crossing where the kidnappers, with the doctor still in their custody, were attempting to shift locations. It was a desperate, chaotic moment. Sensing the trap closing around them, the kidnappers tried to melt into a moving group of Kanwariyas, hoping the religious pilgrims would offer them a human shield.

But there was to be no escape for them.

From the flanks, STF teams, working under Prashant's direct command, tightened the noose with surgical precision, joined by a strike unit from the Delhi Police. The kidnappers were challenged, guns raised, orders barked. For a heartbeat, there was only silence – and then the first shot rang out. The gang opened fire, forcing a brutal exchange. At least three to four rounds cracked through the humid night air. In the short but fierce gunfight that followed, one of the kidnappers took a bullet to the thigh, crumpling before he could disappear into the crowd. The capture triggered a chain reaction. Raids erupted across Meerut and its adjoining districts. Houses were stormed. Safe houses dismantled. The net was thrown wide. Massive operations swept through Daurala, Dadri and the sprawling outskirts – areas that had long served as the safe haven of small-time criminals and growing syndicates. In the days that followed, names started surfacing. Anuj, believed to be one of the prime conspirators, emerged as a key figure behind the operation. Three more – Pradeep, Nepal and Amit – were also identified and picked up in a series of swift raids. Only the cabbie who had initiated the chain of events remained elusive for the moment, but the police were closing in. The message had been delivered loud and clear – there would be no running from this one.

The Assignment After

Earlier, the first real confrontation had erupted in the thick of a sugarcane field near Peerpur village, close to Khatauli. Acting on a tip-off, Prashant Kumar's boys closed in just as the kidnappers, with the doctor still in captivity, were fleeing in a battered WagonR. Spotting the police convoy approaching fast, the kidnappers panicked. In a reckless attempt to escape, they veered off the road, plunging the car deep into a sugarcane field. The vehicle dipped almost five feet into a hidden pit, its tyres bursting on impact. Smoke hissed from the engine. Doors slammed open. And before the stunned officers could react, the kidnappers had melted into the fields, leaving the wrecked car – and the doctor's faint traces – behind.

From that moment, a deadly game of cat-and-mouse began across western UP. Each move from the cops made the kidnappers more desperate, more discreet and infinitely more dangerous. The hostage's life hung by a thread. Every hour that passed without resolution tightened the noose around the abducted doctor.

But if the kidnappers thought the pressure would break the police, they had underestimated Prashant Kumar. Instead of going slow, he turned up the heat. Personally leading the operation from the front, Prashant orchestrated a relentless crackdown – choking off escape routes, detaining family members and flooding the zone with intelligence units. The names of the accused had been identified. Warrants had been issued..

By Wednesday afternoon, a fresh lead surfaced – the kidnappers had been spotted in Shatabdi Nagar, the same area where the previous gunfight had rattled the city. Without losing a second, a heavily armed posse of officers fanned out, sealing exits, closing in from all directions. The kidnappers, with the doctor in tow, made a desperate dash in yet another WagonR. But luck had finally run out. As they tried to race through a railway crossing, the rail gate descended, trapping them. The car screeched, swerved and came to a crippled halt as its chassis scraped against the rising metal barriers.

Cornered, the gang did what desperate men always do: they opened fire. Another gun battle tore through the humid evening. Bullets snapped across the narrow lanes. Officers took cover, returned fire with precision, inching closer with every exchange. And when the dust settled, it was over. At around 5 p.m., the doctor was pulled free – shaken, battered, but alive. The game was over. And this time, it was the law that had won.

The rescue was a shot of adrenaline for the force – a rare clean win in a world that rarely offered clean endings. But even as the cheers faded, a darker undercurrent began to stir. The country was heading into a season of turbulence. Agitations were being planned. Politicians were sharpening their narratives. Activists were rallying their supporters. The old ways of policing were about to collide with a new, restless India.

In the weeks that followed, the rescue became a talking point across police circles and beyond. The precision of the operation, the timing, and the high-profile nature of the case drew widespread attention. In 2017, Prashant Kumar was awarded the President's Police Medal for Gallantry (PMG), one of the country's highest honours for courage in the line of duty. Superintendent of Police Manzil Saini, who had led the field operation alongside him, was also chosen for the same recognition. The award wasn't just a formal decoration, it was also an institutional nod to a moment where instinct, leadership and sheer resolve had turned a potentially tragic case into a story of rescue and redemption.

15

From Lakhimpur Kheri to the Challenge of COVID

There are wars that unfold on national borders – loud, visible, soaked in the colours of patriotism. And then there are wars waged in the narrow lanes of towns, under dim sodium lights, away from the public gaze. From July 2017 to May 2020, the Meerut Zone of UP became one such battlefield. There were no newspaper headlines screaming 'Victory!' – just a quiet, relentless war fought in real time, with bullets, baton charges, intelligence tips and, occasionally, body bags. The person leading this quiet offensive was not a general in uniform but a thinking policeman in khaki – Prashant Kumar, the ADG of Police, a man who didn't speak of success unless it showed up in the crime statistics or in the cautious return of fear in the eyes of gang lords.

Prashant Kumar's area of command wasn't a peaceful one. Spread across ten districts – Meerut, Ghaziabad, Bulandshahr, Baghpat, Hapur, Saharanpur, Muzaffarnagar, Shamli, Bijnor and Amroha – this was a volatile belt, a pressure cooker of caste rivalries, communal undercurrents, political vendettas and deeply entrenched criminal syndicates. For years, these zones had witnessed a dangerous equilibrium – gangsters thrived, politicians looked the other way and the police, outgunned and often demoralized, maintained a fragile status quo. When Prashant Kumar took charge, he refused to accept this narrative. Instead, he launched a concerted crackdown across the entire zone, supported by field units, intelligence operatives and a handpicked network of officers who understood that this would be a war of attrition.

Since 2017, UP Police have conducted nearly 15,000 encounter operations, leading to approximately 30,694 arrests, 9,467 injuries, and 238 deaths among suspects. The Meerut zone, comprising Meerut, Shamli, Muzaffarnagar, and Ghaziabad districts, saw the highest activity—with 7,969 arrests and 2,911 injuries. In the Ghaziabad Commissionerate, alone, authorities recorded 1,133 arrests and 686 injuries. However, the detailed district-wise breakdown for arrests, injuries, fatalities, and police casualties remains unpublished.[65]

The crackdown wasn't random. It was structured, intelligence-driven and determined. In Bulandshahr, Baghpat, Saharanpur and Hapur, illegal arms factories were shut, gang leaders arrested and extortion cartels broken apart. Yet the toughest fight wasn't against the criminals outside – it was against the inertia within. Prashant had to rebuild morale, reinstate belief and reignite a culture of accountability. His leadership was quiet but direct, with a keen eye on ground intelligence and unwavering support for honest officers.

The transformation didn't go unnoticed. Crime figures dipped, business owners who once stayed silent began reporting threats and families stepped out with a little less fear. Even within the force, there was a shift – officers stood taller, spoke firmer and rediscovered pride in the uniform. The Meerut Zone, once seen as volatile, began to resemble a working model for proactive, coordinated policing. But just as the dust began to settle on gang wars and street crime, a different kind of crisis began to take shape – one where the police were no longer chasing fugitives but navigating the far trickier terrain of public anger, political pressure and national scrutiny.

The Ram Janmabhoomi verdict in 2019, and the protests against the Citizenship (Amendment) Act (CAA) and National Register of Citizens (NRC), had already tested the limits of crowd control and intelligence coordination. And he had managed to keep the streets calm during those flashpoints. But nothing compared to what came next. The Lakhimpur Kheri incident was the kind of test that arrived without warning and with no room for error.

A convoy linked to Union Minister of State for Home Affairs Ajay Mishra Teni plowed through protesting farmers in Tikunia. The footage was horrifying. The fallout – explosive. Four farmers, a journalist, and others died. Public rage soared. Opposition parties, activists and media houses seized the moment. The tragedy became a national flashpoint, igniting debates on farmers' rights, administrative accountability and the state of democracy. Demands erupted from across the political spectrum – from street protests to parliamentary uproar – calling for the dismissal of the minister and the arrest of his son, Ashish Mishra.

The Supreme Court took suo motu cognizance of the incident, raising sharp questions about the state government's handling of the case. Under immense pressure, the state administration needed someone to stabilize the volatile situation without worsening the political storm. Chief Minister Yogi Adityanath turned to his most dependable officer – Prashant Kumar.

The ACS had attempted to fly in but had to return as the helicopter couldn't take off. The chief minister then dispatched

Prashant Kumar and the ACS to Lakhimpur to negotiate an increasingly volatile and politically sensitive standoff.

The situation on the ground was nothing short of chaos. Grieving families had preserved the bodies of the deceased in refrigerated boxes, refusing cremation until their demands were met. Chief among those demands was the inclusion of Union Minister Ajay Mishra's name in the FIR even though he wasn't present at the scene where the victims were allegedly mowed down. As the father of the main accused, Ashish Mishra, his name had become a symbol of the families' demand for accountability at the highest level.

The chief minister was on the line every half hour. '*Kahan tak pahunche?*' ('Where have you reached?') he kept asking.

Prashant Kumar, fielding calls and tempers, began negotiations over the phone. The compensation discussions shifted: from ₹50 lakh to ₹10 lakh; from permanent government jobs to contractual or private employment. But nothing moved the needle.

The breakthrough came only after a conversation with Rakesh Tikait, the influential farmer leader. Prashant Kumar reached out to him directly, invoking past interactions with Tikait's father and appealing to his strategic instincts. He warned Tikait that unless he acted swiftly, political leaders from Delhi would descend, take control of the narrative and claim credit.

Tikait was in another location at the time. He agreed to come, but on one condition: The offer had to be acceptable. He would not show up just to walk away empty-handed.

By the next morning, Tikait arrived. The crowd, many of whom wore Bhindranwale T-shirts, listened closely as he spoke. He told them about the negotiated settlement and made an emotional appeal to avoid delaying post-mortems and cremations any further. '*Mitti kharab ho rahi hai*,' he said. The bodies were decomposing.

Still, two families resisted, claiming their kin had died from gunshots. But autopsy reports did not support those claims. It later emerged that members of the convoy had allegedly fired shots while fleeing and, in the confusion, some bullets may have struck the crowd.

The driver of the convoy reportedly acted out of a misplaced sense of impunity, driven by ego and the belief that the road belonged to them. When farmers refused to clear the way, the vehicle surged ahead, running people over. The SUV was later set ablaze and the weapons disappeared – never recovered.

At 3 a.m., in a makeshift police station buzzing with mosquitoes and lit by a dim bulb, Prashant Kumar sat with the Munshi and a single officer, Rahul. Together, they drafted the FIR. Ashish Mishra's name was included.

Backdoor objections came swiftly. Some from the establishment hinted that even naming the minister's son might be excessive. Prashant Kumar refused. 'There are witnesses. Video clips. I can't hide facts,' he said.

He held up the FIR later and said simply, '*Ho gaya. Naam bhi likhwaya.*' ('It's done. I've even had the name included.')

He hadn't slept in thirty-six hours. Mosquitoes buzzed around the lone bulb. His shirt stuck to his back. But the only thing that weighed on him was the FIR. He knew one misstep could turn law and order into chaos and make him the fall guy. Still, he didn't flinch.

In that moment, under pressure from the state, the Centre, the grieving families and his own conscience, Prashant Kumar didn't blink. He mediated, negotiated and delivered. That was his real gallantry.

By January 2024, Prashant Kumar had killed over 300 dreaded criminals, from Sanjeev Jeeva to Mukeem Kala. His calm discipline and strategic clarity had redefined the Meerut Zone. Prashant had also modernized policing, combining his MSc in Applied Geology, MBA in Disaster Management and MPhil in Defence Studies with street-smart policing. He led not with slogans but with structure. Four successive President's Police Medals for Gallantry (2020–23) stand testimony to his courage. In the end, when he moved on, he didn't just leave behind a stronger police force. He left behind a belief – that justice, when backed by resolve, doesn't need to shout. It just needs to show up. But law and order don't take victory laps. Just when one front calmed, another opened. First came the CAA–NRC agitations – loud, polarizing and explosive. And then, as if taking turns in a well-rehearsed relay, in rolled the Kisan Andolan – the farmer protests that turned into a pan-India civil resistance movement.

For Prashant Kumar, it wasn't déjà vu. It was a bigger stage with higher stakes.

This time, it wasn't a few districts on fire. It was a slow-moving but massive show of strength that reached deep into the villages of UP, especially its western belt – Meerut, Muzaffarnagar, Rampur, Baghpat, Sambhal, Gautam Buddha Nagar and yes, Lucknow and Agra too. Highways were jammed, trains threatened, toll plazas monitored. For once, it wasn't criminals but the common farmer holding the state to a standstill.

Heading this charge was none other than Rakesh Tikait, the fiery national spokesperson of the Bharatiya Kisan Union and a son of western UP's soil. Tikait, already riding the momentum of an emotional breakdown–turned–political masterstroke on live TV, now turned his gaze on his home turf. Mission Uttar Pradesh, he called it. And he didn't mince his words.

'We have to stop the country from being sold,' he thundered at a mahapanchayat. 'This is not just about farmers. It's about youth, employees, traders and the future of India.'

And then came the punchline. 'Allah-ho-Akbar' and 'Har Har Mahadev' were shouted from the same stage, by the same man, in the same breath. Tikait wasn't just leading a farmers' protest. He was crafting a political statement – one with enough communal, caste and class symbolism to make any law-and-order officer sit up straight.

Prashant Kumar did more than sit up. He fortified.

In Muzaffarnagar alone, 8,000 police personnel were deployed. Twenty-five companies of PAC, twenty senior officers from Meerut Zone and a sweeping surveillance operation ensured the mahapanchayats were loud but not lawless. Prashant, by now ADG, Law and Order, was clear: protests were not the enemy, disruption was.[66]

'We've deployed forces to ensure no miscreants hijack the farmers' voice,' he told reporters. 'We're not here to silence dissent, but we won't let anti-social elements create chaos either.'

His critics accused the administration of staging a velvet-gloved clampdown. Detentions, roadblocks, heavy surveillance and preventive arrests gave the impression of excessive caution – some called it overkill. The Opposition parties and civil liberties groups weren't impressed. But on the ground, there was calm.

Because Prashant understood something many others didn't. This was a protest against the farmers' law, not Lucknow. 'It's not about us,' he said privately to his core team. 'Handle their leaders smartly. Show them we're listening, even if we're not the ones they're shouting at.'

And it worked. While rail tracks were blocked in Punjab, and Delhi's borders turned into trenches, in UP, farmers marched, rallied, shouted – but violence stayed at bay. No buses were torched. No police stations attacked. Headlines from UP didn't scream. And in the law-and-order game, no headlines is often the best headline.

Even during the Bharat Bandh call, which threatened to choke arterial roads and disrupt the heart of western UP, Prashant's force kept traffic flowing. Assistant superintendents of police (ASPs) like Satyajeet Gupta in Agra monitored toll plazas minute by minute. 'Nothing blocked. All clear,' was the day's silent victory tweet.

The warning, though, remained on loop. 'Miscreants might try to blend in. Keep eyes open. Keep the leaders closer,' Prashant had instructed.

Was it flawless? Of course not. There were moments of near-fissures. Tempers flared in Jhansi. A few barricades fell in Jalaun. But in a storm of this scale, the fact that the boat didn't capsize was its own kind of miracle.

And at the centre of that balance – between letting the people speak and preventing the state from bleeding – stood a man who believed in controlling chaos without killing its voice.

Prashant Kumar's role in the Kisan Andolan wasn't about silencing rebellion. It was about keeping UP from becoming a battleground for someone else's war.

And perhaps that is his rarest gift – knowing when not to fight.

But what truly set UP apart during the Kisan Andolan was not just how it handled its own turf – it was how it held the line when other states faltered.

On 26 January 2021, chaos erupted in Delhi. What was meant to be a symbolic tractor parade turned into a storming of the Red Fort. Protesters deviated from the agreed routes, clashed violently with police, broke barricades and hoisted alternative flags atop the historic monument. Over 300 police personnel were injured, metro stations shut down, and the national capital, for a day, looked like it was slipping into siege.

In Haryana, authorities dug trenches, used water cannons and tear gas and blocked highways to halt farmers marching towards Delhi. The resistance was met with resistance. There was confrontation, aggression and a sense that things were slipping out of hand.

And yet just a few kilometres away, UP remained a study in controlled dissent. That wasn't luck. It was design.

Hindi and vernacular press reported extensively on how the violence in Delhi had sparked outrage among common citizens, particularly over the desecration of the national flag. The sentiment quickly turned volatile. And while the political Opposition sharpened its attack on the Centre, there was growing concern that states around Delhi might become launchpads for more agitation.

It was in this high-pitched environment that ADG, Law and Order, Prashant Kumar took charge. When asked if UP would support Delhi Police's investigation, he responded with quiet authority: 'If Delhi Police needs our help, we'll extend it fully. We will not allow miscreants from that incident to find shelter here in UP.' No bluster. Just decisive reassurance. His statement was echoed in Hindi media as a signal of resolve.

The UP Police immediately activated intelligence networks across western districts. The CCTV footage was analysed, infiltration routes were monitored and clear orders went out: let no one use UP as an escape hatch.

As a result, several groups voluntarily vacated protest sites. Farmers pulled out of Chilla Border and Dalit Prerna Sthal. In Baghpat, officials managed to explain the impact of ongoing infrastructure work, and farmers withdrew silently under the cover of night.

Prashant Kumar also acknowledged the shifting mood. He noted that many local groups felt betrayed by the Delhi incident and wanted to distance themselves from the violence. 'We have been assured by citizens and farmer representatives alike that they will not support any element involved in disrupting the peace,' he told the press.

Meanwhile, Haryana and Delhi struggled to maintain control. The Delhi Police took days to restore normalcy and faced fierce criticism for failing to anticipate the Red Fort breach. In Haryana, aggressive containment triggered clashes, deepening political and civil tensions.

In contrast, Prashant's method of containment without coercion and his ability to keep western UP from boiling over was widely acknowledged, even by political opponents, as a masterclass in calibrated policing. The media, both Hindi and national, described it as a rare example of precision in the midst of unrest. At the heart of this balancing act was a mantra that echoed from the chief minister Yogi Adityanath: '*Samvaad Se Samadhan*' – resolution through dialogue. It wasn't just a slogan but a working principle. As tensions mounted, Prashant engaged directly with all stakeholders – religious leaders, community heads, trade unions, transporters – ensuring that essential services continued uninterrupted and peace was not held hostage to politics.

That may have been his most understated triumph – winning not with power but with posture.

From Lakhimpur Kheri to the Challenge of COVID

Even as the Kisan Andolan simmered, another crisis was already tightening its grip – COVID-19. The virus that had the world on its knees came down on India like a rolling inferno, and for UP, the stakes were apocalyptic.

Prashant Kumar knew this wasn't going to be a law-and-order challenge. It was going to be a test of nerves, imagination, empathy – and stamina.

At the time, Haryana's highways were blocked for weeks due to the protests. Amid that chaos, the country was also reeling from a complete shutdown. Total *bandi*. Businesses shuttered. Movement banned. And yet lakhs of migrant labourers – jobless and desperate – were now swelling at the Delhi–UP border.

The Ministry of Home Affairs had issued standing instructions under the National Disaster Management Act. No movement was to be allowed. But this wasn't a dry file. This was a humanitarian flood.

The chief minister called him. 'What will happen if we open the border?' he asked.

Prashant's reply was blunt: 'It's very, very difficult to keep them here. Let them go to the villages. Factories are closed. No jobs. No homes. How will they survive here on concrete?'

The chief minister took a call that would make history in UP's COVID-19 response – he allowed movement. Quietly, discreetly, with strategy.

Initially, special trains were started. But those too stopped. This meant Prashant had to do something no rulebook had prepared him for: mobilize school buses, private buses, public support and ferry lakhs of migrant workers to their districts. In coordination with Bihar officials, those heading farther east were escorted to the UP–Bihar border.

Not a single death. Not a single act of violence in his jurisdiction.

While some states saw angry crowds and chaos, UP held steady. And the credit, much of it, belonged to Prashant's quiet refusal to treat people like statistics. These weren't violators. These were families looking for home.

But the work didn't end with movement.

The police – on Prashant Kumar's direction – went far beyond their call of duty. They delivered medicines and ration packets; they handled cremations when families couldn't. There were instances where relatives of the deceased were stuck abroad, weeping via WhatsApp video calls. 'We were the last human touch for so many,' he would later say.

And here, in the middle of all this, came an unexpected chapter of compassion.

Prashant's wife, IAS officer Dimple Verma, mobilized an army of women who began stitching cloth masks for the police. Not in boardrooms but on verandas, in schoolrooms, in village homes. Hundreds of them. As the world reeled under personal protective equipment (PPE) shortage and UP's police force fought an invisible enemy, those masks were more than fabric. They were morale stitched into cotton.

Among the few of powers that be out on the streets, Prashant Kumar was one – visiting divisional headquarters, handing out food, patting his constables on the back, talking to doctors and breaking bread with volunteers. He spent long hours with NGOs and charity groups, ensuring that the community itself became the strongest link in the chain of survival.

In the end, close to 30–40 lakh people came back to UP during COVID-19. Many of them were skilled – welders, masons, carpenters, tailors. The crisis became an opportunity. Their services were mapped, indexed and brought into the state's employment networks.

'It got us closer to the community,' Prashant would later say. 'The goodwill we earned can't be measured. But it can be felt.'

COVID-19 didn't just test UP, it also changed its relationship with the people it governed. And it proved that policing, at its best, is about care. But that care had to be fought for, every single day.

The early days of lockdown were a study in controlled chaos. Cities fell silent, but fear roared loud. Rumours spread faster than the virus. Panic-buying began. Ambulances became everyday sounds. And the police – already under strain – now stood between order and anarchy.

It wasn't always pretty. In some districts, baton-happy constables clashed with restless citizens. There were viral videos, accusations of brutality. Prashant Kumar knew that in a war like this, force couldn't lead – it had to follow compassion.

He issued advisories to all zones: 'Don't criminalize panic. De-escalate. Talk. Distribute.'

Meanwhile, the virus didn't spare the khaki. Police personnel fell ill. Some died. Their families were quarantined. Entire thanas were shut. The fear was real. Yet the uniforms kept showing up. When more PPEs were required, Prashant made phone calls – not to suppliers but to hearts. The press never covered it. But in the barracks and chowkis, it was spoken of with reverence.

The UP Police also turned into a humanitarian workforce. In Gorakhpur, constables carried oxygen cylinders on their backs. In Prayagraj, they delivered insulin shots to senior citizens. In Lucknow, they livestreamed funerals for NRI families. It was relentless, exhausting work. And yet there were no parades. No awards. Just long shifts and silent tears.

The second wave hit harder. Oxygen ran out. Tempers flared. Crematoriums overflowed. Reports surfaced of unclaimed bodies floating in the Ganga. Media channels tore into the administration. Some visuals were real; others, exaggerated. But the ground was on fire.

Prashant Kumar didn't respond with press conferences. He responded with movement.

He travelled across divisional headquarters – barebones visits, no convoy drama. He sat with district heads, charted oxygen movement plans and ensured that police patrols did not clash with grieving families.

When asked if the force was exhausted, he said: 'So are the people. We're all tired. But we can't stop now.'

He coordinated with doctors, NGOs, Sikh langar committees, Rotary groups, anyone who had a truck, a kitchen or an idea. Police vans were repurposed into mobile food carriers. Abandoned PCR booths became oxygen supply points.

Meanwhile, opposition leaders slammed the UP model. National dailies called the state underreported, unprepared and overwhelmed. But there was also praise from unexpected quarters.

And through it all, Prashant kept walking. Kept showing up. By the time the worst had passed, the UP Police had distributed lakhs of food packets, escorted thousands of patients to care centres, helped cremate hundreds who had no one left.

For Prashant Kumar, COVID-19 was not just a test of duty. It was a call to reimagine what the police could mean to the people.

In answering that call, he didn't just uphold the law. He restored faith.

PART 5
An Officer and a Gentleman

16
Not a Power Couple – Just Partners

She didn't wear a uniform. She didn't brief the press. She didn't travel with flashing lights or walk into meetings with flanked security. But when the state gasped for breath, when panic made even the police falter, Dimple Verma picked up a needle and began stitching masks.

Not metaphorically. Literally.

An IAS officer by rank and an administrator by instinct, Dimple wasn't just Prashant Kumar's partner at home – she was also a silent strategist in the background. While her husband was busy holding the state's fraying nerves together, she created her own micro-army: SHGs, school volunteers, district-level Mahila Samitis. They didn't make noise. They made cloth masks. Thousands of them.

School classrooms were converted into tailoring hubs, and verandas of homes in Sitapur, Gonda, Raebareli and Jhansi were turned into PPE lines. It was the kind of grassroots mobilization that the system couldn't even draft into a plan – because it wasn't part of one. It was instinct, emotion, duty.

She didn't walk away from power with a press conference. There was no farewell bouquet, no lobby whispering about her next move. She simply stepped out of the system the same way she had walked through it – on her own terms.

But even as she stepped back from government corridors, her resolve to serve didn't waver. Quietly, without fuss, she took on new responsibilities – because stepping aside had never meant stepping away. Her presence continued to echo in every project she had nurtured, every space she had shaped. What she had left behind wasn't a résumé. It was an ecosystem.

In every role she held – no matter how complex, chaotic or controversial – Dimple Verma never settled for the ceremonial. She redefined what the chair could mean. She changed outcomes by changing questions. She showed how leadership wasn't about control but about conviction.

And she did all of that while being married to Prashant Kumar. On paper, they could easily be branded a 'power couple' – both decorated, respected, unyielding in their paths. But Dimple always laughed that off with a mixture of sarcasm and ache. 'If we were a power couple,' she told me once, 'we would've lived together. We would've raised our child together. But none of that happened. So tell me – what kind of power couple lives on different ends of the state, year after year? You call it power. I call it the cost of duty.'

In truth, Prashant Kumar might not have become the towering figure of policing without her. While he took down gangsters, she held up the fort. She never asked him to pull back. She never needed him to shine less so she could shine more. Her support was foundational.

This chapter isn't about her service record. It's about her silences. Her choices. Her resilience. It's about a woman who never asked to be remembered, and yet who will never be forgotten.

Not a Power Couple – Just Partners

Prashant Kumar and Dimple Verma form a 'power couple'.

It is said with admiration, sometimes awe. A decorated IPS officer known for his clinical precision and steel-core discipline, and an IAS officer with a reputation for clarity, compassion and quiet authority. Together, they had risen through the ranks of India's most demanding bureaucracy. Together, they had faced crises, commanded forces, shaped policies and walked corridors of power.

So yes, 'power couple' felt like a natural tag. Except, Dimple Verma hated the phrase.

'Power couple? What does that even mean?' she shot back once, half amused, half annoyed. 'It sounds so manufactured. Like we're some kind of political showpiece. We're not. We're just two people trying to do our jobs right – raising a family, making tough choices and staying sane.'

Her voice didn't rise, but the message landed with precision.

In that moment, the phrase melted away, revealing the far more compelling truth beneath. This wasn't a story of two powerful people basking in success. This was the story of two individuals with very different temperaments – one quiet and deliberate, the other spirited and outspoken – who had managed to find a shared rhythm in the madness of public service.

For all their medals, designations and accolades, they lived by a quieter set of values. Balance. Integrity. Loyalty. And above all, partnership.

It was this understated chemistry between a man whose silences spoke volumes and a woman who spoke with clarity and courage that had become their defining legacy. Not power but poise. Not dominance but understanding.

And perhaps that's what made them stronger than any 'power couple' ever could be.

They came from the same state – Bihar – but from very different worlds within it. Different in geography, temperament, even energy. She was raised in a household that encouraged bold thinking and confident speech. He was shaped by discipline, reticence and quiet precision. But what united them wasn't where they came from – it was what they believed in.

Dimple Verma was the kind of child who always spoke her mind. Outgoing, spirited, confident. She was raised in a home where education mattered and fairness wasn't negotiable. She grew up believing that being a woman was an asset, as long as you knew how to use your voice. She topped exams, debated in school and didn't hesitate to speak up even in rooms where girls were taught to stay quiet.

Public service wasn't just a career goal for her. It was a way to create the kind of impact that lingered long after she left a room. It was about making a difference. Her father, a quiet man of principle, often told her, 'If you do something, do it in a way that no one has to clean up after you.' That advice stuck and would later become the cornerstone of how she approached administration.

When the two of them met at the Lal Bahadur Shastri National Academy of Administration, they were not instantly drawn to each other. If anything, they stood at opposite ends of the social spectrum. Dimple had friends across batches, participated in cultural events and spoke freely. Prashant stuck to his schedule, his books and his morning runs. But perhaps that's where the chemistry began – in difference, not similarity.

Their conversations began around work, grew into mutual respect and matured into something deeper. There were no cinematic gestures, no dramatic declarations. Just a growing realization that in a world filled with noise, they understood each other's silences.

She admired his consistency. He admired her clarity. She could energize a crowd; he could defuse a crisis. She thrived on instinct; he built on analysis. Where she was a voice, he was a presence. Where she questioned, he endured. Together, they were not mirror images, but complementary halves of the same puzzle.

By the time their professional paths began to converge again outside Mussoorie, it was evident to those who knew them, that these two were not just civil servants climbing the ladder. They were building something far more complex and enduring: a partnership that didn't just survive the system but also quietly began to change the way the system saw them.

Marriage for civil servants isn't just a union of two people. It's often a negotiation of geography, ambition and the invisible calendar of state and central postings. For Dimple Verma and Prashant Kumar, marriage wasn't the beginning of a new life – it was the beginning of a complicated dance, sometimes in sync, often in sacrifice.

They didn't get too much time to settle into the comfort of married life. Within months of their wedding, the realities of the job took over. Postings came with no regard for convenience. Files didn't care about anniversaries. The state had plans of its own.

They were often posted in different cities, sometimes hundreds of kilometres apart. There were days when one of them was managing a law-and-order crisis while the other was battling red tape over land acquisition. And yet not once did either of them consider slowing down the other's journey.

She never tried to shrink his ambition. He never stood in the way of hers.

That's not to say it was easy. There were difficult choices. There were job opportunities that had to be declined, department preferences that had to be foregone. There were times when she took on a less high-profile role just to be closer to her child, not because anyone asked her to but because she chose to.

'It's never really sacrifice,' she once said. 'It's just strategy. For the family. For the sanity of the household. And for the bigger picture.'

Her decisions were born of strength – the strength to choose what mattered in that moment, knowing that her career would still speak for itself when it needed to. She didn't need to be visible all the time to stay relevant.

What made the difference, though, was the mutual respect between her and Prashant Kumar. In a world where marriages have power dynamics, theirs was unusually balanced. They didn't compete. They didn't compare. They completed different parts of the same journey.

They were both bureaucrats, yes, but they were also sounding boards. She would ask him to look at a policy draft from a field officer's perspective. He would ask her how the Secretariat might react to a move on the ground. Over long phone calls between districts and quick conversations on rushed weekends, their lives began to mirror the complexity of the system they served.

While Prashant quietly built a reputation as an officer who would never compromise on discipline, Dimple became known for her sharp memory, administrative clarity and people-first thinking. He inspired confidence in his subordinates through resolve. She did it through accessibility.

And when they were together, away from the administrative hum, they didn't talk shop all the time. They spoke about children, books, food, music. But in the background of their life was always the rhythm of responsibility.

Those who knew them closely said they were never showy about their affection, never demonstrative. But it was there in how she would check on him late at night during a law-and-order deployment, in how he would ask if she had eaten after a long review meeting. Not grand gestures, just small consistencies.

As the years went by, their bond was tested by the unpredictability of postings. Sometimes the demands of governance came knocking at the worst times – during exams, illnesses and family events. But they had made peace with it. This was the life they had chosen. And as long as they remembered why they had chosen it, everything else could be managed.

There were also the quiet wins – when they both got promoted in the same year, when their child did well, when a policy they had pushed for months finally passed.

Theirs wasn't a picture-perfect marriage for social media. It was far more meaningful, built on quiet faith, shared values and a deep-rooted understanding that their lives were not about power or prestige. It was about doing their bit – and doing it with dignity.

Dimple Verma's career wasn't built on the back of borrowed identity – she was never 'the wife of a senior IPS officer'. She was, from day one, a civil servant who carried her own gravitas – earned, not inherited.

From her first posting as assistant magistrate in Kanpur, she showed an unusual sensitivity towards issues that many officers dismissed as 'minor'. Women's safety, children's welfare, sanitation gaps, school dropouts – these were not headline subjects, but she treated them with urgency and empathy. When she moved to Gorakhpur as joint magistrate, she carried the same energy – balancing law and administration with a sense of lived responsibility.

What made her different was her ability to listen – really listen. Her office door was always open, her meetings unhurried. '*Aap pehle chai lijiye*,' ('Have tea first,') she would often say to citizens who walked in with fear. She believed that bureaucracy didn't have to feel distant. That power didn't have to be intimidating.

In Mirzapur, one of her most demanding postings, she came face to face with the challenges of rural neglect, mining mafias and a fractured administrative apparatus. Yet she worked with the patience of a surgeon – identifying problems at the root, stitching together unlikely partnerships and empowering officers under her with clarity and confidence.

From there, her trajectory touched multiple verticals – rural development, cooperatives, municipal governance and, eventually, education and child welfare. Each role added a new facet to her leadership. In the Social Welfare Department, she championed transparency in pension schemes and revamped the monitoring of hostels for girls and Scheduled Caste/Scheduled Tribe (SC/ST) students. In the women and children development sector, she strengthened vigilance around Integrated Child Development Services (ICDS) schemes and focused on grassroots impact rather than paper metrics.

By the time she became secretary in the Department of Basic Education, Dimple Verma had evolved into a name that commanded both admiration and comfort. Officers working under her often described her as a 'thinking boss' – not one to micromanage but also never absent. She encouraged innovation but never lost sight of protocol. She allowed room for mistakes but demanded learning from them.

Colleagues remember her walking into dusty classrooms in remote villages, unannounced, to inspect mid-day meals, assess dropout rates or simply sit with schoolgirls and ask them what they dreamt of becoming. These weren't PR exercises. This was Dimple Verma at work – connecting the high table of policy to the chalk-smeared world of implementation.

One of her key achievements was her role in reviving enrolment in backward districts, especially among girls. She led state-wide campaigns to ensure that dropout students were tracked, visited and brought back into the system. The focus wasn't on creating statistics. It was on creating change.

Another milestone was her instrumental role in reforming the recruitment and training processes of basic education teachers in the state, bringing a layer of discipline and quality control that had long been missing.

Her tenure also saw the strengthening of inter-departmental coordination, especially among education, health and nutrition services, addressing the child holistically rather than through fragmented silos.

But perhaps her most defining quality was a complete lack of arrogance. Despite seniority, despite the weight of her CV, she never wielded power like a sword. She wasn't afraid to say, 'I don't know; let's find out.' And that humility, in the world of bureaucracy, was both rare and refreshing.

Even when she attended the prestigious NDC – an institution reserved for top-tier civil servants and military officers – she carried herself with quiet confidence. No flamboyance. No self-promotion. Just curiosity and commitment. Her batchmates from the Army, Navy, IAS and international services found her approachable, focused and deeply grounded.

There were offers for deputations and possibilities of central postings, but Dimple always chose assignments where she could be closer to the people – and, when necessary, closer to home. For her, family and service were not competing priorities, they were overlapping circles. She never felt the need to apologize for choosing one over the other at times.

Her legacy is not in viral headlines or political proximity. It lies in the girls who stayed in school because she refused to allow dropout lists to gather dust, in officers who felt heard in her meetings, in villagers who remember her visit for the eye contact. She rose through the ranks by lifting others as she climbed.

And she did it without ever losing sight of the simple, stubborn purpose that had brought her into the service: to make governance human again.

Behind every successful man, they say, is a woman. But in the case of Dimple Verma and Prashant Kumar, that saying never quite fit. Because she was never behind him. She walked beside him. Always.

Their journey was not one of public displays or performative harmony. It was built in stolen hours between crises, in delayed dinners and hurried conversations across districts, in knowing silences over phone calls when words weren't possible. Theirs is a marriage that carried the strain of public service but never let it cloud the private bond.

If Prashant Kumar was known for his quiet grit and discipline, she brought to their equation a certain lightness and warmth. She could defuse tension with humour, lift moods with a casual anecdote and hold her own in any room – from dusty village panchayats to high-stakes policy reviews. He was measured, reflective. She was expressive, instinctive. But at the core, both were driven by the same ethics – service without compromise.

As their careers progressed, they were often asked how they managed. How two demanding lives with such little overlap in geography could remain anchored in stability. The answer was deceptively simple. They never kept score. If one had to step back for a year or take a lower-profile assignment to ensure the family wasn't uprooted, it was done without resentment. And when the other's time came, they rose to the occasion.

In those early years, when their daughter was young, it was Dimple who often chose postings that kept her closer to home, even if it meant less visibility. She doesn't call it sacrifice. She calls it strategy. 'You can't build a house and climb the mountain at the same time,' she once said. 'Sometimes you anchor. Sometimes you ascend.'

And yet her career didn't plateau. Far from it.

Throughout her career, she held significant positions, including principal secretary roles in departments like Basic Education, Civil Defence and Child Development. At the central level, she served as the chief vigilance officer in the NBCC, Ministry of Housing and Urban Affairs, and as joint secretary in the Ministry of Minority Affairs.

Her commitment to public service was evident even during crises. During COVID-19, she personally operated sewing machines alongside female police personnel to produce masks for frontline workers, showcasing her hands-on approach and dedication.

Colleagues say she is as sharp as ever, with a memory that can recall clause numbers from state acts and the faces of Anganwadi workers from visits years ago. But more than that, she brings a quality that leadership often forgets – listening without judgement.

And through all of this, she remains Prashant Kumar's sounding board. He, the decorated officer with gallantry medals and a towering legacy in policing, often turns to her for counsel because her mind is sharp and uncluttered by ego.

In many ways, their story is not just about individual brilliance. It's about the invisible muscle of companionship that powers their service. He guards the streets; she rebuilds the system. He quells unrest; she nurtures hope. He plans security; she plans futures.

This, perhaps, is their real strength. Not their ranks, not their medals, but the ability to grow without outgrowing each other, to serve without forgetting who they are.

In a system that often devours idealism, Dimple Verma and Prashant Kumar remain reminders that values still matter. That one can rise without trampling. That strength can be quiet. And that sometimes, the most powerful partnerships are the ones that last.

In the corridors of power, it's easy to lose sight of purpose. But Dimple Verma never did. She walked her path without noise, without posturing. Whether as a district magistrate, a central official or a policy leader in the state, she carried her responsibilities with a clarity of conscience that never blurred under pressure. And through it all, she remained the quiet centre of Prashant Kumar's storm. A partner not in shadow but in stride. As one senior official once said, 'In a system like ours, rising is rare. Rising together, even rarer.' Their story is proof that it can be done – not with shortcuts or slogans but with shared values, mutual respect and a daily commitment to something larger than themselves.

17

The Final Badge

In the cold light of a January morning, as one top cop bid farewell to the UP Police, another quietly stepped into his place. But this was no routine handover. On 31 January 2024, the corridors of power witnessed a moment both calculated and consequential. Prashant Kumar was appointed the ADG of Police – the fourth such appointment in just twenty months.

For the media, it was a headline. For bureaucrats, a point of contention. But for those who had watched Prashant Kumar's journey – who had seen his grit, his balance and his quiet wars – it was the inevitable rising to meet its rightful hour.

He was not the seniormost officer on the list. Thirteen names stood ahead of him in the gradation chart. These included stalwarts like Mukul Goel, Anand Kumar, and Subhash Chandra – all senior officers who had once been in contention. Mukul Goel had been removed unceremoniously in 2022 for 'disregard of government duty' and 'indolence'. Anand Kumar was nearing retirement, and others like Aditya Mishra and P.V. Rama Shastri were on central deputation. There were others too: Safi Ahsan Rizvi, Sandeep

Salunke, Daljit Singh Chawdhary, Renuka Mishra and B.K. Maurya – all passed over. The list was long. The murmurs, longer.

Yet none carried the trust of the state leadership like he did. In a system where perception often outruns performance, Prashant was a rare exception. He was both trusted and tested. And he had prevailed. Repeatedly.

'Those who questioned his appointment,' said Rajiv Ranjan Verma, former special director of the Intelligence Bureau and Prashant's friend of over four decades, 'don't come close to matching his calibre. If he's become the DGP today, it's purely on the strength of merit and unwavering self-discipline. I say this from inside the system.'[67]

For nearly four years, he had carried the burden of law and order across the most volatile belt of India's largest state. As ADG, Meerut, and later special DG, Law and Order, he had walked through fires, literal and political. From orchestrating surgical crackdowns on mafia empires to managing religious flashpoints with monk-like precision, Prashant Kumar had been the man in the background while others grabbed the frame.

But in the age of optics, even a well-earned victory is subjected to trial by noise. The appointment drew criticism – another acting DGP, screamed the headlines. Bureaucratic circles whispered about a deliberate bypassing of UPSC guidelines, about officers superseded, about a state thumbing its nose at the Centre. The political undertones were unmistakable: 'Was this the chief minister's way of installing his man before the Lok Sabha elections?'

In the cacophony of rules, precedents and petitions, what got lost was the reality on the ground. The people of UP were not watching the UPSC portal. They were watching their streets, their homes, the pulse of safety in their daily lives. And that, Prashant Kumar had guarded with relentless focus.

Yet the purists were livid. Prakash Singh, the retired IPS stalwart whose Supreme Court petition in 2006 led to landmark police reforms, called this a 'clear violation' of the court's directive. Another petition was filed. Questions were raised in columns and courtrooms. 'Why was no list of eligible officers sent to the UPSC?', 'Why another ad hoc appointment?', 'Why Prashant Kumar?'

But behind the closed doors of power, the answer was simple: trust.

Prashant Kumar had the chief minister's complete confidence. He understood the ground. He didn't blink in a crisis. He had direct communication with the topmost echelons of governance. And most crucially, in a state hurtling towards a national election, he was the crisis manager-in-chief.

Even critics couldn't ignore his record. Under his leadership, the police force dismantled criminal empires. The numbers were seismic shifts. Forty years of unchecked mafia dominance was being rolled back, brick by brick, acre by acre. In towns that once cowered under the weight of extortion, fear now changed sides. The hunter had become the hunted.

It wasn't a clean-up. It was a purge.

Across UP, a total of sixty-eight mafia figures were marked by evidence, surveillance and legal strike; 1,427 operations followed, each one a calculated blow to criminal strongholds. The FIRs weren't gathering dust: 806 were filed and 621 arrests followed, many from fortified hideouts once thought untouchable. From the Goonda Act to the Gangsters Act, from NSA detentions to externment orders, the law was unsheathed, section by section, to pin down those who had mocked its very foundation.

Some went down in gunfights – twenty mafia members and their aides were killed in encounters that thundered through the night. Others found the law catching up after years of impunity – seventy-six convictions, including thirty-two mafia bosses and eighty-four enablers, were recorded. But this wasn't just about shoot-outs and trials.[68]

It was about collapsing an economy of crime.

Over ₹4,076 crore worth of illegal properties were seized, demolished or recovered from mafia control. Lands reclaimed. Mansions flattened. Mining leases cancelled. ₹1,429 crore in annual losses inflicted on illegal businesses that had greased the wheels of terror – from benami firms and rigged tenders to extortion networks and illicit liquor empires. The impact wasn't just felt in jail cells. It echoed in boardrooms, auction houses and construction lobbies.

And still, the crackdown didn't rest: 358 licensed weapons were revoked, 470 history-sheets opened, 114 new gang registrations made. Every act was documented. Every signature traced. Even the absconders – three still on the run – had their faces splashed across the intelligence grid, with rewards on their heads and no shadow safe enough to shield them.

Inside the system, whispers grew louder. This wasn't just another officer. This was a man with the resolve to bulldoze the rot, both literally and metaphorically. His officers didn't just salute him, they followed him into battle. His critics didn't just oppose him, they feared he might succeed.

If the seizure of illegal wealth exposed the financial arteries of the mafias, what came next ripped out its beating heart.

Between 20 March 2017 and 21 May 2025, UP witnessed the kind of sustained crackdown most thought impossible in a democratic setup. Over 14,500 criminals were arrested across its twelve zones and six commissionerates, each one linked to serious offenses, hardened syndicates and terror networks that had survived for decades on muscle and fear.

The Final Badge

This war unfolded in alleys, forests, highways and abandoned godowns; in midnight raids and dawn ambushes, where bullets flew and men bled.

Between 20 March 2017, and 21 May 2025, UP police launched nearly 15,000 crackdowns targeting organized criminal networks that had operated with impunity. Over this period, 30,694 alleged criminals were arrested, 9,467 were injured (mostly shot in the leg) and 238 were killed in security operations. The Meerut zone – including Meerut, Shamli, Muzaffarnagar and Ghaziabad – witnessed the most intense activity, with 7,969 arrests and 2,911 injuries. These confrontations occurred across alleys, forests, highways and abandoned warehouses, often through midnight raids and dawn ambushes – where bullets flew and suspects fought back. Far from an unchecked 'encounter raj', this was a calculated campaign to reassert state authority over crime corridors.[69]

The frontlines paid the price too.

Seventeen police officers were martyred. Bravehearts who stepped into the line of fire knowing they might not return. Their names are not just etched on memorials – they echo in the silence that now hangs heavy in once-lawless *basti*s. About 1,626 police personnel were injured in operations that demanded skill and raw courage. Many took bullets to the chest, some to the leg, and still kept firing to protect their colleagues.

Zone by zone, the stories piled up.

In Meerut, the bloodiest theatre, 4,120 criminals were taken down in operations, 2,766 injured, 76 killed and 450 police officers wounded – the zone became a battlefield where old dons were dethroned, and the rule of law was writ in gunpowder. Agra followed, with 2,262 arrests, 5,442 criminals identified and 681 wounded. The cops here didn't flinch – eight fell in the line of duty, nineteen were injured and the flag still flew high.

Bareilly clocked nearly 2,000 arrests, 868 injured, 15 killed and 418 officers wounded. This was no isolated cleanup – it was a full-blown offensive.

From Gorakhpur to Prayagraj, from Kanpur to Varanasi, every zone bled and every officer stood his ground. Even the newly formed commissionerates – Gautam Buddha Nagar, Lucknow, Ghaziabad – clocked hundreds of arrests and dozens of shoot-outs, showing that the urban mafias were no safer than their rural cousins.

This was pre-emptive strike strategy, executed with military precision, judicial accountability and operational intensity. It pushed criminals to the edge and made a mockery of the myth that law enforcement was toothless in India's heartland.

Because under Prashant Kumar's leadership, the UP Police was no longer chasing shadows. It was lighting fires in the dens of the underworld.

As one senior officer said, 'We weren't just taking down criminals. We were reclaiming the soul of the state.'

Prashant Kumar redefined the idea of law enforcement through results.

Prashant Kumar had his share of controversies too. The Hathras case, in particular, had dented his public image. The Lakhimpur Kheri case too, and the violent CAA protests that engulfed large parts of the state, and even the chaotic early days of the pandemic. But he stood his ground, faced the scrutiny and let the institutions play their course. Leadership, after all, is not defined by the absence of storms but by how one sails through them.

In September 2020, a whisper of terror turned into the loudest test of his career yet.

The Final Badge

The Hathras case erupted like a firestorm. A nineteen-year-old Dalit woman had died after a brutal assault, and the nation erupted in rage. The media, civil society and political Opposition converged on UP, accusing the police of negligence, cover-up and caste bias. The late-night cremation of the victim's body without her family's consent only intensified the fury. Protests surged across India, and the state machinery was under siege.

At the eye of this storm stood Prashant Kumar even as he faced the cameras with a calm assertion, The forensic report had found no semen in the samples collected from the victim, and the post-mortem had indicated death due to neck trauma. He emphasized that the victim's initial statements did not mention rape and cautioned against spreading misinformation that could incite caste tensions.

Critics pounced. Legal experts pointed out that the absence of semen does not conclusively rule out rape, especially when samples are collected days after the incident. The Allahabad High Court questioned Prashant's public statements, noting that he was not directly involved in the investigation and should have refrained from commenting on its findings.

Yet Prashant remained steadfast. He ensured that the investigation proceeded methodically, without succumbing to public pressure. Eventually, the CBI found no evidence of rape, aligning with the forensic findings and dropped charges under Section 376. While the district court criticized the handling of the cremation, it did not find fault with the investigative conclusions while holding one person guilty and acquitting three others.

According to the court, the victim and her mother did not mention sexual assault at the time of her admission to the hospital on 14 September 2020. The first recorded reference to sexual assault came eight days later, on 22 September. Medical evidence submitted during the trial found no traces of semen in the forensic samples, and the court observed that the ligature mark around the neck, while consistent with attempted strangulation, was not the cause of death. The injuries, it noted, were indicative of an attack by a single individual. 'The injuries do not indicate assault by multiple persons,' the judgment stated.

The court further highlighted inconsistencies in the statements made. The victim's account to the doctors differed from what she later told a woman constable. Moreover, videos recorded on the day of her admission and statements made to reporters did not reference sexual assault. Names of other accused persons were introduced later, during her statement to the police on 22 September.

It was a verdict that cut through the noise. For the investigators, for the family, for the public, it left many uncomfortable questions in its wake. But for Prashant Kumar, it reaffirmed something he had leaned on throughout the crisis: procedure. He had waited for the facts to speak, knowing well how rare that patience was in times like these.

As Dimple Verma later told me, 'He has tremendous patience. Then his perseverance, his calm nature... He would never talk about his cases at home. He would quietly pursue his goal and reach the destination. He cannot be shaken just because the nation was shaken.'

Likewise, in Lakhimpur Kheri, when a union minister's son was accused of mowing down protesting farmers, all eyes were on the police brass. It was a tinderbox – one misstep and the entire western belt could have exploded. But Prashant didn't flinch. He reached the district, took charge of the investigation framework and ensured that FIRs were filed against the powerful, that due process didn't collapse under political weight. Amidst VVIP

The Final Badge

visits, national media frenzy and court-monitored investigations, he kept the needle steady.

During the anti-CAA protests, when parts of UP flared up in rage, Prashant – then ADG, Meerut Zone – was on the ground, helmet on, baton in hand, dodging stones, taking blows. He was injured during one of the flare-ups in Muzaffarnagar. But he refused to be evacuated. 'The men need to see their officer standing,' he reportedly said. The image of a bloodied senior cop restoring calm with a mic in hand became symbolic of how he operated: with presence, with persuasion, with purpose.

And then there was the pandemic. When fear spread faster than the virus, when lockdowns turned highways into human rivers of despair, and law enforcement became the first – and often only – line of civil control, Prashant led from the front. He organized quarantine facilities inside police lines. He personally monitored logistics of food and oxygen supply to remote thana areas. He ran a control room that never slept. A silent general in an invisible war.

In each of these flashpoints, he did not emerge unscathed. But he emerged undeterred. That's the thing about Prashant Kumar. The harder the hit, the straighter he stands.

To those who knew him intimately, this was destiny asserting itself. A quiet man who had spent his life shunning the limelight was now the torchbearer of the force. Not through lobbying, not through loud politics, but through sheer merit, immovable discipline and an uncompromising sense of duty.

Inside the police ranks, there was celebration of justice. Young officers whispered stories of his late-night check-ins at vulnerable outposts, his eye for detail, his silent presence in moments of crisis. And somewhere deep in his heart, one imagines, there was no celebration. Just a fresh logbook, a sharpened pencil and a quiet line drawn: a new mission begins. Because that is who Prashant Kumar is. While others campaign for power, he prepares for responsibility.

Much later in life, when I asked him how he remained so steady under pressure, he didn't have a textbook answer. But, in a rare moment of reflection, he said, 'I was a very small boy when one day I saw my father crying, something had happened during a marriage in the family… I don't know what… But he was crying. I cannot forget that scene, somehow.

'Then, my second brother, who was a bit naughty, would often be scolded by my father. I somehow did not like to see my brother getting scolded.

'My mother was a good cook yet she would hear a lot of criticism from my father if something in the preparation went even marginally wrong… "*namak kyun kam hai*"… "*masala kitna jyada dal diya tumne.*" I used to feel very bad. Poor lady was working 24/7 for the family… No helping hand, no gas, no proper tap water. Yet she would have to take the brunt every now and then while she had dedicated her everything for the happiness of her kids and husband, her extended family. Yet!

'Now having said that, it was also true that my father had no one to take out his frustrations on. He too, just like my mother, had dedicated his life for his children. Where would we be today without his guidance? He sacrificed his life for us and made sure we become something in life.

'So, that taught me one thing – not to make a fuss about anything in life. *Mila toh mila, nahin mila toh nahin mila!*' ('If you get it, great. If you don't, then so be it!')

His reflections on childhood pain and family sacrifice were shared. And few understood that journey better than his elder brother, Susheel Kumar, a senior IAS officer, who had always played more than a brother's role in his life. 'He's seven years younger to me,' Susheel said. 'And my feelings for him are... more than just brotherly. When the age gap is wide, you look at your sibling somewhere between a brother and a son. That's how I always saw him.'

No wonder, Susheel Kumar saw something others didn't. 'When his turn came, Physics had become overcrowded. I told him and our father to choose a less competitive subject where he could stand out. More importantly, I insisted he leave Hajipur and come to Delhi, even though he was deeply attached to home. I fought with our parents because I knew he needed the exposure.' Prashant eventually joined Hansraj College, where his elder brother Susheel Kumar had studied years earlier. Though Susheel had long moved on, his time at the hostel still held an emotional connect. Seeing his younger brother now walk the same corridors stirred memories. He felt a sense of duty as he recalled. 'That hostel had shaped a part of me, and now it was his turn. The least I could do was guide him towards making the most of it.'

Prashant, of course, didn't need much hand-holding. He found his rhythm quickly and excelled, eventually becoming a gold medallist. Interestingly, it wasn't Susheel who nudged him towards the civil services. That ambition, like so much else with Prashant, came from within.

'He simply observed and followed – that was his nature,' Susheel said.

Their bond only grew stronger.

'When I was posted in Gonda and Ranikhet, he'd visit often. My wife, Poonam, gave him the same affection I did. For his friends, I was "Bhaiya" and she was "Bhabhi". We were family then – and still are.'

'Back in college, his room was like a yogi's quarters,' Rajiv Ranjan Verma recalled. 'Clean. Sparse. Purposeful. Nothing flashy. He lived like he policed – disciplined, focused, untouched by indulgence. We all drifted now and then. He never did.'

That stillness – of not fussing over outcomes, of not complaining – had been forged early.

'Prashant was clear about his goal right from childhood,' said Dr Anil Kumar, now a senior physician, who studied with Prashant until the twelfth grade. 'We were just boys, but he was already the most disciplined among us. Time wasn't flexible for him – it was sacred.'

He recalled how Prashant never missed a deadline, rarely strayed from his schedule and often turned down casual outings. 'If he ever came along, it was only because we pressured him – and even then, he'd feel guilty about wasting time.'

His discipline was built on conviction. 'He had a strong sense of honesty and fairness. Once, when I told my father I'd topped in Chemistry, Prashant didn't interrupt. But later, he quietly said, "You didn't check properly. It's not right to tell your father something that isn't true." He didn't scold me. He just made me see what was right.'

There was courage too – measured, instinctive. 'We were once cycling home from coaching classes when a stone crashed near us from a rooftop. I panicked. But Prashant told me, "You go ahead. I'll find out what's going on." He was more concerned about my safety than his own.'

That sense of duty, of moral compass over convenience, was always there. 'Even as schoolboys,' Dr Anil said, 'we knew he wasn't like the rest of us.'

If Dr Anil saw his sense of duty, Nishi – another childhood friend – remembered the softer spark. 'We were neighbours and family friends, and later attended the same tuition classes from the ninth grade,' she said. 'His father was a well-known science teacher, and the pressure to perform was constant. But Prashant never made excuses. He just did the work with quiet discipline.'

He was reserved, thoughtful, patient. But not distant. 'He had a certain innocence, a soft, romantic side until the tenth grade. He was warm-hearted, sincere and incredibly fair in how he dealt with people. He loved music – those old ghazals and melodies – and often dreamed of meeting the singers behind them.'

'Time's turned the tables,' she laughed. 'Back then, he hoped to meet celebrities. Now, they hope to meet him.' Something shifted after matriculation. 'A switch flipped,' she said. '"*Agar mujhe life mein kuchh karna hai, toh karna hai*" ('If I have to do something in life, then I have to do it,') – he told me. That was it. No Plan B. He was on a mission.' His elder brother's success inspired him, no doubt. But the obsession, the will, that was all his. 'Even as teenagers,' Nishi said, 'we knew. This boy was going places.'

One of the few who observed that transformation up close was Colonel Sanjay Sahay, his wife Dimple's sister's husband, and once a fellow Hansraj College hostel mate.

'When I met him at my wedding,' Sanjay recalled, 'he was quiet, introverted – almost shy. But once we discovered our families were distantly connected, the bond deepened. And then came the college memories.'

They had both lived in the same North Campus hostel, a few years apart. 'In our hostel, if you were from Bihar and aimed for the civil services, your path was fixed,' he said. 'No movies. No parties. No distractions. You studied, you ate, you slept and you repeated. And Prashant took to that life like a monk to silence.' Coming from strict parents and following in the footsteps of an IAS elder brother, Prashant had clarity and zero appetite for detours. 'He was teased by rich Delhi boys for being a "Bihari", invited to parties that could've derailed many. But he stayed rooted. Focused. And when his results came – top of the class – that's when he found unshakable confidence.'

Sanjay laughed while recalling one of his favourite moments. 'A girl from his class once gave him a Cadbury chocolate. For most people, it's just a sweet. But for Prashant – it was a moment. He didn't eat it. He didn't unwrap it. He just lay on the bed, chocolate pressed to his chest, staring at the ceiling like he'd been handed a secret dream.

'That was who he was. That was where he came from.'

Perhaps that's why he never made noise, even when standing at the edge of chaos. Like in December 2024, when a whisper of terror turned into the loudest test of his career yet. The Punjab Police had been hit hard. A police outpost in Gurdaspur district was attacked with grenades by three wanted Khalistani militants. Armed with modified AK rifles and foreign pistols, they had vanished into the night, slipping into the dense sugarcane belts of UP. The men were part of the Khalistan Zindabad Force (KZF) – seasoned, radicalized and determined to strike again. But they had entered a state that now had a new resolve.

In Pilibhit's Puranpur area, alarms had started ringing. The surveillance grid was buzzing – alerts of a stolen motorcycle and three armed men cutting through village tracks, evading CCTV blind spots, darting past checkpoints like ghosts. But these ghosts had left behind a trail – fuel receipts, digital pings, grainy frames of a helmeted rider – feeding into a war-room where officers didn't sleep.

The breakthrough came at the edge of dawn.

A skeletal bridge near the Madhotanda canal turned into a choke point. It was still under construction, its exposed rods jutting out like claws – an unintentional fortress. Two units – the Punjab Police and UP STF – flanked it with machine precision. Loudhailers screamed through the fog: 'Drop your weapons. You are surrounded!'

What followed was chaos unleashed.

The militants responded with a barrage of bullets, indiscriminate and wild. Two policemen collapsed, hit by ricocheting metal. But the STF didn't flinch. They returned fire with deadly accuracy. For nearly eight minutes, the canal banks echoed with gunfire. When silence returned, it carried the weight of finality. All three militants lay dead – bodies sprawled beside the very bike that was meant to disguise them. The weapons, ammunition and other technology they carried were lethal and symbolic: AK-47s shortened for indoor killing, Glocks traced to cross-border routes, magazines duct-taped together for speed and a GoPro camera possibly to record the carnage they never got to commit.

For Prashant Kumar, it was only the tip of something far more sinister. The real storm had a name: Lazar Masih.

He had slipped through many nets before. But in early 2025, his shadow grew longer and darker. He was known to be an arms courier, a sleeper cell operative and a suspected conduit for ISI-backed Babbar Khalsa International (BKI). But above all, he was a ghost with a plan – one that aimed to strike at the soul of India. His target: the Maha Kumbh in Prayagraj.

It was a plot born across continents. From the alleys of Lahore to the quiet suburbs of Sacramento. Masih wasn't working alone. His handler, known in surveillance intercepts as 'Kaka', was based in the US. Kaka was later identified as Harpreet Singh alias

Happy Passia, a designated BKI terrorist and a long-time ISI asset. Happy had been supplying grenades, Chinese pistols and heroin to Masih through a porous pipeline involving smugglers, drones and dead drops.

When Lazar was finally pinned in UP, he was shifting between three safehouses – Kaushambi, Kanpur and Lucknow – changing phones, faces and aliases. But the STF was closing in.

On the cold morning of 6 March 2025, at 3.20 a.m., a sleepy turnoff near Kokhraj in Kaushambi became the setting for one of the most significant counter-terror operations in India's recent memory.

Masih was in a white SUV, en route a new safehouse. The STF vehicles boxed him in with clinical precision. There was no firefight this time. The man who once trafficked in terror now sat still, his eyes hollow, his mission undone.

What they found on him could have brought down an entire congregation. Three live hand grenades, two gelatin sticks and live detonators were recovered from his vehicle. A Norinco M-54 Tokarev pistol – Soviet-era, 7.62 mm calibre – loaded and ready. Thirteen live S&B bullets, designed for quick penetration. A Samsung M14 smartphone still pinging tower locations across UP and Punjab. And most disturbing – a fake Aadhaar card, foreign IDs and evidence of encrypted chats linking him to terror nodes in Portugal, Germany and Pakistan.

During the interrogation that followed, Masih didn't try to deny. His confession was ice-cold. He admitted his links to ISI handlers Sultan Jatt and Rana, whom he had been speaking to directly. His recruitment had been facilitated by Harvinder Singh alias Rinda, another BKI–ISI operative based in Pakistan, and Happy Passia, who until days ago was operating freely in Sacramento before being arrested by the FBI and US Homeland

Security on 17 April 2025, after a formal red alert issued by Indian intelligence agencies.

Masih revealed chilling details – how drones were used to airdrop weapons over the Punjab border, how ISI operatives paid him through cryptocurrency routed via Dubai, how the Maha Kumbh was chosen for its religious symbolism and global attention. The plan was to attack police deployment with grenades, create stampedes and then vanish into the crowds. But Masih underestimated the machine he had entered – an UP under the watch of Prashant Kumar.

Prashant had turned the state into a digital battleground. Cyber cells tracked conversations in real-time. Artificial intelligence–based facial recognition systems picked up Lazar's images from old SIM registrations. Local informants were incentivized. Coordination with the Punjab Police became seamless. And once the net was cast, the margin for escape was zero.

The KZF bust was more than a mission. It was a turning point. It reminded the world that India's soft targets were no longer soft. And that UP was not what it used to be. Yet like every shadow war, the operation came with whispers.

Human rights activists questioned the STF's methods. Some journalists speculated that this was another 'encounter' pushed under the radar. But amidst the noise, the facts stood clear. A major terror attack on the Maha Kumbh had been foiled. A multi-nation, ISI-backed plot had been crushed before it could draw blood.

The KZF bust was a defining moment for the UP Police under Prashant's leadership – a thrilling, high-stakes drama that showcased their ability to confront terrorism with unwavering resolve. Prashant's strategic foresight, from leveraging inter-state collaboration to deploying cutting-edge tech like AI facial recognition, was pivotal. Yet whispers of controversy lingered – activists questioned the operation's transparency, and his encounter-heavy past fuelled speculation of excessive force. But in the shadow of a thwarted catastrophe, he stood tall, a guardian who had stared down the abyss and emerged victorious, ensuring that the KZF's deadly dream died in that cold night.

Months later, during a small barbecue dinner hosted in honour of Prashant Kumar's niece Radhika and her husband, the same attention to rhythm, flow and unseen detail played out. 'The food arrived in waves. The timing, the warmth, the pacing – everything moved like clockwork,' said Shaurya Sahay, Prashant Kumar's nephew and a lawyer in the Supreme Court. 'There was no shouting, no delegation. But the tone was set. That's how he leads a police operation too. Everyone knows their role. Everyone moves in rhythm. Because the man at the top doesn't need to bark orders. He sets the tempo.'

Even as the dust from the Hapur anti-terror operation had settled, Prashant's focus never wavered. With the Lok Sabha elections approaching and the Maha Kumbh around the corner, the war against organized crime had to continue without pause. He intensified the government's long-standing campaign against the mafias, breathing fresh momentum into a drive that had already disrupted criminal empires across UP.

'Many officers have done encounters,' said Rajiv Ranjan Verma. 'But often carelessly, some even landed in jail. Prashant went beyond that – he managed entire cases. He ensured watertight investigations, monitored prosecution and secured convictions against mafia lords. That's real policing.'

The ATS, too, maintained its pace. From 2017, it had arrested 130 terrorists, and 171 Rohingya and Bangladeshi operatives tied to illegal infiltration and criminal activity. Though detailed disclosures from 2024 remained classified, the command chain stayed active. Intelligence-led crackdowns, Prashant's hallmark, continued to prevent large-scale disasters. Between 2017 and 2024, over 650 potential heinous crimes had been stopped before they could be executed. That trend didn't slow under his leadership.

Then came the legal shift of the decade. On 1 July 2024, India transitioned to the Bharatiya Nyaya Sanhita, replacing the colonial-era Indian Penal Code. For a state like UP, with its size, diversity and administrative complexity, the potential for disruption was enormous. Yet Prashant ensured the changeover was seamless. The first FIRs under the new law were registered in Amroha and Raebareli without procedural delay. Ongoing investigations under the old regime were preserved, while new cases were taken up with trained personnel, upgraded software and airtight chain-of-command instructions. Where others saw the possibility of confusion, he saw only a challenge of execution – and he met it with the same quiet efficiency that had defined his career.

Of course, no story of power is ever without its critics. Prashant Kumar's career remained under scrutiny for its enduring association with encounter-style policing. Over 300 such operations had been conducted under his leadership in earlier postings. Though no controversial encounters were officially reported during his tenure as DGP, civil rights groups continued to demand greater transparency and oversight. Some viewed his style as uncompromising, even excessive. Others, particularly within the ranks and among communities once plagued by crime, viewed it as necessary.

And somewhere between those opposing truths stood Prashant Kumar – unapologetic, unsentimental, and untouched by noise. 'He had never chased applause. He didn't need vindication. He just kept showing up,' Rajiv Ranjan Verma said. 'Real police leadership is not about VIPs. It's about the common man. That's what he grasped early. Under him, the force felt morally empowered. And that's why his men followed him – not out of fear but respect.'

Yet the controversy around his appointment remained unresolved. Critics claimed the government had 'tailor-made' new appointment rules to secure his elevation. They cited seniority violations and bypassing UPSC norms. Contempt petitions in the Supreme Court were still pending when he retired. But to Prashant, these were distractions. He knew his record would speak longer than public noise.

He wasn't a man of theatrics. Those who served under him recall a leader who asked for no deference, demanded results and led by example. Subordinates remember him walking into volatile zones without backup, choosing the front line over conference calls. Officers admired his ability to switch from a crisis manager to a human being in a moment – visiting injured constables, calling up bereaved families or sitting late into the night with team members who had faltered but showed remorse.

For all the commanding presence he held in the field, those closest to him knew another side – quieter, softer, impossibly understanding.

'He's always been a supportive father,' his daughter Shivani said. 'Never one to impose his will or expectations. Even when others assumed I'd follow in his footsteps – he never pushed.

He just stood by, quietly supporting my dreams, even when they seemed unconventional.' In fact, she remembered once telling him, half in jest, that she wished to meet Shah Rukh Khan. 'It was more a wish than a plan. But he made it happen. I met the superstar on the set of *Jawan*. That's the kind of father he is. If he can make something happen, he will – without a fuss, without fanfare.'

Shivani described him as someone who listens more than he speaks. 'He won't intrude. He won't argue. He just understands. When I told him I didn't have the patience for UPSC, he just smiled. He didn't need words to show support. He just quietly stood by.'

In that reflection, one sees the whole arc of the man. Even at home, he governed with silence, not control. With patience, not pressure. 'A person who is silent creates his own aura,' said Shaurya, his nephew. 'He doesn't command attention. He alters the atmosphere by simply being there.'

Shaurya remembered spending his early law years under his uncle's roof. What struck him then – and even more now – was how Prashant's presence never needed assertion. Even as a child, Shaurya never saw him as a commanding officer but as someone who observed more than he spoke. 'I once declared we should name our new German Shepherd "Skipper" – a name I read in a storybook. He just said, "Done. That's the name." My cousin Shivani had another suggestion. But he didn't budge.' It wasn't a grand gesture. But it stuck.

But the gesture that stayed with Shaurya didn't come during a grand event or in the middle of a crisis. It happened in an ordinary moment. Years after law school, as he prepared to begin his practice, Prashant Kumar returned to him something he had all but given up on – a radiogram, gifted by Shaurya's grandfather, long broken, thought irreparable. Without ever being asked, without even mentioning it, Prashant had it restored. Fully functional. Quietly, thoughtfully.

'That gesture said everything I ever needed to know about him,' Shaurya said. 'He fixes what's broken. He doesn't announce it. He just does it. That's who he is. That's why he leads the way he does. He values people, not just rules. Humanity, not just hierarchy.'

Testimonials from colleagues, friends, and juniors all echo the same chord: Prashant Kumar was the kind of officer people followed not out of fear, but out of faith. 'In college, hostel mates borrowed his notes,' Rajiv Ranjan Verma laughed. 'Today, senior officers borrow his preparation. That tells you everything about the man.' He may not have worn the permanent DGP tag, but in the eyes of many, he didn't need to. His command was never about designations. It was about delivery. To many in uniform, he was a commander. But to those at home, he was something far more enduring. 'Though Mausiji was more boisterous and fun-loving,' said their niece Radhika, referring to Dimple Verma, 'summer vacations were somehow always more fun at Mausaji's place.'

For Radhika and her brother Shaurya, growing up between cantonment towns and bureaucratic homes, Prashant Kumar's presence brought something different – quiet reassurance without rigidity. 'While Mausiji's home meant more homework and structure,' she recalled, 'Mausaji's place offered a gentler, more relaxed atmosphere. That's where the real vacation felt like a vacation.'

Over the years, he became more than an uncle. 'He's always been a father figure. Whenever I've faced struggles – academic, professional, personal – he's been my go-to. He doesn't just listen. He gives clarity. And somehow, the clarity always turns out to be the solution I didn't know I needed.'

His presence left an imprint on even the youngest in the family. 'My three-year-old daughter,' Radhika said with a smile, 'recognizes only two people without fail: her uncle Shaurya and "Muchhad Uppa" – the moustached grandpa she instinctively bonded with.'

And then there was his style. Always understated, always just right. 'He used to affectionately call me "Stylo" as a child,' she added. 'Now I call him that. Because if anyone defines grace in simplicity, it's him.'

'If I ever write an autobiography,' she said, 'Mausa would feature in every chapter. He's been that present. That integral.' So, when his critics speculated, he strategized. When his detractors doubted, he acted. He let results do the talking.

On the day of his retirement, accolades poured in from all quarters, but none more telling than that from O.P. Singh, former DGP of UP, and one of the most respected voices in the IPS:

'Shri Prashant Kumar, UP DGP, signed out yesterday. He is perhaps the most recallable face of UP Police in its fight against entrenched mafias. With life expectancy on the rise, I wish him decades of productive life ahead.'

As a tribute, Singh posted a verse by legendary poet Ramdhari Singh 'Dinkar', a reflection not just of Prashant Kumar's accomplishments, but of the resolve that defined his journey:

Hai kaun vighn aisa jag mein,
Tik sake aadmi ke mag mein?
Kham thonk thelta haia jab nar,
Parvat ke jaate paon ukhad.

Maanav jab zor lagata hai,
Patthar paani ban jata hai.
Gun bade ek se ek prakhar,
Hain chhipe maanavon ke bheetar.
Mehendi mein jaise laali ho,
Vartika-beech ujiyali ho.
Batti jo nahi jalata hai,
Roshni nahi vah paata hai.

Singh didn't need many words – he simply handed over Dinkar's verses, knowing full well that those who understood the weight of those lines would understand the man they described.

This isn't a swan song, it's a salute to a fellow captain who never shouted to be heard. He just showed up and led.

From H.C. Awasthy, another former DGP of UP, who led the force during the high-voltage Vikas Dubey manhunt, came a message laced with warmth and deep admiration:

'Deep down in my heart I know that it is your sheer hard work, decency, polite behaviour and unmatched professional competence, which are behind your massive accomplishments. It was my good fortune to have a dependable younger brother like you as my colleague. I consider myself fortunate. You still have a lot of fundamental work to do for the police and I am sure that opportunity will come soonest.'

On 31 May 2025, Prashant Kumar officially signed off from active service. The corridors of UP PHQ felt a little heavier that day – not from ceremony but from the silent acknowledgment that an era had just ended. Messages poured in from officers, bureaucrats, journalists and citizens alike. For many, it wasn't just the retirement of a DGP – it was the pause of a force field. Across the state, the buzz was that his departure had left a huge void – one that would be difficult to fill.

The Final Badge

But Prashant Kumar didn't deliver a long farewell speech or appear in a glittering send-off. He did what he had always done – he let his actions and his quiet words speak for themselves. And this time, it came in the form of a message that moved many to tears:

'From the very first day in uniform to this moment of parting, I have lived each day with a single purpose – to serve the people, uphold justice and stand by my force. What we do is not just a job, it is a calling. And I have been privileged to respond to that call with all of you by my side. To the constable who stood in the rain to manage traffic, to the officer who cracked cases through sleepless nights, to the teams that innovated – you are the true soul of this force. I have only been a thread in the grand tapestry of UP Police, and you made me feel like its fabric.'

As tributes poured in, one sentiment echoed across police lines and civilian circles alike: Prashant Kumar may have left the office, but he hadn't left the mission.

And perhaps the best way to sum it up comes from another arena altogether. I remember Mukesh Ambani once said at a felicitation ceremony for Sachin Tendulkar: 'Sachin's best is yet to come.' Few could imagine how much was still left in the legend's tank. Months later, Tendulkar went on to score the first-ever double century in one-day international cricket.

With the same quiet fire, Prashant Kumar steps into his post-uniform life. He may no longer command a battalion, but his presence will still command respect, inspire reform and anchor the conscience of a generation of officers yet to rise.

Because for men like him, service is not defined by the badge.

It is defined by purpose.

And that purpose? It's still unfolding.

Acknowledgements

Mrs Dimple Verma, IAS and wife of Prashant Kumar; Additional SP, Rahul Srivastava, UP Police; Inspector Ramesh Kumar Singh, PS to Mr Prashant Kumar.

Notes

1. PTI. 'Up Dgp Denies Allegation of Caste-Based Encounters, Says No Partiality Is Practised.' ThePrint, 9 September 2024. https://theprint.in/india/up-dgp-denies-allegation-of-caste-based-encounters-says-no-partiality-is-practised/2259073/.; Kumar, Pravin. '"Contrary to Perception, up Police Not Trigger-Happy Force."' The Times of India, 20 October 2024. https://timesofindia.indiatimes.com/city/lucknow/uttar-pradesh-police-defends-its-actions-amid-encounter-controversy-is-the-trigger-happy-perception-misleading/articleshow/114404878.cms.
2. Ibid.
3. 'CM Yogi Adityanath Visits Kanpur to Pay Tribute to Martyred Policemen'. *Times of India*. 3 July 2020. https://timesofindia.indiatimes.com/city/kanpur/03k-cm-yogi-adityanath-visits-kanpur-to-pay-tribute-to-martyred-policemen/articleshow/76777311.cms.
4. Pandey, Alok, and Deepshikha Ghosh. 'UP Cop, Accused of Helping Gangster-On-Run Vikas Dubey, Arrested'. *NDTV*. 8 July 2020. https://www.ndtv.com/india-news/suspended-up-cop-vinay-tiwari-accused-of-tipping-off-gangster-vikas-dubey-on-raid-arrested-2259286.
5. 'Police Should Kill My Son, Says Mother of Main Accused in Kanpur Encounter Case'. *ANI News*. 3 July 2020. https://www.aninews.in/news/national/general-news/police-should-kill-my-son-says-mother-of-main-accused-in-kanpur-encounter-case20200703221612/;

    Abraham, Bobins. '"Kill Him in Encounter": Mother of Gangster Vikas Dubey Who Orchestrated Killing of 8 up Cops'. *Indiatimes*. 4 July 2020. https://www.indiatimes.com/news/india/mother-of-gangster-vikas-dubey-who-led-to-killing-of-8-cops-says-kill-him-in-encounter-517166.html;

    PTI. 'Police Officer, Suspended for Alleged Role in Vikas Dubey Case, Moves SC Seeking Protection'. *Times of India*. 12 July 2020. https://timesofindia.indiatimes.com/india/police-officer-suspended-for-alleged-role-in-vikas-dubey-case-moves-sc-seeking-protection/ articleshow/76924635.cms?utm_source=chatgpt.com;

Bajpai, Namita. 'Bikru Massacre Fallout: UP Govt Suspends IPS Officer over Links with Gangster Vikas Dubey'. *New Indian Express*. 13 November 2020. https://www.newindianexpress.com/nation/2020/ Nov/13/bikru-massacre-fallout-up-govt-suspends-ips-officer-over-links-with-gangster-vikas-dubey-2223232.html?utm_source=chatgpt. com.

6. Ibid.
7. Pandey, Alok, and Deepshikha Ghosh. 'UP Cop, Accused of Helping Gangster-On-Run Vikas Dubey, Arrested'. *NDTV*. 8 July 2020. https:// www.ndtv.com/india-news/suspended-up-cop-vinay-tiwari-accused-of-tipping-off-gangster-vikas-dubey-on-raid-arrested-2259286.
8. Siddiqui, Faiz Rahman. 'Up: Slain Dsp Mishra's Daughter Found His Letter, Call Recording'. *The Times of India*. 7 July 2020. https:// timesofindia.indiatimes.com/city/kanpur/slain-dsp-mishras-daughter-found-his-letter-call-recording/articleshow/76843626.cms?utm_source=chatgpt.com.
9. Singh, Rohit K. 'Kanpur's Controversial Ex-Ssp Transferred Days after Massacre of Cops | Latest News India – *Hindustan Times*'. Hindustan Times, 7 July 2020. https://www.hindustantimes.com/india-news/ kanpur-s-controversial-ex-ssp-transferred-days-after-massacre-of-cops/story-LPIkl1ae21ZWeAWLoPkLFK.html?utm_source=chatgpt.com;

Sanyal, Anindita, ed.'Former Kanpur Top Cop Who Ignored Murdered Officer's Letter Shunted'. *NDTV*. 7 July 2020. https://www.ndtv.com/ india-news/former-kanpur-top-cop-who-ignored-murdered-officers-s-letter-shunted-2258850?utm_source=chatgpt.com;

PTI. 'Entire Police Station under Scanner over Kanpur Ambush; 68 Personnel Shunted Out'. *Economic Times*. 8 July 2020. https:// economictimes.indiatimes.com/news/politics-and-nation/entire-police-station-under-scanner-over-kanpur-ambush-68-personnel-shunted-out/ articleshow/76849554.cms?utm_source=chatgpt.com&from=mdr.

10. 'Vikas Dubey News Latest Updates: Gangster Killed in Shootout; Opposition Leaders Raise Questions', *CNBCTV18*, 2020. https:// www.cnbctv18.com/india/vikas-dubey-encounter-news-latest-updates-gangster-vikas-dubey-killed-in-shootout-as-he-tries-to-escape-in-kanpur-6299611.htm.
11. Nair, Arun, and Deepika Pundir, eds. 'Vikas Dubey Encounter News Highlights: UP Gangster Was Asked to Surrender, Killed in Retaliatory Firing, Say Police'. *NDTV*. 11 July 2020. https://www.ndtv.com/india-news/up-gangster-vikas-dubey-killed-while-being-taken-to-kanpur-say-reports-updates-2260206?utm_source=chatgpt.com;

'Dubey Shot in Startling Encounter'. *The Pioneer*. 11 July 2020. chrome-extension://efaidnbmnnnibpcajpcglclefindmkaj/https:// www.dailypioneer. com/uploads/2020/epaper/july/delhi-english-edition-2020-07-11.pdf?utm_source=chatgpt.com

12. Jaiswal, Pankaj, 'Vikas Dubey Was "Silenced", His "Encounter Staged": Who Said What after Kanpur Encounter, *Hindustan Times*, 2020. https://www.hindustantimes.com/india-news/vikas-dubey-was-silenced-his-encounter-staged-who-said-what-after-kanpur-encounter/story-SL93D4NR3R3kdVRKMlGg7O.html.

13. 'Vikas Dubey Killing: Trinamool Congress Says "Justice Killed" in UP, CPM Calls It "Cold-Blooded Murder" by Cops', *The Indian Express*, 2020. https://indianexpress.com/article/india/vikas-dubey-killing-trinamool-congress-says-justice-killed-in-up-cpm-calls-it-cold-blooded-murder-by-cops-6500128/.

14. 'In Video, Vikas Dubey Discloses His Political Links'. *National Herald*. 6 July 2020. https://www.nationalheraldindia.com/india/in-video-vikas-dubey-discloses-his-political-links?utm_source=chatgpt.com;

Deka, Kaushik. 'The Rise and Fall of Vikas Dubey'. *India Today*. 9 July 2020. https://www.indiatoday.in/india-today-insight/story/the-rise-and-fall-of-vikas-dubey-1698770-2020-07-09?utm_source=chatgpt.com.

15. Chakraborty, Pathikrit, 'Vikas Dubey Encounter: Judicial Panel Gives Clean Chit to Police', *The Times of India*. https://timesofindia. indiatimes.com/city/lucknow/dubey-encounter-judicial-panel-gives-clean-chit-to-police/articleshow/85502462.cms.

16. 'Atiq Ahmad Admitted to Having Links with Pakistan's ISI, LeT, Says FIR'. *Business Standard*. 16 April 2023. https://www.business-standard. com/india-news/atiq-ahmad-admitted-to-having-links-with-pakistan-s-isi-let-says-fir-123041600569_1.html?utm_source=chatgpt.com;

'Explained: Gangster Atiq Ahmed and His Links to Pakistan, in Life and Death'. *Firstpost*. 17 April 2023. https://www.firstpost.com/explainers/atiq-ahmed-killing-pakistan-isi-lashkar-e-taiba-zingana-12464492. html?utm_source=chatgpt.com.

17. Mani, Rajeev, 'Former Top Cop Lalji Shukla Paid Price for Taking on Atiq Ahmed', *Times of India*, 2023. https://timesofindia.indiatimes.com/city/ allahabad/this-former-cop-paid-price-for-taking-on-atiq-ahmed/ articleshow/99628933.cms.

18. Chakraborty, Pathikrit. '"Up Crime Rate Much below National Average"'. *Times of India*. 6 December 2023. https://timesofindia. indiatimes.com/city/lucknow/up-crime-rate-much-below-natl-average/ articleshow/105767860.cms?utm_source=chatgpt.com.

19. Chakraborty, Pathikrit. 'Epicentre of Techtonic Shift in State Policing'. *Times of India*, 9 October 2023. https://timesofindia.indiatimes. com/city/lucknow/

epicentre-of-techtonic-shift-in-state-policing/articleshow/104275248.cms?utm_source=chatgpt.com.

20. Srivastava, Samarth, and Ashish Srivastava, 'Jailed Gangster-Politician Mukhtar Ansari Dies of Heart Attack', *India Today*, 2024. https://www.indiatoday.in/india/story/jailed-gangster-politician-mukhtar-ansari-dies-after-being-admitted-to-hospital-2520532-2024-03-28.
21. PTI, 'Mayawati Demands Probe into Death of Gangster-Politician Mukhtar Ansari', *NDTV*, 2024. .https://www.ndtv.com/india-news/mayawati-demands-probe-into-death-of-gangster-politician-mukhtar-ansari-5332222.
22. PTI. 'Mayawati Demands Probe into Death of Gangster-Politician Mukhtar Ansari'. Ndtv.com, 2025. https://www.ndtv.com/india-news/mayawati-demands-probe-into-death-of-gangster-politician-mukhtar-ansari-5332222?utm_source=chatgpt.com.
23. PTI, 'After Mukhtar Ansari's Death, Akhilesh Yadav Demands Supreme Court Probe', *NDTV*, 2024. https://www.ndtv.com/india-news/after-mukhtar-ansaris-death-akhilesh-yadav-demands-supreme-court-probe-over-doubtful-cases-5332665.
24. 'Mukhtar Ansari's Death: "My Father Was given Slow Poison", Claims Son Umar Ansari', *Hindustan Times*, 2024. https://www.hindustantimes.com/india-news/mukhtar-ansari-death-news-my-father-was-given-slow-poison-claims-son-umar-ansari-march-29-101711669437087.html.
25. Verma, Sanjeev, 'Mukhtar Ansari Had Comfortable Stay in Ropar Jail for over 2 Years during Congress Regime', *The Times of India*. https://timesofindia.indiatimes.com/city/chandigarh/mukhtar-ansari-had-comfortable-stay-in-ropar-jail-for-over-2-years-during-congress-regime/articleshow/108859445.cms.
26. Ojha, Arvind, 'Exclusive: कृष्णानंद पर चल रही थी गोली, अभय सिंह से बोला था मुख्तार अंसारी -काट लीन्ह!', *Aaj Tak*, 2020. https://www.aajtak.in/crime/story/mukhtar-ansari-up-bjp-mla-krishnand-rai-2005-murder-phone-call-recording-with-shooter-abhay-singh-1110748-2020-08-10.
27. Jha, Anuja, ed. 'Mukhtar Ansari's Viscera Report Rules out Poisoning, Brother Questions Findings'. India Today. 24 April 2024. https://www.indiatoday.in/india/story/mukhtar-ansari-viscera-report-rules-out-poison-his-brother-questions-findings-2531240-2024-04-24?utm_source=chatgpt.com;

'Viscera Test Results of Mukhtar Are Meaningless: Afzal Ansari,'. *Times Of India*. 24 April 2024. https://timesofindia.indiatimes.com/city/varanasi/viscera-test-results-of-mukhtar-are-meaningless-afzal-ansari/articleshow/109576868.cms?utm_source=chatgpt.com.
28. Ibid.

29. 'U.P. Police Conducted 10,713 Encounters in Yogi Adityanath's Tenure', *The Hindu*, 16 March 2023. https://www.thehindu.com/news/national/other-states/up-police-conducted-10713-encounters-in-yogi-adityanaths-tenure/article66627130.ece.
30. 'Improvement in Law and Order, Policing Standards, and Quality of Enforcement Since 2017'. Report prepared by the DGP's office.
31. 'Strong Law & Order Makes up Ideal Place for Investment: WB Chief', *The Times of India*, 9 May 2025. https://timesofindia.indiatimes.com/city/lucknow/strong-law-order-makes-up-ideal-place-for-investment-wb-chief/articleshow/121037680.cms.
32. Ibid.
33. Chakraborty, Pathikrit, 'UP Police Attached Assets Worth Rs 2000 Crore of 64 Gangsters since 2021,' *The Times of India*, 21 March 2023. https://timesofindia.indiatimes.com/city/lucknow/up-police-attached-assets-worth-rs-2000-crore-of-64-gangsters-since-2021/articleshow/98844103.cms.
34. 'Pradesh mein Kukhyat Mafiao ka saashan wa police mukhyalay star par chinhitkaran wa karyabahi'. Report prepared by Prashant Kumar's office to be sent to his seniors;
    'Action against 69 Mafiosi, 1153 Gang Members since Jan 2020: Police'. *Hindustan Times*. 2 July 2023. https://www.hindustantimes.com/cities/lucknow-news/crackdown-on-lucknow-mafiosi-69-arrested-16-killed-properties-worth-3516-cr-seized-in-3-years-says-police-101688237968639.html?utm_source=chatgpt.com.
35. Internal police report issued by the office of DGP Prashant Kumar.
36. 'Pradesh mein Kukhyat Mafiao ka saashan wa police mukhyalay star par chinhitkaran wa karyabahi'. Report prepared by Prashant Kumar's office to be sent to his seniors. Page 5.
37. 'Atiq Ahmed's Property Worth ₹50 Crore Transferred to UP Government'. Hindustan Times. 17 July 2024. https://www.hindustantimes.com/india-news/atiq-ahmeds-property-worth-rs-50-crore-transferred-to-uttar-pradesh-government-101721213727973.html?utm_source=chatgpt.com.
38. 'Pradesh mein Kukhyat Mafiao ka saashan wa police mukhyalay star par chinhitkaran wa karyabahi'. Report prepared by Prashant Kumar's office to be sent to his seniors. Page 6.
39. Ibid.
40. Pattanayak, Banikinkar. 'UP Beats West Bengal, Emerges 3rd Largest to House "Active" Companies in India'. *Economic Times*. 29 October 2024. https://economictimes.indiatimes.com/news/company/corporate-trends/up-

beats-west-bengal-emerges-3rd-largest-to-house-active-companies-in-india/articleshow/114743826.cms?utm_source=chatgpt. com&from=mdr.
41. PTI. 'Flats Build on Land Seized from Atiq Ahmad Allotted to Poor in Prayagraj'. *EconomicTimes*. 9 June 2023. https://economictimes.indiatimes. com/news/india/flats-build-on-land-seized-from-atiq-ahmad-allotted-to-poor-in-prayagraj/articleshow/100882440.cms?from=mdr.
42. Dixit, Kapil. 'Prayagraj Administration Razes House Where Atiq Ahmed's Wife, Sons Lived'. *Times of India*. 1 March 2023. https://timesofindia. indiatimes.com/city/allahabad/prayagraj-administration-razes-house-where-atiq-ahmeds-wife-sons-lived/articleshow/98342842.cms.
43. From one of the DGP's reports titled 'UP Police Vision Statement', which was sent to the Chief Minister in December 2024.
44. Butt, Riazat, 'This Year's Hajj Was the Lowest Attendance for 30 Years Excluding the Pandemic', *AP News*, 5 June 2025. https://apnews. com/article/saudi-arabia-hajj-pilgrims-arafat-5bf6f65b4ad0c53b69fc5 1589989a202?utm_source=chatgpt.com.
45. 'Millions of Hajj Pilgrims Celebrate Eid'. *Al Jazeera*. 27 October 2012. https://www.aljazeera.com/news/2012/10/27/millions-of-hajj-pilgrims-celebrate-eid?utm_source=chatgpt.com;

Usman, Bilal Aftab. 'Hajj Pilgrimage: Years with the Highest Footfall'. *WorldAtlas*. 29 May 2017. https://www.worldatlas.com/articles/hajj-pilgrimage-years-with-the-highest-footfall.html?utm_source=chatgpt. com.
46. '7-Tier Security for Maha Kumbh 2025, over 37,000 Policemen to Be Deployed'. *The Statesman*. 19 October 2024. https://www.thestatesman. com/india/7-tier-security-for-maha-kumbh-2025-over-37000-policemen-to-be-deployed-1503355310.html?utm_source=chatgpt.com
47. Sheikh, Saaliq. 'Maha Kumbh Mela 2025: Millions of Pilgrims Take Holy Dips in India's Mega Hindu Festival'. *AP News*. 14 January 2025. https:// apnews.com/article/india-maha-kumbh-hinduism-527170e00730b5e2a 61a70b7423493ad.
48. 'Maha Kumbh 2025 Kicks Off: AI Enhances Security and Pilgrim Experience'. *Economic Times*. 13 January 2025. https:// economictimes.indiatimes.com/tech/artificial-intelligence/maha-kumbh-2025-kicks-off-ai-enhances-security-and-pilgrim-experience/ articleshow/117192221.cms?utm_source=chatgpt. com&from=mdr.
49. Mohan J., Anand, 'Maha Kumbh Goes Digital: 2,700 CCTVs, AI to Track Crowd, Underwater Drones', *The Indian Express*, 10 January 2025. https://indianexpress.com/article/long-reads/maha-kumbh-goes-digital-2700-cctvs-ai-to-track-crowd-underwater-drones-9770545/.

50. Singh, Namita, 'Report Suggests 79 Pilgrims Died in Kumbh Mela Stampede, Far Exceeding Official Toll', *The Independent*, 6 February 2025. https://www.independent.co.uk/asia/india/kumbh-mela-stampede-death-toll-b2693367.html.
51. Srivastava, Samarth, 'Kumbh 2025: UP Government Plans 7-Tier Security, 37,000 Cops to Be Deployed', *India Today*, 19 October 2024. https://www.indiatoday.in/india/uttar-pradesh/story/maha-kumbh-mela-2025-yogi-adityanath-uttar-pradesh-government-plans-security-policemen-deployed-cctv-2619712-2024-10-19.
52. 'Kumbh to Boost up Economy by Rs 3L Crore: Yogi Adityanath'. *Times Of India*. 14 February 2025. https://timesofindia.indiatimes.com/ india/kumbh-to-boost-up-economy-by-rs-3l-crore-yogi-adityanath/ articleshow/118259159.cms?utm_source=chatgpt.com;
Roy, Robin. 'Maha Kumbh's Economic Ripple: Rs 25,000 Crore Revenue Boost'. *First India*. 29 January 2025. https://firstindia.co.in/ news/life-style/maha-kumbhs-economic-ripple-rs-25000-crore-revenue-boost?utm_source=chatgpt.com;
'The Economic Impact of Maha Kumbh Mela 2025: Revenue, Employment, and Growth'. 10 July 2025. https://www.kotaksecurities.com/investing-guide/articles/maha-kumbh-mela-2025-economic-impact/?utm_source=chatgpt.com.
53. 'Rs 2 Lakh Crore Revenue, GDP Boost: The 'Maha' Impact of Maha Kumbh 2025', *Moneycontrol*, 13 January 2025. https://www. moneycontrol.com/news/india/rs-2-lakh-crore-revenue-gdp-boost-the-maha-economic-impact-of-maha-kumbh-2025-12909243. html?utm_source=chatgpt.com#google_vignette.
54. John, Kenneth, 'Amid Build-Up, Past Data Indicates Mahakumbh to Be a Money Spinner', *Hindustan Times*, 6 January 2025. https://www.hindustantimes.com/cities/others/amid-build-up-past-data-indicates-mahakumbh-to-be-a-money-spinner-101736186620583.html?utm_source=chatgpt.com.
55. 'Mahakumbh 2025: Larger Area, Advanced Security Measures -Hindustan Times'. Hindustan Times, 24 September 2023. https:// www.hindustantimes.com/cities/others/mahakumbh-2025-larger-area-advanced-security-measures-101695560453766.html?utm_ source=chatgpt.com.
56. Ojha, Srishti, 'IIT Baba's Ganja Case: Here's What the Law on Narcotics & Psychotropic Substances Says', *India Today*, 3 March 2025. https:// www.indiatoday.in/india/law-news/story/iit-baba-ganja-case-what-law-narcotics-psychotropic-substances-says-2688344-2025-03-03.
57. PTI. '"Boatmen among Biggest Beneficiaries": UP amid Row over Rs 30 Crore Earning in Kumbh'. *NDTV*. 6 March 2025. https://www. ndtv.com/india-news/boatmen-among-biggest-beneficiaries-of-maha-kumbh-mela-2025-uttar-

pradesh-amid-row-over-rs-30-crore-earning-7865059?utm_source=chatgpt. com;'Maha Kumbh Transforms Lives of Boatmen'. *Times of India*. 6 March 2025. https://timesofindia.indiatimes.com/city/allahabad/maha-kumbh-transforms-lives-of-boatmen/ articleshow/118768489.cms?utm_source=chatgpt.com.

58. 'Anupam Kher Takes Holy Dip at Maha Kumbh, Shares Video: Tears Started Flowing'. *India Today*. 23 January 2025. https://www.indiatoday. in/movies/celebrities/story/anupam-kher-takes-holy-dip-at-maha-kumbh-2025-shares-video-2668999-2025-01-23?utm_source=chatgpt. com.

59. 'Vicky Kaushal Visits Mahakumbh 2025 in Prayagraj ahead of Chhaava Release'. *HindustanTimes*.13 February 2025.https://www.hindustantimes. com/entertainment/bollywood/vicky-kaushal-visits-mahakumbh-2025-in-prayagraj-ahead-of-chhaava-release-101739441313127.html?utm_ source=chatgpt.com.

60. 'Kumbh Not about Hindus & Muslims, Will Take Dip in Sangam: Kabir Khan'. *Times of India*. 28 January 2025. https://timesofindia.indiatimes. com/city/allahabad/kumbh-not-about-hindus-muslims-will-take-dip-in-sangam-kabir-khan/articleshow/117653250.cms.

61. 'Rs 10,000 Bonus, Medal, 7-Day Leave: Reward for Cops on Kumbh Duty'. *NDTV*. 27 February 2025. https://www.ndtv.com/india-news/rs-10-000-bonus-medal-7-day-leave-reward-for-cops-on-maha-kumbh-duty-7809726?utm_ source=chatgpt.com.

62. 'Rs 10,000 Bonus, Special Medal, 7-Day Leave for 75k Cops on Maha Kumbh Duty'. *Business Standard*. 27 February 2025. https://www. business-standard.com/india-news/rs-10-000-bonus-special-medal-7-day-leave-for-75k-cops-on-maha-kumbh-duty-125022701162_1. html?utm_source=chatgpt.com.

63. As told to the author by Prshant Kumar in an interview.

64. As told to the author by Neelam Katara in an interview in March 2020.

65. Bajpai, Namita. 'UP's 'Zero-Tolerance' Policy: 238 Criminals Killed, over 9,000 Injured since 2017'. *New Indian Express*. 17 July 2025. https://www.newindianexpress.com/nation/2025/Jul/17/uttar-pradeshs-zero-tolerance-policy-238-criminals-killed-over-9000-injured-since-2017?utm_source=chatgpt. com;

'UP Saw 895 Police Encounters in '17; 26 Killed, 2,186 Arrested'. *Times Of India*. 30 December 2017. https://timesofindia.indiatimes.com/city/ meerut/up-saw-895-police-encounters-in-17-26-killed-2186-arrested/ articleshow/62310533.cms?utm_source=chatgpt.com.

66. Bajpai, Namita, 'Thousands of Farmers Attend "Kisan Mahapanchayat" in Muzaffarnagar', *The New Indian Express*, 5 September 2021. https:// www.newindianexpress.com/nation/2021/Sep/05/thousands-of-farmers-attend-kisan-mahapanchayat-inmuzaffarnagar-2354651.html?utm_ source=chatgpt.com.

67. As told to the author in an interview.
68. '8 Years of Yogi Govt: 222 Dreaded Criminals Killed, 8118 Injured in Police Encounters', *Hindustan Times*, 16 March 2025. https://www.hindustantimes.com/cities/lucknow-news/8-years-of-yogi-govt-222-dreaded-criminals-killed-8118-injured-in-police-encounters-101742153658050.html?utm_source=chatgpt.com.
69. Scroll Staff.'Over 30,000 'Criminals"Held,238 Killed in 14,900 Gunfights since 2017: UP Police'. *Scroll.in*. 18 July 2025. https://scroll.in/latest/1084643/over-30000-criminals-held-238-killed-in-14900-gunfights-since-2017-uttar-pradesh-police?utm_source=chatgpt.com;

'Over 30,000 Criminals Held, 238 Killed in 14,000 Encounters since 2017: UP Govt'. *Indian Express*. 17 July 2025. https://indianexpress.com/article/cities/lucknow/criminals-killed-encounters-2017-up-govt-10133399/lite/?utm_source=chatgpt.com;

Bajpai, Namita. 'UP's 'Zero-Tolerance' Policy: 238 Criminals Killed, over 9,000 Injured since 2017'. *New Indian Express*. 17 July 2025. https://www.newindianexpress.com/nation/2025/Jul/17/uttar-pradeshs-zero-tolerance-policy-238-criminals-killed-over-9000-injured-since-2017?utm_source=chatgpt.com.

Mairi MacMillan lives on the wet and windy west coast of Scotland, brewing dark tales and even darker cups of tea – despite her son's advice that five minutes is the maximum steeping time required. After an intentionally dramatic time at university, she left Glasgow's urban sprawl many years ago, and now spends her days weaving romances containing characters that may or may not be inspired by some of her quirkier kinfolk.

When not corrupting perfectly good characters with morally grey choices, she can be found wild-swimming in a sea-loch described locally as 'baltic', ice-skating, or nose-deep in books with heat levels to compensate. She's currently plotting her escape from the everyday grind in a yet-to-be-acquired camper van, much to the amusement of her nearly-grown children. Her husband remains hopeful that one day she'll get around to sorting out her clutter – and that he might be invited along on any trips!

https://substack.com/@mairimacmillan

facebook.com/Mairi-MacMillan-Author
instagram.com/mairi_macmillan_author